A·B·C Et Cetera

BOOKS BY

ALEXANDER AND NICHOLAS HUMEZ

Alpha to Omega
The Life & Times of the Greek Alphabet

Latin for People / Latina pro Populo

The Boston Basin Bicycle Book
(WITH EDWARD AND JANICE GOLDFRANK)

A·B·C
ET
CETERA

The Life & Times
of the Roman
Alphabet

---

by Alexander &
Nicholas Humez

David R. Godine · Publisher

BOSTON

First hardcover edition published in 1985,
first softcover edition in 1987 by
David R. Godine, Publisher, Inc.
Horticultural Hall
300 Massachusetts Avenue
Boston, Massachusetts 02115

Library of Congress Cataloging in Publication Data
Humez, Alexander.   ABC et cetera.
Includes index.
1. Latin language—Alphabet.
2. Latin language—Glossaries, vocabularies, etc.
1. Humez, Nicholas D.   II. Title.
PA2125.H86   1985   937   85-70148
ISBN 0-87923-587-X   (hc)
ISBN 0-87923-664-7   (sc)

First softcover printing, April 1987

Printed in the United States of America

In memoriam
Warren Cowgill, a good friend
in any language

Contents

Preamble

This is a book about the Roman alphabet and the people who used it as a medium for the transmission of their civilization. Primarily, this means the Romans and their Italic subjects, speakers of Latin who disseminated the language, and the culture of which it was an expression, throughout Europe and the coasts of the Mediterranean Sea: at its height, the Roman empire included what is today Italy, Switzerland, Austria, France, Spain, Portugal, Rumania, Greece, Asia Minor, Syria, Libya, Tunisia, Morocco, the islands of Sardinia and Sicily, and the greater part of Britain and the German Rhineland. A traditional story has it that Romulus, legendary founder of Rome, was promised a twelve-hundred-year future for his city. As it eventually turned out, this promise was fulfilled: counting from the legendary founding of Rome in 753 B.C. to the overthrow of the last emperor by Odoacer in 476 A.D., the city just squeaked by, though if one adds on the days during which the Byzantine Empire (formerly the Eastern Roman Empire) actively perpetuated Roman culture, another thousand years goes into the tally. Moreover, the establishment of Christianity with its seat at Rome provided a vehicle for the perpetuation of at least some aspects of Roman culture down to the present day, for Latin remains the lingua franca of the Roman Catholic Church and the official language of papal encyclicals. Which is by no means to suggest that Latin is otherwise extinct: over the years, the language has not-so-quietly transmuted itself into the Romance languages of to-day – Catalan, French, Italian, Portuguese, Provençal, Rhaeto-Romance, Rumanian, Sardinian, Spanish, and their numerous dialects. Or, put another way, the language of the Romans is alive and well in the form of Latin's temporally far-flung dialects, the modern Romance languages.

As speakers, readers, and writers of English, we are greatly indebted to the long line of purveyors of Latin in its various forms. We have borrowed the alphabet from them not once but twice – the Runic scripts of Ireland, England, and much of Scandinavia were offshoots of the Roman alphabet that eventually replaced them and that we use, in only slightly expanded form, today – and we have rarely missed an opportunity to appropriate handy Latin linguistic terms and idiomatic phrases when given the chance, making them our own to the tune of some sixty percent of our present working vocabulary. This has meant liberally helping ourselves in the early days to the small change of linguistic currency during the Roman occupation of Britain and, in the later days during which Latin served as the European lingua franca par excellence, to seconds from Late Latin. The Norman invasion brought an updated version of the language that permeated much of English life, and subsequent contact with the world of Romance has yielded us further linguistic bounty of a Latinate persuasion. And it has always been fair game to grab some Classical Latin nuts and bolts when a new technical term has cried out to be invented.

When words are borrowed, concepts come with them – what else, after all, are words for but to express ideas? So, if we have borrowed a wide variety of Latin words, it follows that we have also borrowed a great deal of the cultural stuff that they encase, even allowing for some mislabeling, repackaging, and inventory shrinkage during the process of transmission. This book takes a look at what the authors consider to be some of the more intriguing cultural/linguistic goodies that have crept willy-nilly into the English language over the ages from the Latin cornucopia. The approach is appropriately abecedarian: each chapter of the book concerns a different letter of the canonical Classical Roman alphabet; the accompanying narratives look at English words that derive, more or less directly, from Latin words beginning with the letter at hand and explore the aspects of culture that lurk behind those words. The final chapter treats the letters X, Y, and Z (and a few others for which the vast majority of Romans apparently never felt a pressing need), and a bibliography offers suggestions as to where to look for more.

A *note on Latin spellings:* all Classical Latin words now rendered commonly with *j* are here spelled with *i*. Words with *u/v* are given here with V for capital *u/v* and *u* for lowercase. For more on these conventions, see the chapters on *I/J* and *U/V/W* below. This usage follows that of the *Oxford Latin Dictionary* (see bibliography).

A·B·C Et Cetera

A

IS FOR *ATAVISM, AFFINE, AGNATE, AVUN-cular,* and *aunt,* all of Latin ancestry. In fact, all are de-scended from one or another of the many Latin terms that served to define the Roman kinship system, a system that most modern ethnographers would give their eyeteeth to have been able to investigate at first hand (and somehow live to tell the tale). And why not? Aside from the fact that living to tell the tale after having done fieldwork among the Romans would entail either mastery of time travel or the discovery of the secret of eternal graduate-studenthood (per-haps not such a boon as all that), kinship systems and the terminologies that reveal their individual structures are in-trinsically interesting – and not just to the professional eth-nographer, since we all are intimately and inextricably bound up in the tangle of our own personal kinship ties and can use all the enlightenment that we can get by looking at how other people manage or have managed to stay on at least speaking terms with what Russell Hoban's Riddley Walker terms his "nexters," without completely hobbling our tongues – and the Roman system is in many respects a particularly tantalizing one.

Ethnographers have traditionally zeroed in on a society's kinship system-cum-terminology for a couple of reasons be-yond the factor of personal immediacy. Floyd Lounsbury (in *Explorations in Cultural Anthropology*) put his finger on perhaps the more important of these when he wrote that "the primary function of kinship terminologies is to deline-ate the relation of ego to . . . kindred in such a way as to express some socially or legally important aspect of these relationships." In other words, kinship terminology func-tions as a sort of shorthand for locating the individual in society in a number of significant ways. If you understand the local kinship terms and the social network they describe, you have a pretty good handle on how that society works – what you and your mother's sister's daughter or son must refrain from doing (at least with each other), how much your brother-in-law owes you (and how much you have to take from him), who gets together at Grandpa's birthday (or at ex-Aunt May's latest wedding), and why you never throw a lighted lamp at Mother.

Another reason for studying kinship is that, unlike a good many other aspects of society, it tends to resolve itself into a closed system, so you can study it (and hope to get your degree before forgetting just what it was that you went there to study in the first place, lo those many years ago). In 98 A.D., Cornelius Tacitus, after picking the brains of several of his friends (including those of his father-in-law Agricola and Pliny the Younger), and having served on the Roman empire's northern frontiers, published his famous monograph on the Germans which recorded, among other things, that the various Germanic tribes seemed to have a propensity for blood feuds. What Tacitus did not say (whether because his informants didn't think to mention it or, if they did, because he was too busy scribbling away in his notebook to catch it) was that in order to contain such quarrels, the more enlightened tribes allowed a settlement in blood money instead of actual blood and gore: if you killed someone, you paid a graduated sum to all the living relatives of the deceased, as far as fourth cousins – and were expected to assess your own kin accordingly, out to your own fourth cousins, to help pay it all off. One can well imagine the flurry of genealogical calculations whenever anybody got murdered – most speakers of English today would be hard pressed to define the chain of kinship connection between oneself and one's second cousin, let alone one's fourth cousin, whoever he or she might be. Apparently, all of this information was more readily accessible to the Germans than it is to the ordinary twentieth-century speaker of English, though in a society in which there were fewer people and most of them were related by blood, this may not be altogether amazing. Among the Romans, the obligations of kinship may have been less explicit than among their neighbors to the north, but the ties were surely there, and some of them still lurk in our own language and culture.

"Home," as Robert Frost once put it, "is the place where, when you have to go there, they have to take you in." (It has also been said that the paradigmatic nuclear family consists of five people: a mother, a father, two children – one of each sex – and an ethnographer.) To the Romans, the Latin word *familia* meant "family-plus-everybody-else-attached-to-the-household," a sense best preserved in our use of the word *familiar* (both as the noun designating the sorcerer's faithful spirit-servant, conventionally disguised as a coal-black kitty, and as the more familiar adjective referring to the stuff sufficiently close to home that it doesn't strike us as strange) and in the direct borrowing of *paterfamiliās*, which meant much the same to speakers of Latin as it does to us (though we tend to use the term tongue-in-cheek in a way that they mostly did not) – male head-of-household – to which the Romans do not seem to have seen fit to coin a corresponding *māterfamiliās* to designate a female head-of-household. (*Note*: Asterisks precede unattested words; for more on the asterisk or *splat*, see page 187.)

But then, the structure of Roman society – like that of all the other Indo-European societies of the time, as far as one can tell – was aggressively and unabashedly patriarchal, a fact suggested by the kinship terminology of the language and, for those of a less subtle turn of mind, hammered home by the law: to be a Roman *paterfamiliās* was to have the right to expose your children at birth, if you thought them too sickly or born of adultery, or to sell them into slavery, or even to kill them if they offended you seriously enough; and you also had absolute control (in most cases) over your wife and her property, and a good deal of control, besides, over your sons' wives. You were also religious head of the household, on whom fell the principal obligations to care for and lead the worship of your particular household gods, the *Larēs* and *Penātes;* and it was you whom the government would come looking for when it was time for general taxation.

Latin *pater* and *māter* are cognate with English *father* and *mother,* as they are with the standard formal terms for these relatives in virtually all of the Indo-European languages we know, though Roman kids were probably more likely to call their fathers *tata* or *pappa* and their mothers *acca, amma,* or *mamma,* just as American kids are more likely to call their fathers "Dad" or "Pop" and their mothers "Mummy" or "Mom." *Frāter* and *soror,* whatever else their Roman siblings may have called them as they jockeyed for position in the eyes of their parents, are also familiar Indo-European terms, cognate with English *brother* and *sister* – a *sibling* being the diminutive flavor of Old English *sibb* (kinsman, from the Indo-European root meaning "one's own" that underlies English *self* and the *sui-* of *suicide*). *Sibb* forms the second half of the word *gossip,* originally *godsib,* the linguistic offspring of one's godmother and godfather, i.e., people whom one treats like immediate family in some ways, such as in the free exchange of scurrilous rumor about everyone's nearest and dearest, even though they may well not be actual blood relatives at all.

While it would be reasonable to guess, on the basis of the widespread agreement among the Indo-European languages on the words for father, mother, brother, and sister, that the words for daughter and son would be cognate from India to Balto-Slavic to Greek to Latin to Celtic to Germanic, the major subfamilies of the Indo-European community, this guess, as it happens, would turn out to be wrong: English "daughter" and "son" have no etymological connection with Irish *ingen* (daughter, literally, "one born into [the family]") or *mac* (son, which turns up in numerous Celtic "son-of" surnames, like *MacDonald* and *McCarthy*), Greek *hyiós* and *hyia,* or with Latin *filius* and *filia* (which seem to come from the same Indo-European root that underlies *fēcundus* [fertile, fruitful, prolific] and the verb *fēlāre* [to suckle]) from which the *Fitz-* of *Fitzgerald, Fitzpatrick,* and *Fitzwilliam* is derived by a commodius vicus of recirculation. On the other hand, *filly* (young female horse) is related to none of the above, but is rather the offspring of an Old Norse term derived, ultimately, from an Indo-European root meaning "small."

Outside of the nuclear family (with or without its resident ethnographer, the *ethno-* part of whose moniker, incidentally, comes from the same root as *sib-* and *self*), the terms designating one's Indo-European kinfolk tend to become even more scattered, though all the more worthy of scrutiny for all of that, as the scattering is by no means random. Our words *uncle* and *aunt*, for example, are derived through French from Latin *auunculus* (mother's brother) and *amita* (father's sister), suggesting that these particular kinds of uncle and aunt were especially important (as they are in many societies), the Latin terms for the other kinds – *patruus* (father's brother) and *mātertera* (mother's sister) – eventually falling through the cracks at some point in the ever-expanding woodwork, presumably because these people didn't play as big a role in the normal course of familial follow-the-leader as the others. Similarly, *cousin* comes (again through French) from Latin *consobrīnus* (cousin on the mother's side) while *patruēlis* (cousin on the father's side) has left no heirs. Note, incidentally, that each of these Latin kinship terms is more or less transparently derived from some other: *patruēlis* and *patruus* are both spin-offs of *pater*; *mātertera* is *māter* plus suffix; *consobrīnus* (which even in Roman times had begun to be used as the generic term for cousin) is an elaboration of *sobrīnus* (cousin on the mother's side) which is itself from **sororīnus*, that is, *soror* plus diminutive suffix; *amita* is a diminutive form of *amma* (mommy); and *auunculus* is a diminutive form of *auus* (grandfather).

Auus probably originally meant "old person" and only later got the specific meaning of grandfather (on either side of the family). A great-grandfather was a *proauus*, a great-great-grandfather an *abauus*, and a great-great-great-grandfather an *atauus*, a term more commonly used in the

sense of ancestor, and from which *atavism* (the reappearance in an organism of a characteristic that one might have
thought to have disappeared for good – or ill – generations
ago) is derived, *atauus* itself being apparently the combination of the child's word for grandpa – *atta* – plus the
grown-up word – *auus*. A male grandchild was a *nepos* and
a female grandchild was a *neptis*. In classical times, these
terms came to be used in the sense of nephew and niece –
indeed, English *nephew* and *niece* are borrowings of the
French versions of *nepos* and *neptis*. (Modern Italian uses
nipote for nephew and niece, and diminutive forms of *nipote* – *nipotino* and *nipotina* – for grandson and grand-
daughter.) *Nepotism* seems first to have been used as the
standard term for wangling a job for your relative during the
bad old days of the Renaissance when clergymen powerful
enough in the hierarchy – perhaps "hire-archy" would be
more apt here – would arrange for suitable appointments
for their "nephews" (i.e., illegitimate sons) when the latter
came of age.

It is the second-degree terms "uncle," "aunt," "cousin,"
"nephew," and "niece" that replaced whatever the indigenous peoples of the British Isles called these relatives, and
it is a conspicuous commentary on the societies that came
to speak English (or, for that matter, any of the Romance
languages) that they felt no apparent need to distinguish
father's brother from mother's brother, father's sister from
mother's sister, or paternal cousins from maternal ones.
Moreover, the amount of generational skewing found in the
use of Latin kinship labels is certainly suggestive: by deriving *auunculus* from *auus*, the Romans implied that there
is something shared by mothers' brothers and grandfathers,
and by their nephews and nieces and grandchildren, a sharing echoed not only in the double use of *nepos*/*neptis* as
nephew/niece and grandson/granddaughter but in the subsequent Spanish use of *sobrino* (from *sobrīnus*) to mean not
cousin, but nephew and first cousin once-removed (i.e.,
the child of one's first cousin).

We know from Suetonius's racy history of the first twelve Caesars that nieces were allowed a great deal of familiarity with their uncles: in the case of the emperor Claudius and his niece Agrippina, this option was exercised to passionate effect, with the result that Claudius got the senate to pass a law exempting uncle–niece marriages from the existing legal prohibitions against incest, and married her forthwith. Few seemed to care to follow Claudius's example of uncle marrying niece, however: two cases are reported – one of a freedman, and the other of a chief centurion, guests in attendance at the latter's wedding including none other than Claudius and Agrippina. Cassius Dio, writing in 229 A.D., reports that the law allowing uncle–niece marriage nevertheless remained on the books for fifty years until excised by the emperor Nerva. Inasmuch as Claudius's matrimonial union with Agrippina assured the succession of her son Nero, the people of Rome might well have clucked their tongues and said, "See what happens when you fool around with the kinship system?" in light of the calamities over which Nero presided. In any case, while nieces and their uncles presumably continued to enjoy each other's company after Nerva, sexual relations between them were once again considered incest in the eyes of the law, and marriage had nothing to do with it.

Marriage, of course, entails its own set of rules and its own set of quasi-kinship terms. Many societies are clearer than ours on the difference between one's kinsmen proper (i.e., one's blood relations) and one's affines (i.e., relatives by marriage) – *affine* being ultimately from Latin *adfinis* (neighboring), literally "near (*ad*) the border (*finis*)," hence, connected (by marriage) – and what sort of behavior is prescribed (or proscribed) toward members of one group as opposed to members of the other. (Do you still call Uncle Harry "Uncle Harry" after he and your father's sister get divorced, assuming, of course, that Uncle Harry isn't also your mother's brother?) The Romans simplified these matters somewhat by their tendency to focus their attention on the male line (a tendency echoed in ethnographic terminology, in which there is a word for kinsman through the male line – *agnate* – but no comparable word designating kinsman through the female line, *affine* generally being used instead): the *gens* (clan, house-and-lineage) was reckoned through the male ancestors, and when a woman married, she would adopt her husband's *gens* name. Thus, when Publius's second daughter married G. Cornelius, she became Publia (Secunda) Cornelii, presumably dropping the "Secunda," since her husband's *gens* name would ordinarily have been sufficient to distinguish her from her sisters (unless, of course, one of them also married a member of the *gens* Cornelius). The husband would refer to his wife as his *uxor* (whence English *uxorious* and *uxorial*), while she would refer to him simply as her *uir* (man).

Beyond this, it was the woman who got to use nearly all the specialized vocabulary in referring to her new family: her *glōs* was her husband's sister, her *ianitrix* was her husband's brother's wife (literally, "female door-keeper"), and her *lēuir* was her husband's brother – whence the anthropological term *levirate*, used to denote marriage, whether ceremonial or physical, to the wife of one's deceased brother. (The Romans themselves seemed to believe that *lēuir* was related to *laeuus* [left-hand], though this is probably not so, however tempting it is to compare the French expression *mari de la main gauche* [man with whom one lives as though married; quasi-common-law husband, literally "left-hand husband"].) The legally questionable practice that W. S. Gilbert characterized as "that annual blister/ Marriage to deceased wife's sister" is termed *sororate* and left at that.

The term *socer* (father-in-law) seems originally to have applied exclusively to the woman's husband's father but later came to be used to refer to the man's father-in-law as well. Unlike *glōs*, *ianitrix*, and *lēuir*, *socer* did not completely fall by the wayside on the road to Modern Romance: it is virtually intact in meaning and form in Rumanian and is also found in Spanish thinly disguised as *suegro* and in Italian as *socero.* The standard terms for the other two in-laws for whom the Romans had discrete terms are also alive and well: *gener* (son-in-law) appears in Spanish as *gerno,* in Italian as *genero,* and in French as *gendre;* and *nurus* (daughter-in-law) appears in Spanish as *nuera* and in Italian as *nuora,* the French having ditched Latin *nurus* in favor of a Germanic word cognate with English *bride.*

Actually, French, like English, has a preference for identifying in-laws with a standard add-on: to English mother-in-law, father-in-law, son-in-law, daughter-in-law, brother-in-law, and sister-in-law correspond French *belle-mère,* *beau-père, beau-fils, belle-fille, beau-frère,* and *belle-soeur,* the terms that the French also use to designate their "step" kinsmen, *belle* and *beau* (beautiful, handsome, nice) having presumably been attached to the terms for the members of the nuclear family as a form of respectful fond address to the members of one's family-by-marriage, whether the marriage was one's own or that of one's mother or father. (The *step-* of English stepmother, stepfather, and the like – no relation to the *step-* of stepladder – comes from an Indo-European root meaning "push, shove, strike" that seems to have taken on the specialized sense of "bereave[d]" in Germanic.) The Romans, for their part, had separate terms for their stepkinsmen: a stepfather was a *uītricus* or a *patraster,* a stepmother was a *nouerca* or *mātrastra,* and a stepchild was a *priuīgnus/priuigna* or a *filiaster/filiastra,* the *-aster/ -astra* suffix denoting a "resemblance," sometimes with a mildly pejorative connotation – the wicked stepmother in a French fairy tale is more likely to be a *marâtre* than a *belle-mère.*

Adoption was a frequent practice in Rome, chiefly as a means of transmitting property – Juvenal speaks scathingly of legacy hunters whose M.O. involved getting themselves adopted by the elderly childless rich – and power: of the first five Roman emperors, four were adopted sons, and for three of them their foster-father's legacy was no less than the empire. (Augustus adopted Tiberius, who adopted Caligula; and Nero was adopted by Claudius after the latter's marriage to Agrippina.) Sometimes, of course, Roman adoptions worked out for the best: Pliny the Younger was adopted by Pliny the Elder, who was his *auunculus*, and the former's patron, Trajan, was the second of the "Five Good Emperors" (Nerva, Trajan, Hadrian, Antoninus Pius, and Marcus Aurelius), all but the last of whom adopted the next in line in plenty of time to forestall a recurrence of the bloody succession struggles that had characterized the infamous "Year of the Four Emperors" (69 A.D.).

In light of the alarming mortality rate among males of senatorial rank during the early days of the empire, the Romans did well to exercise so generous a system of adoption, for it was not uncommon to lose all one's heirs in a purge, let alone in death by disease or misadventure, in the army or at sea: to keep the family name alive and to perpetuate the family fortunes, many an aging *paterfamiliās* adopted a grown man for an heir. Nor did the Romans stint when it came to providing their foster-relations with individualized kinship terms, all, like the English word *foster*, having some etymological connection with *feeding* and being *fed*: a foster-mother was a *nūtrix, nūtricis* (the basis of English *nurse* and *nutritious*), a foster-father a *nūtricius*, a foster-sibling was a *conlacteus* or *conlactea* (literally a milk-sharer, from a combining form of *cum* [with, together] and *lac, lactis* [milk]), and a foster-child was an *alumnus* or *alumna* (from the root underlying the verb *alere* [to feed, nourish], whence also English *alimentary*).

Alumnus and *alumna* are, of course, more familiar to us today in their later Latin sense of "(sometime) student," i.e., one whose intellect is nourished (by one's *alma māter*, i.e., one's nourishing mother). But then, speakers of English have always enjoyed playing fast and loose with kinship terminology when confronted with a promising opportunity for metaphor, especially if it doesn't tweak somebody too close to home: "father" and "mother" are fairly sacrosanct, being used chiefly in the solemn context of religion or government – Mother Superior, Father of his country – when used in other than their literal meanings. "Brother" and "sister" are a little more flexible – brothers and sisters can not only be members of religious orders but may belong to college fraternities and sororities or to even larger groups proclaiming the power of sisterhood or the brotherhood of man.

It is "uncle," "aunt," and "cousin" who do the bulk of the linguistic boon-work. If you've *gone to visit your uncle*, this can mean either that you've deserted your wife shortly after marrying her or else that you've simply gone to visit the W.C. – a woman would have said that she had gone to see her aunt in the latter circumstance. In Cockney rhyming slang, your bed is your *Uncle Ned*, bread is your *Uncle Fred*, and silly is *Uncle Willie. Uncle Sam* wants you to enlist in the armed forces and to pay your taxes, while a *Dutch uncle* asks neither what he can do for you nor what you can do for him (other than go out for a *Dutch treat*, such expressions as *Dutch uncle, Dutch treat, Dutch courage*, and the *dutchman* that the carpenter uses as a shim all coming from the prolonged arm-wrestle between the English and the Dutch, beginning in the seventeenth century, the winner to beat the other out of control of a lucrative maritime trade, at least for a while, and the loser to be subject to linguistic ignominy in the other's language). *Saying uncle* as an ad-mission of defeat is probably a spin-off of the ambiguously honorific use in English of both "uncle" and "aunt," which are still used in the American Southeast by whites toward their black elders, just as children in other parts of the U.S. are encouraged to call their parents' (usually childless) friends "Uncle Ralph" and "Auntie Jane" – "aunt" used to be a euphemism for prostitute, while in Russell Hoban's mythic *Riddley Walker*, Aunty is simply Death.

And as for cousins, they come in a variety of flavors: King Henry IV instituted the practice of referring to Peers of the Realm as "cousins" (as, indeed, many of them literally were), and the sense of cousin as one of the family (though definitely second-class in comparison with "real" family) is still with us – Americans speak of their "Canadian cousins" when the latter grant amnesty to draft resisters or complain about acid rain, but metamorphose these same people into "Canadian brothers and sisters" when it's a question of working out a deal on hydroelectric power or a collective nose-thumb at the commie boycotters of the Summer Olympics. Plus there are the *country, poor,* and *kissing* varieties of cousin, the last being variously understood as "people who, if they are related to each other at all, are so distantly related that they are allowed to kiss each other without anybody's worrying about incest taboos" and "kin who are right on the fringe of promiscuous fooling around with the social order," an ambiguity reflected in the variation in American state law which has some states allowing marriage with one's first cousin and others not – Massachusetts only recently repealed a law prohibiting a woman from marrying her ex-father-in-law (while leaving on the books a law prohibiting a man from marrying his ex-mother-in-law).

Why kinship systems, like the languages that express their workings, are apparently inherently subject to change if they are to survive is a mystery. And it would be smug to say that most people aren't aware of these changes: not everybody may be keeping track of the increasing numbers of folks who think it's O.K. to use *which* for *that* (as in "The river which runs by my house is smelly" which many an old curmudgeon might insist should be "The river that runs by my house is smelly" or "The river, which runs by my house, is smelly"), but Miss Manners is rightly prominent in contemporary America's daily newspapers as she deals with such questions as what to say when introduced to a gay couple ("How do you do?" "How do you do?") or how to refer to the man or woman with whom your daughter is currently romantically involved ("This is John/Jane, and this is my daughter Suzie" or the like) and how to deal with the sleeping arrangements when the kin and quasi-kin come home to roost, problems with which the Romans, with all their elaborate kinship structure, seem to have become off-handed at some point, allowing their kids to go off and become speakers of the various languages of Romance with not much more than a "What would your mother say?"

B

IS FOR *BELLICOSE, BELLIGERENT,* AND
the *-bell-* of *rebellion,* all ultimately from Latin *bellum*
(war). Latin *rebellāre* originally meant "to engage in renewed warfare" and referred specifically to the annoying
slap-and-tickle routines in which people indulged after suitable periods of rest, recuperation, refreshment, and general
regrouping when it turned out that their hearts and minds
had not in fact been won by their Roman conquerors, public proclamations to the contrary notwithstanding. The Roman attitude toward uprisings by the disgruntled denizens
of "secure hamlets" is suggested by another use of the word
rebellāre, namely to signify the renewed outbreak of a disease, whether native or brought back from the latest front.

   Revel is an Old French offspring of Latin *rebellāre.* A
revel is traditionally a boisterous get-together, as often as not
involving the participants' getting loaded and having a
grand old time tearing the place apart. It is just this sort of
activity, traditional on the Feast of the Epiphany (Twelfth
Night), that Shakespeare's Sir Toby Belch has in mind when
he says to Malvolio, "Dost thou think, because thou art
virtuous, there shall be no more cakes and ale?" The
"cakes" of "cakes and ale" fame were presumably the bean
cakes customarily consumed at Twelfth Night revels: a cake
would be baked with a bean hidden inside, and if you got
served the piece of cake with the bean inside, you got to be
the Bean King for what it was worth – if nothing else, first
dibs on the liquid refreshments and the Alka-Seltzer. "Beer
and skittles" seem to have replaced "cakes and ale" as the
common linguistic combo for good times, "skittles" being a
quite inedible form of nine pins.

   Bellum – whence *bellicose* (from *bellicōsus* [warlike, fond
of warfare]), *belligerent* (from *bell-* plus *gerens, gerentis*
[war-waging]), and *Bellōna* (the Roman goddess of war who

lent her name to the club at which all the unpleasantness transpired in Dorothy Sayers's *Unpleasantness at the Bellona Club*) – is derived from Old Latin *duellum* (whence English *duel*), the sound change from *dw* to *b* being the same as in *duonus* to *bonus* (good, a modern-day *bonus* being a good thing) and **dwi-peds*, **dwi-pedis* to *bipes, bipedis* (two-footed), **dwi-* being the Proto-Latin form of the prefix *duo* (two) and **ped-* being the contemporaneous form for foot.

This is not to lead up to saying that Latin *duellum/bellum* comes from the word for "two," though phonetic shape and semantic content certainly tempt one to think that it should. (Indeed, there was unusual agreement among the community of Latin-speaking etymologists over the centuries that *duellum* did in fact come from the word for "two," but etymologists aren't always right – even if they agree that they are.) The fact is that the ordinary everyday words for "war" in the Latin, Greek, Celtic, and Germanic branches of the Indo-European family are all from different roots, the Latin and Greek ones being of obscure origin, all of which suggests that the original Indo-Europeans simply didn't have a single word for "war" as their offspring (and their neighbors) came to know it, i.e., as the organized and continued armed conflict between two distinct political communities. It has been suggested that war as we know it was impossible until there was such a thing as sides, i.e., a degree of political organization in the societies to which the combatants belonged. This seems plausible enough and is certainly not contradicted by the fact that the standard Latin word for "fight" – which does not have cognates in the other Indo-European languages – comes from the word for "fist" or "punch" – *pugnus*, whence English *pugnacious, pugilist, pounce, puncture,* and *expunge.*

The English word *war* represents a Middle English borrowing of Norman French *werre*, which in turn seems to have come from a Germanic root meaning "discord, confusion." The same root yields Standard French *guerre* and Spanish *guerra* (whence *guerrilla*), the initial *gu-* of the Romance languages being a fairly reliable tip-off that we're dealing with a borrowing of a Germanic form with an initial w-: compare French *Guillaume* (William), Italian *guarda* (ward, as in "watch and ward"), and such doublets as *guarantee* and *warrantee*. It has been suggested that the speakers of Late Latin borrowed *guerra* from Germanic in order to have something with which to replace *bellum* (which was felt to look too much like *bellus, bella, bellum* [beautiful], and so might confuse people into thinking that war was a lovely thing), but this seems pretty unlikely. Far more plausible is the notion that the Latin legions borrowed the term from their latest slam-dance partners, the invading Germanic tribes, as the English were later to borrow *war* from the Normans under similar circumstances.

The Romans went through several stages of warfare in their rise to and fall from supremacy in Europe and the Mediterranean. Initially, it was the Latini versus the neighboring Italic tribes, a period lasting at least from the legendary founding of the Roman republic in 509 B.C., to the third century B.C. or thereabouts. This was followed by the Punic Wars, in which Rome and Carthage, whose respective territorial hegemonies collided in Sicily, slugged it out for control of the Mediterranean trade. As a consequence of the second Punic War, the Romans also became embroiled in a civil war in Greece, the upshot being that what started out as "helping" one side against the other wound up with the "helpers" in control of the whole ball of wax, a scenario still popular today, at least among the heavy rollers.

A third phase in Rome's military life might be called "wars of consolidation," starting with the war against the Numidian king Iugurtha, continuing with the Social War – wars fought between the Romans and their allies on the Italic Peninsula who wanted something closer to full citizenship for their military services, *sociī* (whence *social* and *society*), meaning "allies, army buddies" – and ending with the civil wars of the first century B.C., the last of which placed Augustus Caesar on the throne as emperor. A fourth phase might be termed "wars of imperial expansion," a period that overlapped somewhat with phase three, since Julius Caesar's expansionary campaigns against Gaul and Britain came between two fits of civil war. The last major war of Roman expansion was Trajan's conquest of Dacia (modern-day Rumania). The fifth – and final – stage, which spanned the years from approximately 200 A.D. to the bitter end, might as well be called "wars of imperial attrition," during which the outlying provinces slipped one by one from Roman control and Rome itself was finally bagged by the unfriendly Odoacer in the fifth century.

With each different period of Roman war-mongering came a different combination of tactics and strategy. The common form of battle array all around the Mediterranean in the early days of organized hostility seems to have been some form of the Greek phalanx – a square of spearmen spaced so closely that their shields locked, with spears of the second through fifth ranks projecting forward from the front line, the standard Greek spear at the time of the Persian Wars being apparently some twenty-one feet long. Each phalanx was made up of heavy infantry with armor (the hoplites), augmented by bands of light-armed troops (the peltasts), whose job it was to provide harrying action on the wings. Cavalry was used sparingly by the Greeks and then only as a response to the use of mounted archers by the Persians. The Greeks did have navies, the richer citizens being obliged by law to outfit and staff a warship each when it came time to gear up for yet another war; but, apart from outsailing or ramming their adversaries, the Greeks seem to have regarded naval battles as occasions on which parties of marines fought enemy marines hand to hand on the deck of somebody's boat. With minor local variations, more or less everyone worth fighting wars with in the Mediterranean community fought wars in this way until about 200 B.C.

The Romans, after getting knocked about a bit, improved on the phalanx by turning it into the legion. (*Legion* comes from Latin *legiō*, which is itself from a root meaning "gather, choose," though what being in the army had to do with choice is not clear.) A legion was made up of ten *cohorts*, each cohort being made up of three *maniples*, and each maniple being made up of two *centuries*. *Cohors, cohortis* originally meant "farmyard, enclosure in which farm animals are kept" and was somewhat jocularly applied first to a military encampment and then to the soldiers enclosed therein; a *manipulus* was literally a handful – from *manus* (hand) – and a *centuria* was, at least nominally, a group of a hundred soldiers. The generic term for soldier, while we're at it, was *mīles, mīlitis* – whence *military, militia*, and the like. The term is possibly of Etruscan origin, which is to say that nobody really knows where it came from. A regular soldier was either a *pedes, peditis* (foot-soldier, infantryman) or an *eques, equitis* (horseman, member of the cavalry). Indeed, the expression *equitēs peditēsque* (cavalry and infantry) was used to designate the whole body of Roman citizens since, foreign auxiliaries excepted, to be a Roman soldier you had to be a Roman citizen.

What was overwhelming about the Roman legion was not the amount of Latin vocabulary that the enemy had to learn in order to tell who was what, though this was formidable enough, but the fact that the Roman legionnaires were deployed in a new and improved way, at least from the point of view of military strategy. In fact, the legion was deployed in a number of new and improved ways at various times and in various terrains, generally in three lines of cohorts, either staggered checkerboard fashion or with the first and second lines so staggered with the third more tightly packed (with the more experienced veterans), all of which allowed a greater mobility than the solidly packed ranks and files of the rectilinear phalanx. (The *rank* of military *rank* or labor's *rank and file* comes through Old French from a Germanic word meaning "circle, ring," from an Indo-European root meaning "bend," and originally referred to a left-to-right line of soldiers. *File* comes through Old French from Latin *fīlum* [thread] and originally referred to a front-to-back line of soldiers.)

The rear guard of the Roman legion had not only the older and wiser among its ranks to help hold the line but the troops called *uēlitēs* or "fast guys" (from *uēlox* [speedy] whence *velocity*) as well. These latter were the successors to the Greek peltasts and were generally assigned to the wings, as were the cavalry and whatever auxiliaries the Romans had managed to graft onto the legion. The auxiliaries – literally "helpers" – were native troops recruited from the local population whose knowledge of local fighting methods was very handy when the Romans came, as they increasingly did, to military dealings with exotic foes and tactics. In this form, the legion proved extremely versatile in comparison to the phalanx, for whereas the latter was only really good on a nice, level plain, the legion could be deployed to exploit terrain unsuitable for conventional battle. Another significant improvement of the legion over the phalanx was that the Roman soldier in cohort formation had three feet of elbow room on either side, while the phalanx, being tighter, lacked maneuverability and the space for hand-to-hand fighting, and had to rely instead on the initial shock of collision. Moreover, while a tightly packed phalanx could easily be broken up into confusion if borne down upon by an elephant or a scythe-bearing chariot, the Roman cohort had plenty of room to get out of the way.

The Romans have been justly praised for their ability to adapt to new types of warfare. Besides enlisting auxiliaries whose tactics were similar to the enemy's, Rome was quick to learn from Carthage the value of a true naval force: Carthaginian ships captured early in the second Punic War were used as models for a brand-new Roman navy, the Roman ships prior to this time having been little more than commercial vessels with a few marines posted to them. And bizarre though Hannibal's elephants must have seemed when the Romans first encountered them in battle, by the end of the second Punic War the Romans had managed to acquire a few of their own. Moreover, much of what the Roman army learned about artillery – *tormenta*, as they called it – was as a result of having seen it used against them during their siege of Syracuse, whose chief consultant engineer on such matters was none other than Archimedes of "Eureka!" fame and the father of the Archimidean screw.

That the Roman soldier who slew Archimedes in a fit of pique when the city finally fell should have been put to death by his commander is the more comprehensible when one considers how valuable the great engineer would have been to the winners. (If an overzealous infantryman had blown away Wernher Von Braun in 1945, it is doubtful that any congratulations would have come down the chain of command.) Engineers were in fact the single greatest feature of the Roman army, making the best use of the technology of the day. Thanks to Caesar's *Gallic War* (*Commentarii*), we know something of the engineering which went into the design of the Roman army camp, a new one of which was built at the end of every day's march between fortified towns. Surrounded by a ditch and an earth rampart, with branches and stakes facing outward and a palisade wall, the Roman *castra* – the *-caster/-chester* of such English place names as *Lancaster* and *Dorchester* – was very difficult to take by storm and almost impossible to take by surprise. On the march, the army found rivers no great obstacle: their engineers could and did build serviceable bridges on short notice. Siege operations brought into play the engineers' skills as towers on wheels were built, under cover of which a wall could be attacked. The artillery ranged from the *catapulta, ballista,* and *scorpiō,* which threw heavy spears and light stones, to the *onager,* which threw heavy rocks and was so called for its kick when fired, *ónagros* being Greek for wild donkey. (*Catapulta, ballista,* and *scorpiō* are also borrowings from Greek, attesting to the source of much of Rome's knowledge of such matters.) Furthermore, once the enemy was subdued, Roman engineers saw to the building of roads that made possible the rapid deployment of troops in the likely event of rebellion in the provinces or trouble at the borders. Some of these roads survive to this day – Watling Street in Britain and the Via Appia Antica in Italy, to mention only two.

It is no surprise that the author of one of the first Roman books on tactics – the *Stratagems*– should also have written another book called *Aqueducts:* Sextus Julius Frontinus, who was provincial governor of Britain around 75 A.D. (He was largely responsible for subjugating the warlike Silures of Wales and was succeeded by the equally able Agricola, Tacitus's father-in-law.) By 78 A.D., Frontinus was serving as commissioner of aqueducts for the city of Rome. A century before him, Marcus Agrippa, who had already distinguished himself in the civil wars as a naval commander, oversaw the construction of the Julian aqueduct, running twelve miles into Rome from the southeast. The ideal commander, as Polybius pointed out in his history of the Punic Wars, was a general who not only understood what the troops were capable of doing on what sort of terrain, but also had a scientific education, preferably in geometry and astronomy. Veterans might scoff at a military victory that "smelled of the lamp," i.e., that had been planned out on paper, but the fact remained that Roman victories were won as much by cagey technology as by brute force.

Military historians like to make much of the use of cavalry, perhaps because the cavalry charge is such an exhilarating tableau to the imagination. Real life is, of course, another story – the word from which *cavalry* ultimately derives, Latin *caballus*, originally meant "nag," though the Roman cavalry itself, the *equitēs*, took their name from the more respectable name for horse, *equus;* they could afford to, since each member of the Roman cavalry was obliged to supply his own horse at his own expense and had to be pretty well-heeled in order to be able to do so. In any event, it is with regret that we must note that the mounted soldier, Roman or other, has rarely if ever decided a battle. The Romans made use of the cavalry in much the same way as they employed the *uēlitēs:* as a means of fast harrying on the wings, and ensuring the possibility of encircling the foe and striking from the rear. The shock charge was not possible until the introduction of the stirrup, unknown in Europe until the fifth century A.D., and even then its value was far greater psychologically than physically. (A former U.S. cavalryman informs us that horses, while they can be ridden straight at the enemy if the rider is good enough, will balk at actually riding down infantrymen, let alone being shot to horseburger by the enemy.) The mounted soldier is, in fact, quite vulnerable, his main defense being the speed with which he can escape. The horsemen of antiquity were useful as scouts and messengers between battles, but in the battles themselves, they were essentially frosting on the cake. Hannibal's cavalry was primarily Numidian, and in the centuries that followed, the Romans continued to use Numidian auxiliaries in the same way.

A great deal of the American mystique concerning the cavalry arose from tactics borrowed from the Plains Indians, who had themselves been accustomed to horses for only a few generations by the mid-1880's. Custer's last stand is a classic example of how not to use the cavalry: to dismount and dig in when surrounded by vastly superior numbers of mounted warriors is to invite the enemy to cut you to pieces, which is precisely what happened. (It is only fair to say that Custer graduated near the bottom of his class at West Point.) Horses are helpful, to be sure, when there's lots of baggage to haul from bivouac to bivouac, but even here a mule is probably a better bet: the mule is more sure-footed on steep hills because its eyesight is better – a horse can't focus on its own feet – and indeed many a mule rendered noble service lugging artillery and shells up to hilltops during the campaign in the Alps in World War II.

The last American cavalry unit was disbanded at the outbreak of that war, and its soldiers were reassigned elsewhere. The "airborne cavalry" of the Vietnam War attests to the survival of the unit in name only. Actually, combat cavalry had long since been rendered obsolete by the proliferation of the machine gun, though well before World War I the way had been pointed by such disasterous blunders as the charge of the Light Brigade at Balaclava and had been foreshadowed centuries before that when the French knights were mowed down by British longbowmen at Crécy and

Poitiers during the Hundred Years' War. Indeed, the only campaign in which cavalry may have made any significant difference was that of the Spanish conquest of Mexico: while Bartolomé de las Casas's contemporary account probably overstates the case – ". . . in one hour's time, a single horseman could spear 2,000 Indians" – Cortés's biographer, Francisco López de Gómara, was probably right enough when he said that "they were astonished and frightened by the horses, whose great mouths seemed about to swallow them, and also by the speed with which the horses overtook them, although the Indians were themselves swift runners. Moreover, since they had never before seen a horse, the first one that attacked them terrified them, even though it was alone; and when it was joined by many more, they could not stand against the shock and strength and fury of their charge. They thought that man and horse were one."

As far as the Romans were concerned, cavalry was just part of the military mix. It is a strategic truism that excessive reliance on one type of soldier lays you open to the exploitation of that one type's weakness, and the Romans knew this as well as anybody today. Heavy infantry packs a wallop but moves slowly and cannot be maneuvered easily once a battle is in progress. The classic battle, whether phalanx against phalanx or legion against phalanx, consisted of heavy fighting at the center plus attempts at outflanking, as with the *uēlitēs* or light-armed auxiliaries on the wings. Here the Romans excelled, though they were occasionally thrown for a loop: they suffered at least one major military disaster at Hannibal's hands (at Cannae) by being enticed forward by a center that deliberately gave only token opposition, whereupon Hannibal's wings encircled the Romans and slaughtered them. (It was in the third stage of battle, the mop-up, that Hannibal's Numidian horsemen could work to deadly effect, for by then the Roman line was in total disarray, and the Numidians had the easy task of cutting down individuals rather than a massed legion.)

This was, however, the exception rather than the rule, and trickery had more to do with the outcome than force:

Hannibal's other major victory over the Romans (at Lake Trasimene) was accomplished by getting the Roman infantry into an indefensible position (between a cliff and the water) and charging down onto them from positions concealed by a heavy fog. Frontinus's *Stratagems* cites numerous examples of How to Outwit Your Enemies, including snappy comebacks for when your foe has holed himself up in his citadel, says he has enough creature comforts to last him ten years, and gives you the raspberry, as the Lusitanians did when besieged by Tiberius Gracchus. (Gracchus – the son-in-law of Scipio Africanus – calmly responded that he would get them on the eleventh year, which so terrified the Lusitanians that they gave up immediately.) Vergil contrasts the honesty of Aeneas with the sneaky underhandedness of Odysseus, but Frontinus and others in the business of military survival did not underestimate the value of bamboozling the foe by such devices as dummies dressed up to look like soldiers, campfires left burning while the enemy secretly hightails it by night, false tunnels to give the besieged the impression that their walls are being undermined, spies sent as spurious "deserters" to gain entry to the opposing camp, and so on.

Because the Roman commanders held military posts as part of the regular career of public men in civilian life, they tended to bring to the job a level of education, expertise, and general noblesse oblige rarely found in the ranks of any other army, and it is no coincidence that the Scipios were largely responsible over several generations not only for the defeat of Carthage but for the introduction of Greek literature to Rome. A capable general was vastly helped, however, by the high degree of organization within the army. The noncommissioned officers – the *centuriōnēs*, literally "commanders of a hundred," and their minions, the *decuriōnēs*, literally "commanders of ten" – were elected by the troops and in turn chose the *optiōnēs* – the "chosen" ones – who functioned more or less like today's quartermasters: the *optiōnēs* handled administrative matters for the *decuriōnēs* and *centuriōnēs*. In addition, each legion had attached to it six military tribunes who were voted in by the citizens of Rome as part of the general election process. The function of the military tribunes was initially similar to that of the civilian tribunes, namely, to act as a plebeian advocate in a force whose leaders were largely patricians. In short, the Roman commander presided over an army that allowed for an effective chain of command that was at the same time firmly rooted in the civilian state: it may well be that no society in history has taken such precautions as the Romans did to safeguard the civil rights of its soldiers while maintaining a rigorous sense of discipline, all of which made the Roman legion formidable beyond its numbers.

So why, one might ask, did the Roman empire eventually fall apart if the army was as versatile, well-organized, technologically adept, and well-commanded as any in Europe in its day? One fly in the ointment was the discovery, early in the days of the empire, that emperors could be made elsewhere than at Rome – the year 69 A.D. saw no fewer than four emperors, three of them with backing from the boonies: Nero was toppled by Galba at the head of troops from Spain; Galba's successor, Otho, was overthrown by Vitellius with the backing of the army in Germany; and Vitellius was in turn succeeded by Vespasian, who had been commanding a force in the Near East. Although the army played little part in the succession of the Flavians, and none in the careful series of adoptions of rightful heirs by the first four of the so-called "five good emperors" – Nerva who adopted Trajan who adopted Hadrian who adopted Antoninus Pius who adopted Marcus Aurelius who was so foolish as to sire the barbaric Commodus who eventually picked a fight with someone bigger than himself and ended his reign in an exhibition punch-out – a pattern had already been established that was easy enough to follow after the death of Commodus: provincial armies came to be almost as much involved with putting their man on the throne as they were with protecting the frontiers.

A more insidious source of decay was simply that the empire and its army grew too big. In the old days, when it was merely a question of the citizens of Rome protecting their own and beating up a bit on their neighbors during the slow part of the agricultural year, all went reasonably well. When it became a question of grabbing far-flung territories with the aid of noncitizens, things went somewhat less well, at least from the point of view of the citizen-soldier who might well not get to make it home in time for the planting or harvest. But when the provincials began to make a regular practice of hassling the army of occupation and that army had come to have fewer and fewer "citizens" with a vested interest in keeping the peace, it was basically the beginning of the end.

Bb

27

C

IS FOR *CRANIUM, CAPITAL,* AND *CAP-
itol,* the first of these having been borrowed into Latin from
Greek. *Cranium* is related to Latin *cornū* (horn), the relation between head and horn being an intuitively obvious
one to any cattle-raising society. From *cornū* the French get
cornet, as in *cornet à glace* (ice cream cone), while we get
cornet – the musical possibilities of horns have been recognized from time immemorial – and both the sort of *corn*
that characterizes the unicorn and the more pedestrian variety that grows on your foot. (The kind of *corn* that grows
in a field springs from a different Indo-European root, the
same one that gives us *kernel, grain,* the *-gran-* of *pome-
granate,* and the *gren-* of *hand grenade.*) A more direct steal
from Latin is *cornucopia* (horn of plenty). In Roman military parlance, *cornua* (horns) were the wings of battle array,
a likely enough image since the lighter-armed and more
mobile wings tended to stretch thin in an attempt to out-
flank and envelop the enemy. One type of brass instrument
now used mostly for jazz work is the *Flügelhorn* – from
German meaning "wing-horn": originally a battle trumpet,
it was used for signaling between the wings – *Flügeln* (cf.
fliegen [to fly]) – and the massed infantry at the center.

Cranium refers, of course, to the skull per se as opposed
to the head as a whole. Cranial capacity is a favorite index
in anthropological measurement and has been used (and
misused) for over a century, a popular method of calcula-
tion being to fill the empty skull with lead shot. A pioneer
in this field was Pierre Paul Broca (1824–1880), after whom
*Broca's aphasia, Broca's area, Broca's center, Broca's convo-
lution, Broca's fissure, Broca's formula, Broca's plane, Bro-
ca's pouch,* and *Broca's space* are all named. Having co-
founded the Anthropological Society of Paris in 1859,

Broca shortly found himself embroiled in a controversy over the relation of cranium size and brain weight to intelligence. Starting with the preconception that whites were superior to blacks and Asians, men to women, and French to other Europeans (and especially Germans), Broca adduced his painstaking and copious measurements of cranial capacity and cerebral mass to back up his assumptions.

Undismayed by actual measurements of Alaskans and convicted criminals, both of whom yielded bigger brain sizes than comparable measurements of bourgeois Parisians, Broca managed to reconcile the facts with his prejudices through the use of tortuous logic. When confronted with measurements of the denizens of a city morgue close to the Seine, Broca reasoned that the high cranial capacities, relative to those of respectable folks, were indicative of (a) a larger than usual number of drowned people who (b) may largely have been suicides, many of whom were probably (c) insane and, as Broca already knew, (d) insane people, like criminals, often had larger-than-usual brains.

A less dedicated empiricist might have been led to fudge the data – archaeologists refer to this as "salting the dig" – or to become less concerned about the accuracy of measurement. Indeed, this is what happened fifty years later in the laboratory of a Virginia doctor named Robert Bennett Bean. Bean published a study in 1907 showing that, according to his measurements, the relative size of the front and back sections of the corpus callosum (the fibrous area between the left and right cerebral hemispheres) was different for blacks and whites. Since it was generally accepted at the time that most of the intellect was centered in the front of the brain while the sensory-motor functions rode in the back, Bean's data – which showed a higher ratio of front-end (*genu*) to back-end (*splenium*) for whites than for blacks – were interpreted as evidence of the intellectual inferiority of blacks. Bean wrote an editorial that same year for *American Medicine* in which he concluded that black people were not amenable to higher education and should be denied the right to vote.

Bean's old teacher at Johns Hopkins, Franklin P. Mall,

smelled a rat, however, and in attempting to replicate Bean's study (using some of the original subjects) found that Bean's measurements were simply wrong: the spread of data from the eighteen brains that Mall used overlapped entirely, with no statistically meaningful difference between white or black or, for that matter, male or female. Mall's results were published in 1909 – but, of course, by this time the damage had been done and refutation could only partly undermine a conclusion that most white physicians undoubtedly considered a capital one.

Capital in all its various senses derives from Latin *caput, capitis* (head), cognate with English *head*. A chapter treating all of the *caput* derivatives in English would be an achievement – indeed, a *chef d'oeuvre* – but our authorial principles forbid our doing the publisher a mischief by taking up too much paper, so a modest flex of the literary biceps will have to do as we take our caps off to the principals in a sort of linguistic "Hail to the Chief." *Chapter, achievement, mischief, chef,* and *chief* all come to us kindness of the French – as, incidentally, does *kerchief* – from Latin *caput, capitis.* (*Principle* and *principal* – and *prince* – also come through French, from Latin *princeps* [foremost, literally "first head"], the *prin-* part being from *prīmus* [first] and the *-ceps* part being a combinative form of *caput.*) Starting with the most recent borrowing: a *chef d'oeuvre* is a "crowning achievement," literally, the "head of (one's) work" – an *hors d'oeuvre* is a little something outside of the work performed by a *chef de cuisine* (head of the kitchen). To *achieve* was originally to "bring to a head," i.e., to a successful conclusion; *mischief* was a "bad head" for things to be brought to, the *mis-* being not the Greek negative prefix found in *misanthrope* and *misogynist* but, rather, a truncation of Latin *minus* (less); and a *kerchief* was originally a *couvre-chief* (covering for the head) – a *neckerchief* is something designed to cover a French head but to be worn around an English neck, while a *handkerchief* is something designed to cover a French head and be held in an English hand but is actually used to blow your nose.

Chief was "head" in Old French where it got used in the

sorts of ways that we now use head in English, namely, to designate, first and foremost, the noggin or old bean, and, secondarily, anything or anyone in a position of prime importance. A *chieftain* was the head of the clan, much as the *captain* – same word – was the head of the troops. (Compare German *Hauptmann* [captain], literally "head man.") A *corporal* – originally *caporal* – was the head of some of the troops, while a *cadet* was literally the "junior head" of the family, i.e., the second son whom the Gascon French with pretensions to noblesse oblige sent off to do military service at the Court in Paris (while his older brother got to inherit the farm and his younger brother got to join the clergy). *Cadet* (in its later sense of military trainee) underlies both *caddie* (of the golf variety) and *cad* (of the ne'er-do-well persuasion, a *cad* being originally an abbreviation of *cadet/caddie* with the sense of "assistant" and later being used in university parlance to designate a member of the local community who might run errands for the students – a low-born gofer, hence, a disreputable person). There is a moral in here, of course, redolent of noble sentiment and the sniff of capital letters: Never Be A Second Son If You Can Help It.

Capital and its younger sibling *chapter* come from Latin *capitālis* (of or pertaining to the head), the latter in the sense of "(written) material under the same heading." *Capital* in its fiscal sense is a great deal older than Marx: the Romans, who referred to a person's social persona as his *caput* (much as Americans of the 1960's might have referred to a nice guy as a "good head"), termed *capitālia* those items of property that attached to his or her legal status. *Capital punishment* is a literal rendering of *poena capitis*, which in Roman times meant "top-of-the-line punishment" and was just as likely to spell banishment as death.

Considering the number and variety of ways in which people have killed each other by judicial license down through the ages, it is a little surprising that in almost all of them the proximate cause of death is the same: asphyxiation, i.e., brain death due to oxygen deprivation. This is so whether the condemned is drowned, hanged, or strangled (loss of oxygen to the lungs), shot through the heart (interruption of circulation), beheaded (both of the above), burned (smoke inhalation where the oxygen ought to be), electrocuted or injected with a lethal drug (paralysis of the nervous system controlling respiration), or forced to drink hemlock (ditto). Probably *decapitation* – beheading – is the most merciful of the lot, if the queasy stomachs of the observers are disregarded: certainly it was the mode of highest status in Europe at the time Dr. Joseph-Ignace Guillotin invented his "infernal machine." While the ostensible motive was to make French executions more humanitarian, the guillotine democratized them as well. (It was, ironically, that arch-Democrat Thomas Jefferson who has provided the most cogent argument against judicial murder: "I shall oppose the penalty of death," he wrote, "until the infallibility of human judgment has been demonstrated to me.") Until the middle of the eighteenth century, the distance between England's Tower Green (where the rich and famous were beheaded) and Tyburn (at the then edge of town where the hangman Thomas Derick – whence *derrick* – was employed to dispatch the poor and nonfamous) was as much social as physical.

No death-row movie scene would be complete without the *chaplain*, who was originally simply the cleric attached to a *chapel* – *chapel*, like *chaperone* and *cape*, coming through French from Late Latin *cappa* (hooded cape). *Chapel* gets its name from the shrine in which the cape of Saint Martin of Tours was preserved, while a *chaperone*, the protector of a maiden's virtue, was originally, like *cappa*, the protector of one's head from the elements. And, in case you were wondering, no: the *-head* of *maidenhead* is not etymologically related to the *head* on your shoulders but is, rather, a variant of the *-hood* of *statehood*, *womanhood*, and *knighthood* (as in "when knighthood was in flower and maidens lost their heads") which is in turn unrelated to either the *hood* of "Little Red Ridinghood" (a straight translation of *"Le Petit chaperon rouge"*) or the *hood* that abbreviates the word *hoodlum*. The origin of this latter word is obscure indeed, though several interesting possibilities have been suggested: first, that *hood* comes from Old English *hōd* (covering for the head, whence the hood of a parka or car), the idea being that the original hoodlums wore hoods so that their victims couldn't identify them later. The word *"hat"* is related to the hood that covers your head, though "head" is not.

Another possibility is that *hoodlum* is from a German dialect in which *hodalum* means "ragamuffin," or, as Marx might have said, "member of the *Lumpenproletariat*," *Lumpen* being "rags to be used and then thrown away" (like Yiddish *shmatte*). By far the most ingenious explanation of *hoodlum*'s origin, though, is the suggestion that the word is a corruption of *noodlum*, itself underworld backwards-cant for *Muldoon*, the head of a turn-of-the-century Irish-American gang that specialized in beating up Chinese in San Francisco. If this sounds a bit far-fetched, it is perhaps no more so than the certain derivation of *loaf* in the sense of head or the *raspberry* in the sense of Bronx cheer from Cockney rhyming slang: your wife is your *trouble and strife*, your old man is your *pot and pan*, your head is your *loaf of bread*, and a flatus is a *raspberry tart*, all reducible to their first (nonrhyming) elements – your wife is your *trouble*, your old man is your *pot*, your head is your *loaf*, and probably the less said about *razzing* in polite company the better.

Other respectable Latinate *head/hood* words include *Capuchin, cap, capot,* and *capitol*. The *Capuchins* were so called because of the distinctive pointed hoods of their monks' robes, notwithstanding the medieval adage *"Cucullus non facit monachum"* ("The cowl doesn't make the monk"). *Cap* (hat) is straight from Late Latin *cappa* (and is not to be confused with the *cap* of *cap-à-pie* [head to foot], *cap* here being Latin *caput, capitis* [head] filtered through Old Provençal and French and *pie* being, ultimately, *pēs, pedis* [foot]). *Cappa* also appears (in mufti) in the words *escape* and *képi*. To *escape* was originally to take off one's cloak, the idea being that a cloak hinders one's freedom of movement (especially when one's captors are holding onto it). A *képi* is the flat-topped military hat worn by members of the uniformed French police and, formerly, of the French Foreign Legion. *Képi* was borrowed into French from Swiss German in which the word, in slightly different form, is the diminutive of German *Kappe* (cap, from Old High German *Kappa* [cloak], a borrowing of Late Latin *cappa*).

A *capot* is a sweep at the game of piquet, a two-player card game whose name translates literally as "little sting." Just what the connection is between *capot* (sweep) and *capot* (hood) is not clear, though it probably has to do with pulling the wool over one's opponent's eyes – *hoodwinking. Capot* in its card-playing sense underlies German *kaput* (finished, done for). A variant of *capot* – *capote* – is a long, usually hooded, coat which, in French, rears its head in the expression *capote anglaise* (condom, literally "English cloak") to which the English response seems to have been to make snide remarks about the "French disease" while dubbing the contraceptive diaphragm the *Dutch cap.*

Capitol comes from Latin *Capitōlium*, the term used originally to designate both the Capitoline Hill and the temple, dedicated to Jupiter, Juno, and Minerva by King Tarquin in the first year of his rule, that crowned its summit. (The neighboring Quirinal Hill, which had formerly been the site of such a temple, was sometimes referred to as the *uetus Capitōlium* [old Capitol].) *Capitōlīnus* was an epithet of Jupiter the Greatest and Best (*Iuppiter Optimus Maximus*, or *O.M.* for short – the same *O.M.* that appears on bottles of Benedictine, *D.O.M.* standing for *Deō Optimō Maximō* [to God, the Greatest and Best]). Since the Capitoline Hill was used for a variety of state functions, it is not surprising that many state houses built during the Greek Revival period in America were called *Capitols* as well, especially so the national seat of legislature in Washington, D.C.

Lowercase *d.c.*, as in the musical notation *d.c. al fine*

(take it from the top and play through to the end), is short for Italian *da capo*. *Capo*, from Latin *caput*, is sometimes used in the sense of head (cranium), as in *capogiro* (dizziness, a *giro* being a turn, gyration), but more often *capo* has the sense of head (chief), as in *capobanda* (bandleader), *capocaccia* (master of the hounds), *capofabrica* (foreman), and *capofamiglia* (head of the family). The more commonly used word for head (cranium) in Italian is *testa*, which comes from Latin *testa*. *Testa* originally meant "shell, carapace," and it is in essentially this sense that English has borrowed *testa* (hard outer covering of a seed) and, in slightly abbreviated form, *test* (hard outer covering of an insect). The other variety of English *test* also comes, somewhat more circuitously, from *testa*. *Testa* in its original sense also formed the basis of Latin *testūdō*, *testūdinis* (tortoise, cf. Latinate English *testudinate* [of or pertaining to a tortoise or turtle]). *Testūdō* was later used to designate, first, a military formation in which soldiers locked their shields over their heads so as not to get pelted by the enemy while covering an advance, and, subsequently, a movable wooden shelter with a similar function.

From the sense of "shell," *testa* also came to mean clay or earthenware vessel or vase; then shard, fragment of broken pottery; and, still later, head (cranium), this last being the meaning underlying Italian *testa* and Old French *teste* – whence English *testy* (which originally meant headstrong) and Modern French *tête*, which chiefly means head (cranium), but is used in a number of extended senses as well: *faire une tête* is to make a face, *se creuser la tête* is to rack one's brains, a *casse-tête* (literally, head breaker) is a jigsaw puzzle, a *tête-à-tête* is a cozy get-together, and *tête-bêche* characterizes side-by-side postage stamps that have been printed upside-down in relation to each other. (*Tête-bêche* comes from *tête* plus *bis* [twice] plus *chevet* [head of a bed], another *caput* derivative, which turns up in English as the architectural term for the extreme east end of a church.)

Just what the connection was thought to be between an earthenware container (or shards thereof) and the human cranium is not clear, though Germans call the head a *Kopf* (cup) and Americans call it a *noggin* (whose literal meaning is "small cup") and refer to the photographic front and side views of the convict's head as *mug shots*. The suggestion that *testa* (and *Kopf*) got to mean "head" from the practice of using empty skulls as drinking vessels can pretty safely be dismissed as ghoulish fancy. The possibility that the head was thought to be as fragile as a bit of crockery is perhaps somewhat less fanciful, though still not utterly convincing.

And the other Romance languages, old and new, have little light to shed on the question: Rumanian uses *ţeasta* for cranium and *cap* for head, Old Provençal used *testa* for head, as did Old Spanish and Old Portuguese, but Modern Provençal uses *cap* for head and *testo* for forehead. Modern Portuguese uses *testa* for forehead and the *caput* derivative *cabeça* for head (cranium), reserving the French borrowing *chefe* for boss. It is, however, Modern Spanish that offers the headiest linguistic mixture: *jefe* (boss) is a borrowing of French *chef*; *testa*, which appears dialectally in the sense of head (cranium) and face, front (of something), was borrowed from Catalan or Provençal during the days in which those languages used *testa* for head; a *tiesta* is the edge of a barrel heading, while a *tiesto* is a flower pot or pot shard, no relation to *tieso* (tight, taut, stubborn), which comes from a now-lost past participle to the verb *tener* (to hold fast); *cabeza* and *cabo* – both from *caput, capitis* – top it all off, *cabeza* being the standard word for head (cranium), and *cabo* being extremity or end, as in the expression *al fin y al cabo* (after all, literally "at the end and at the end").

D

IS FOR DOCTOR, DOCTRINE, DISCI-
pline, dignified, decorum, ductile, ducal, and the *-duc-* of
education. In Latin, *dux, ducis* means "leader" and, as
such, forms the basis of the late Benito Mussolini's sobri-
quet, "*Il Duce*" (much as Hitler was called "*Der Führer*,"
the Leader), and of the English word *duke* in all of its senses
but that of "fist" (as in "Put up your dukes and fight like a
man"), which comes from Cockney rhyming slang, your
Duke of Yorks being rhyming slang for your *forks*, i.e., your
fingers. *Education* does not come, as some have suggested,
from Latin *ēdūcere* (to lead forth, as Socrates led forth the
Pythagorean relation from the mind of a slave) – this would
be *eduction* or *educement* – but rather from a related Late
Latin verb, *ēducāre*, which means "to train (an animal,
such as a bear)," all of which suggests that teachers and
school administrators who call themselves "educators" may
be doing the members of their profession – and their
charges – a disservice, however more fancy the Latinate
educator may sound to the discerning ear than the plain old
Anglo-Saxon "teacher."

The ordinary Latin word for teacher was *doctor*, the verb
"to teach" being *docēre*. *Docilis* – whence English *docile* –
was, therefore, "of teachable disposition." The verb "to
learn" was *discere*, which is related to Greek *didáskein* (from
which English *didactic* and *paradigm* are derived) but not
to the *disc-* of *discothèque*: *discothèque* is a Gallic combination of *disc* (record, from Greek *dískos* [discus]) and the
-thèque of *bibliothèque* (library, place where books are
housed, from Greek *biblío[n]* [book] plus *thḗkē* [case, con-
tainer]), *dískos* being from the Greek verb *dikeîn* (to throw,
i.e., to direct an object), and the verb, in turn, being from
the Indo-European root meaning "show, signal, sign" or the

like that underlies English *(be)token* and *teach* (and possibly *tetchy*, if this peculiar word comes from French *tache* [spot, blemish], since *tache* does come from the Germanic word that underlies *token*). This same root underlies Latin *digitus* (finger) – presumably because that was what you pointed things out with – and *dīcere* (to say) – presumably because saying is verbally pointing out or showing. *Dīcere* shows up in all sorts of English words, among them *dictate*, *edict*, *indict*, *dedicate*, *ditty*, and, believe it or not, *preach*.

Doctrine and *discipline* were originally synonyms, but through the phrase *disciplīna mīlitāris* (soldierly learning), *discipline* came to be understood specifically as the keep-your-powder-dry-and-do-as-you're-told sort of knowledge deemed appropriate to the regulars in the armed forces. (Compare *discipulus*, which originally meant "student" and later took on the particular flavors associated with the word *disciple*.) Both *docēre* (whence *doctor* and *doctrine*) and *discere* (whence *discipline*) are related to the verb *decēre*, which is attested almost exclusively in its third person singular present active form, *decet* ([it] is fitting), often in the formula *decet et opportet* (it is meet and right). *Decēre* also gives us *decent* and, with a little fiddling, *decorum*, as in Horace's dictum "*Dulce et decōrum est prō patriā morī*" – "It is a sweet and fitting thing to die for one's country," to which perhaps the most compelling response was given by General George S. Patton, Jr., who said that the important thing was rather to make the other guy die for *his* country. *Dignus est* was recognized (by, among others, Plautus) as being both equivalent and etymologically related to *decet*. *Indignation* is the reaction of one whose *dignity* has been affronted, that is, one's sense of *decency* impugned. *Dignus* also lurks in the word *condign*, as in *condign* (i.e., appropriate) *punishment*, which in these enlightened times is as likely as not to involve an attempt at some sort of rehabilitation or reeducation of the malefactor.

Roman education started in the home: Roman mothers generally saw to a child's upbringing until the child was old enough to be packed off to school or to be tutored at home.

(The Romans had two words for school, both of them borrowed: *schola* was a borrowing of Greek *scholē* – leisure time, leisure time spent in study, hence, a place in which studying happens; and *lūdus* was probably a borrowing from Etruscan and meant "pastime, game, exercise, practice," hence, "a place for practice." A *tūtor* was originally a "protector.") After the vigorous philhellenism of the Scipios and others that marked the beginning of Roman involvement in Greek affairs in the aftermath of the second Punic War, much of the tutoring and teaching of Roman youth was done by transplanted Greeks – either slaves taken in war or free-lancing freedmen. A child's basic education included learning the Twelve Tables of Roman law by heart, and preliminary instruction in arithmetic and the Greek language, in literature, grammar, and rhetoric – the last frequently by means of set pieces (*suāsōriae*) of this sort: "Resolved: that the piper who played a tune in the Phrygian mode at a sacrifice, so that the officiant went mad and threw himself off a cliff, should (should not) be prosecuted for manslaughter."

Nor was logic neglected: among the favorite teaching devices were the Horn Syllogism – You have what you have not lost; you have not lost horns; *ergo*, you have horns – and the Crocodile Problem – A crocodile, pouncing on a boy, told the hapless child's mother, "I will let him go if you tell me the truth," to which the mother replied, "You won't let go of him"; must the crocodile let go of the child? – a variant of the famous Epimenides's Paradox: " 'All Cretans are liars,' said Epimenides the Cretan." Quintilian the rhetorician gives these and other examples in his *Institutio Orationis*, the first three books of which are devoted entirely to a discussion of the education of Roman youth: benign, sensible, and quite sophisticated observations on the psychology of children, Quintilian's remarks on what is right and wrong in Roman education are of equal interest to the historian and the pedagogue, both terms being borrowings into Latin from Greek, in which a *historía* (originally "inquiry") was "knowledge, information," hence, "an account, a narrative of (past) events," and a *paidagōgós* was someone in charge of "leading" (*agōgós*) "children" (*paidía*). The Latin *paedagōgus* was a slave put in charge of a child's lessons to make sure that he did his homework and got to and from school safely, and was held answerable to the master of the household for the child's behavior.

The foregoing covers the education of middle-to-upper-middle-class Roman children. Roman girls generally got less of this than Roman boys, as they did of much else that society had to offer, generally getting married off at an early age to run the considerable risk of death in childbirth shortly thereafter. (One of Pliny's most poignant letters concerns a friend's daughter who fell sick and died just weeks before her wedding at the age of fourteen.) Boys would assume the *toga uirilis* at the age of fifteen and then would be sent out to serve a kind of apprenticeship under some family friend active in public service, rather as congressional pages are sent off to Washington today. Such an apprenticeship was called a *tīrōcinium*, a *tīrō* being, basically, a neophyte, the sense that the term has in English, whether spelled *tiro* or *tyro*. After serving as a public figure's page for a time, the tiro would usually do a stint in the army, serving a *tīrōcinium mīlitiae* as aide-de-camp to a military friend of the family. When this hitch was up, the boy was considered fully educated and ready, if he so chose, to begin the *cursus honōrum* by standing for his first public office.

Of plebeian education we know a great deal less, but it seems reasonable to assume that tradespeople went to work in their parents' shops as soon as they were old enough to do so. One cannot help thinking of the prostitute in Petronius's *Satyricon* who, when it was objected that a little girl proposed for mock marriage with a slave-boy, Giton, was too young for such sport, laughingly retorted that she was no older than these children when she had her first man. Certainly slaves went to work as soon as they were considered old enough – and one wonders if children were among the slaves whom the tutor of Herodes Atticus's son cleverly dragooned to bear in procession the twenty-four letters of the alphabet, each on a big placard, to help the child learn his ABC's.

Still, it is one thing to carry a letter and another to learn it, and education for any but the wealthy must have been a perfunctory affair. Indeed, the gap between the folks with formal education and those who worked with their hands was well-nigh total, not least because of the disdain with which manual labor was regarded by the former, the philosophy of *labōrāre est ōrāre* (to work is to pray) being a strictly Christian-era phenomenon for which Claude Mossé (in *The Ancient World at Work*) provides an enlightening gloss: "Late imperial Rome was a vast consumer, supplied at the expense of the provinces, a parasitical society with special labour problems arising from the need to support an idle and disorderly population which pretended to a large influence in the affairs of the Empire, which, for all its adherence to Christianity, was unenthusiastic about the ideal of work as preached by the Church. So deeply rooted in men's minds was the idea that work is unworthy of a free man."

Not to say, naturally, that book learning and social productivity have ever really been mutually exclusive, as anyone will attest whose life has been saved by the timely ministrations of a doctor. *Doctor* in the sense of physician comes from the academic degree *Medicīnae Doctor*, literally Teacher of Medicine, which, like other doctorates, is an offshoot of the medieval university system whose lineal descendants are still with us today. Indeed, the universities of the Middle Ages produced a number of "doctors" worthy of mention: the *Admirable Doctor* – also known as the *Wonderful Doctor* (Roger Bacon, ca. 1214–1294), the *Angelic Doctor* (Saint Thomas Aquinas, ca. 1225–1274), the *Divine* – a.k.a. *Ecstatic* – *Doctor* (Jan van Ruysbroeck, 1293–1381), the *Illuminated Doctor* (Raymond Lully, 1235–1315, or Johann Tauler, ca. 1300–1361, take your pick), the *Irrefragable Doctor* (Alexander of Hales, ca. 1175–1245), the *Mellifluous Doctor* (Saint Bernard of Clairvaux, 1090–1153), the *Singular Doctor* (William of Occam, ca.

Dd

43

1300–1349), the *Subtle Doctor* (Duns Scotus, ca. 1265–1308), and the *Universal Doctor* (Alain de Lille, ca. 1128–1202, or Albertus Magnus, ca. 1206–1280). Albertus Magnus referred to his student, Thomas Aquinas, as "The Dumb Ox" who "one day will fill the world with his mooing." Chief among Aquinas's other detractors, when he tried to reconcile certain discrepancies between faith and reason in his *Summa Theologica*, were Duns Scotus (whence, ironically, English *dunce*) and the *Singular Doctor*, William of Occam, who was also known as the *Invincible Doctor*, perhaps because he was known to go about armed with Occam's Razor ("*Entia non sunt multiplicanda praeter necessitatem*" – "Don't invent new beings unless you really have to").

Nowadays, it is generally considered putting on airs for nonmedical doctors to go about clothed in their doctoral titles: after all, nobody was ever cured of a fever by writing a doctoral dissertation; and the unique reverence with which the general public regards members of the medical profession – as it has since time immemorial – is proportional to the life-and-death importance of the training that goes to qualify them for their license to practice their art. Roman medicine seems to have been a hodgepodge affair, but certain theorists and actual practitioners contributed materially to the body of medical knowledge still taught to today's healers. Despite an alarming tendency in Roman education to accept written testimony as more authoritative than the evidence of one's own senses when these were in conflict, much practical experience was gained by those attached to the Roman army's field hospitals, the *ualētūdināria*. (*Valētūdō* is Latin for good health, and comes from the same Indo-European root that gives Irish *flaith* [sovereignty], Old High German *waltan* [to rule], and Tocharian B *walo* [king].) Famous Roman medics – the common Latin term for physician was *medicus* (from the Indo-European root that gives English *meet*, as in *meet and right*, and that seems originally to have meant something like "fix") – included Pedanius Dioscorides, who was a field surgeon in Nero's army and wrote a treatise on medicinal plants that continued to be a standard reference work for the next fifteen hundred years, and Galen (Claudius Galenus), who flourished under the Five Good Emperors of the second century A.D., acquiring hands-on experience in a *ualētūdinārium* in his native Pergamum (in Asia Minor) which specialized in patching up wounded gladiators.

The encyclopedist Aulus Cornelius Celsus, who was born around 25 B.C. and who wrote his *De Medicina* during the reign of Tiberius, says that physicians should shrink neither from dissection of the dead nor from learning what they can from the happy (for them) accident of wounds: "for sometimes a gladiator in the arena, or a soldier in battle, or a man set upon by highwaymen, is wounded such that in one way or another his interior parts are exposed." Certainly Galen's reputation as an anatomist – literally "one who cuts up" – rests in part on practical knowledge gained in just this fashion in the *ualētūdinārium* at Pergamum, but it should not be overlooked that he had previously trained at Alexandria, where, far from squeamish about what a Roman would have considered defiling the dead, Egyptian funerary practice in his time still included mummification, an essential part of which entailed the removal of the internal organs for separate embalming and consignment to the so-called Canopic Jars.

It is significant that another great physician of the era, Soranus, who practiced at Rome during the reigns of Trajan and Hadrian, had also studied first at Alexandria. To him we owe a treatise (in remarkably straightforward Greek) on diseases of women that correctly described the anatomy of the uterus, noted that the *os uteri* dilates during menstruation and sexual intercourse, and accurately described the function of the clitoris – although, curiously enough, he seems to have been unaware of the existence of the hymen, which, as one commentator (Neuberger) delicately observes, "throws an interesting light on the conditions of Roman life at this period." Soranus advised that conception could be prevented by blocking the entrance to the uterus with cotton or fatty ointments or both – the contraceptive sponge is only now being publicly rediscovered and cautiously marketed – and he was the first to suggest in print that children *in utero* receive nourishment by way of the umbilical cord.

As a general rule, the physicians of the late Republic and early empire all received their professional training in Greek cities, coming to hang out their shingles in Rome only later in their careers. Cato the Censor, who violently opposed the hellenistic leanings of many educated Romans in the period between the second and third Punic wars, claimed that cabbage was a panacea and that the ancient Romans were healthy enough without the aid of physicians, by Hercules! In his treatise on agriculture, he recommended the treatment of fractures by splinting and the utterance of the magical (and nonsensical) formula *huat, hanat, huat, ista, pista, sista, domina, damnaustra, luxato* (or, to paraphrase Petronius, "he muttered some claptrap that he later tried to pass off as Etruscan"). With native folk medicine in this shape, Rome needed all the help it could get.

In the area of public health, however, the Romans were much better off: in addition to the *ualētūdināria* – remains of which have been uncovered at strategically central locations all over Europe – the Tiber island of Aesculapius had a shrine staffed by healers; and the Roman sewer system was of great antiquity, having been built starting under the Etruscan kings (the *Cloāca Maxima* [great sewer], which originally served as both sewer and storm drain, is still extant). Provincial capitals were improved along similar lines: one of Trajan's letters to Pliny begins, "*Permittit confornicārī cloācam*" ("The vaulting-over of the sewer is hereby authorized.") Public baths on a sumptuous scale were considered a necessary part of civic architecture, along with temples and amphitheaters, and great ones were built at Rome under Diocletian and Caracalla, as well as in many far-flung outposts from Asia Minor to England (where *Bath* is not so called for nothing). Moreover, on account of the ever-present scourge of malaria, Rome throughout the Republic allocated no small amount of money and muscle to land-filling projects. Indeed, it may well have been a Roman who first remarked that when you're up to your ass in alligators, it's hard to remember that your original objective was to drain the swamp.

Dd

E

IS FOR *ETRUSCANS, ETC.* ETRURIA – MOD-
ern Tuscany – lay to the north of the Tiber and extended up
the west coast of Italy beyond the River Arno. The Etruscans – known to the Greeks as *Tyrsēnoí* or *Tyrrhēnoí*
(whence the name of the *Tyrrhenian Sea* designating that
portion of the Mediterranean bounded by Corsica, Sardinia, Sicily, and southwestern Italy) – seem to have come
into prominence starting in about 800 B.C., though whether
they were indigenous to the peninsula or immigrants from
Lydia in Asia Minor (or from somewhere else) has been a
matter of debate since ancient times. Evidence favoring a
Lydian origin for the Etruscans is scanty and tantalizing,
ranging from Egyptian inscriptions of the twelfth century
B.C. referring to a seafaring folk called the *Tyrsha*, and the
Assyrian root *har-* (liver) which could be identical with the
har- of *haruspex* (a diviner who read the portents visible in
the entrails of sacrificial animals, an Etruscan specialty), to
the testimony of Latin writers that the Etruscans themselves
believed in their Lydian provenance.

That they were seafarers is undoubted, for Tyrrhenian
pirates terrorized the Italic coast down to the fifth century
B.C. – it is said that around 500 B.C. they had even planned
an expedition beyond Gibraltar but were warned off by Carthaginian fleets eager to protect their hegemony in the western Mediterranean. Also certain is that, in addition to their
naval prowess, the *Etruscī* (or *Tuscī*, as the Romans also
called them, their name for themselves being *Rasenna*)
could boast of a talent for metal-working, the refinement of
which was facilitated by their early exploitation of the considerable mineral resources of Etruria's interior hills. Etruscan tombs have yielded a great many items of precious-
metal jewelry (not always wrought with a living wearer in

mind, to be sure). Indeed, the Etruscan passion for burying ornaments with the dead may have been a consideration when the framers of Rome's early legal system prohibited gold and silver funerary offerings in the Twelve Tables. Gold dental prostheses, which the Twelve Tables specifically exempted from the ban, have been found in the skulls of many of the Etruscan dead.

In addition to gold and silver, both iron and bronze were worked with skill and in quantity: when Scipio Africanus was outfitting his expedition to Spain in 205 B.C. to put the heat on Carthage from its own front yard, he requisitioned iron and bronze weapons from Etruria to a total of fifty thousand pieces in addition to the fittings for forty triremes. So extensive were the ironworks at Populonia that the slag heaps left behind have proved commercially workable sources of ore in the present century. Clearly, Etruria was in a position not only to supply local needs but to export its metalwork to the rest of the Mediterranean, and these items were almost certainly what got traded for the many luxury goods of Greek origin that started to appear in quantity in Etruscan tombs from the middle of the seventh century B.C. onward and that profoundly influenced native Etruscan style in the arts and crafts as well.

It is this vigorous, prosperous culture that distinguishes the Etruscans from the other Italic peoples who were eventually swallowed up in the expansion of Rome – the Veneti at the head of the Adriatic Sea; the Oscans and Umbrians on the far side of the Appenines; the Siculi of Sicily; and the Ligurians, who lived at the foot of the Alps and inhabited Corsica and part of Sardinia (the rest of which having been the home turf of the Sardi, about whom we know very little indeed). While the Greeks and Carthaginians were settling the coast of lower Italy and Sardinia respectively, and trying to wrest an exclusive toehold in Sicily from each other, disrespectively, the Etruscans had managed by 500 B.C. to extend their sway over much of northern Italy, well into the Po valley, and for a while called the shots not only in Rome but down the coast into Campania (until they were thrown back by the Greeks). A great naval battle, in which the Etruscans and the Carthaginians fought on the same side, for once, against a Greek force, took place off Sardinia around 540 B.C. and left Corsica for the nonce in Etruscan hands while Carthage felt free to subjugate Sardinia; but in 524 B.C., a land force of Etruscans and their allies failed to take Cumae, which was successfully defended by the Greek general Aristodemus. Moreover, even alliance with Carthage could not arrest the rapid growth of Greek influence in Sicily, and the defeat of Carthage by the Syracusans at Himera in 480 B.C. was followed six years later by the destruction off Cumae of an Etruscan naval force, in token of which Hieron of Syracuse sent several bronze Etruscan helmets to the temple of Zeus at Olympia.

With Rome no longer a part of the Etruscan power bloc after the expulsion of Tarquin the Proud, Etruria began retrenching – Greek imported goods become scarcer and scarcer from this point on – and soon the Etruscans had to cope with onslaughts from the north as well, as the first of the Celtic invasions began which would culminate in the overrunning of Tuscany and the sack of Rome itself in the early fourth century B.C. The Etruscans seem never to have had an internal organization going much beyond a loose confederation of sovereign city-states, much like that of Greece, and this was to prove their undoing as city after city slipped away from the alliance to be absorbed by the growing power of Rome. Despite an alliance with Gaul, Etruria lost out to Rome during the course of the third Samnite War, the Samnites having been an Oscan people engaged in their own futile stand against early Roman expansionism. A decisive defeat was inflicted on the Etruscans and their allies in 295 B.C. near the town of Sentinum – tradition has it that one of the Roman consuls, Publius Decius Mus, offered himself up as a ritual human sacrifice to the gods of the underworld and of the earth for their efforts.

Volsinii, the last great Etruscan town to hold out, was taken over by Rome when a slave revolt broke out and the Romans, called in by the Volsinian patricians, won the town by assault and leveled it, relocating the inhabitants to a new site nearby – without imposing walls. Etruria came so totally under Roman domination that Hannibal was unsuccessful in subverting it during the second Punic War (as he was, at least temporarily, elsewhere in Italy), and the last gasp of Etruscan independence was smothered in the confiscations and proscriptions of Sulla after some of the Etrurian towns had rashly sided with his rival Marius during the power struggle that followed the Social War of the early first century B.C. From then on, Etruria as such ceased to exist except as an ethnic district, like the province of Brittany in modern-day France.

We are severely hampered today in studying the Etruscans by the near impenetrability of their language: so far, a stroke of luck comparable to the discovery of the library of Assur-bani-pal or the Rosetta Stone has eluded us. Most of the Etruscan texts we do have are funerary inscriptions and, as has been pointed out, visitors from another planet would be hard pressed to discover very much about contemporary American society if all they had to read was our gravestones. The Etruscans did write plays, though apparently at a late date and heavily influenced by Greek models; but, unfortunately, all of these are lost; as is the emperor Claudius's history of the Etruscans. We have a couple of bilingual inscriptions, notably a forty-word text in Etruscan and Punic recording the establishment of a shrine to Astarte on Tuscan soil during the brief period of Carthaginian–Etruscan détente at the end of the sixth century B.C. We also have isolated words glossed in the writings of various Latin writers, as when Suetonius mentions a portent of the death of the emperor Augustus: a bolt of lightning struck and melted the C at the beginning of the word CAESAR on one of his dedicatory inscriptions, which some took to mean that he would live only another hundred (C) days, and then be dead and deified, *aesar*, according to Suetonius, "being Etruscan for god." (The word is attested elsewhere as *ais*.) Varro and others claim Etruscan origin for a number of military and theatrical terms: *mīles* (soldier, whence *military*), *satelles* (bodyguard, whence *satellite*), and *histriō* (actor, whence *histrionic*) being three of the more noteworthy. Also of apparent Etruscan origin is the word *fenestra* (window), which survives as German *Fenster* and French *fenêtre* and appears in the English word *defenestration* (a throwing out of a window), the *Defenestration of Prague* being the proximate cause of the Thirty Years' War.

By far the largest number of Etruscan words attested with any degree of assurance are proper names – *Atella* (the town where the celebrated bawdy Atellan Farces were put on), *Tarquinii* (the town where the Tarquin family lived before they became kings of Rome), and the *Mons Velius* (Velian Hill). There are a large number of family names which ended in *-u* in Etruscan and got changed to *-o* in Latin, including those belonging to the censor *Cato*, the orator *Cicero*, the conspirator *Piso*, and the grammarian *Varro*.

Inasmuch as internal consistencies of the extant Etruscan inscriptions have so far failed to point even to a known language family to which Etruscan might have belonged, it is fortunate that these enterprising folks were so generous in providing for their dead: their tombs are filled with actual day-to-day implements and, more to the point, with pictorial and sculptural representations of daily life. From these we can deduce that men and women were on a congenially equal footing – perhaps the strongest prima facie evidence against a Lydian origin of the Etruscan people, or at least against an origin from that part of Lydia overlorded by the more fiercely patriarchal Greeks.

We know that the Etruscans had a multitude of gods, goddesses, nymphs, demons, and so on – a brass model of the liver, used presumably as a memory (or training) aid for the *haruspex*, divides the liver into sixteen sections, each corresponding to a particular part of the sky and its tutelary deity – and we know from other sources that the Etruscans were considered experts in diagnosing from thunder and lightning how things would go for the consultant, depending on what direction the thunder came from or what sort of lightning bolt had been observed. We know, further, that the iron-working city of Populonia had as its patron the fire-god *Velchans*, almost certainly cognate with Roman *Vulcan*. And it is clear that the Etruscans adopted, early on, the practice of venerating Hercules, invoking his aid when going to war. But, as a general rule, whereas the history and habits of the Romans are a full text, we must regard what we know of the Etruscans as – at best – an abbreviation.

As far as abbreviations go, Latin underlies many of the ones in use today, *etc.* being one of the most common. Short for *et cētera* (and the rest [of these things]), *etc.* has become so familiar to us that we tend not to think of it as Latin anymore and so don't bother to italicize it (except, of course, when calling special attention to it). Not so, theoretically at least, with the following (which tend to be confined to the murk of academic footnotes): *ibid.*, which is short for *ibidem* (itself a contraction of *ibi* [there] and *idem* [the same]), used when the cited source is the same as in the preceding footnote; *op. cit.*, short for *opere citātō* (in the work cited), placed after an author's name when you have mentioned his or her work a few footnotes back, and used more or less interchangeably with *loc. cit.*, the *loc.* being short for *locō* (in the place), although properly *op. cit.* means "same work" and *loc. cit.*, "same *page* of same work." Even more vague in reference is *pass.* (for *passim* [here and there], literally "scattered"), a handy device for saving the writer the trouble of listing a whole bunch of page numbers on which a given reference occurs. A similar invitation to browse is the abbreviation *et seq.* (and the following), from Latin *et sequens* or, in the plural, *et sequentia*, for which the abbreviation *et sqq.* is used by selective sticklers for detail. A more popular stand-in for *et seq.* is *f.* (following), from Latin *foliō* (on the [following] page), the way of designating that more than a single page follows being to write *ff.* – no relation to the logician's *wff* (well-formed formula), which is pronounced *woof* and from which logically follows a digression on the subject of acronyms.

An acronym is a special variety of abbreviation, namely, one that is made up of the parts of a series of words and is pronounced as though it were a real word rather than a simple string of letters: the garden-variety abbreviation *s.o.b.* is pronounced *ess-oh-bee* while the acronym *fubar* is pronounced *fyoobar* or *foobar.* (The *foobar* pronunciation of *fubar* – "effed up beyond all recognition" – is the basis of Computerese *foo*, an all-purpose naming device used when a hypothetical example of something has to have a name, as "the data description file *foo.dmd*," "the attribute *foo*," "the text string *foo*," and so on.) Sometimes acronyms sneak into the language as real words: the computer *bit* (binary digit) from which have evolved the *byte* – typically eight bits – and the *nibble* – half a byte, or four bits; *laser* (light amplification by stimulated emission of radiation), *radar* (radio detecting and ranging), and *snafu* (situation normal: all fouled up).

Sometimes acronyms are uppercased: *FORTRAN* (formula translation) and *COBOL* (common business-oriented language, or, according to people who actually have to program in the language, compiles only because of luck). (*PASCAL*, a younger, rather more laid-back programming language, sometimes gets capitalized because it's a programming language like its older siblings FORTRAN and COBOL even though it happens to be named after the shower-of-sparks *Blaise Pascal* and isn't an acronym at all. *APL* – a programming language – is a dark figure whose components transposed spell the German word for "nightmare": *Alp.*) Other uppercase acronyms include the *WAVES* (women accepted for volunteer emergency service – into the Navy); and *AWOL* – absent without official leave. AWOL and its lowercase variant *awol* are both pronounced as though a single word, while A.W.O.L. and *a.w.o.l.*, their more formal representatives, are drum-rolled out letter by letter.

AWOL/awol/A.W.O.L./a.w.o.l. raises the question of how one is supposed to know, on first eyeballing, whether a peculiar-looking string of letters is an abbreviation, an acronym, or a regular, everyday word. In the best of all possible worlds, abbreviations would end in a period, acronyms would be uppercase and not end in a period, and regular, everyday words would be neither of the above (except at the end of a sentence). Unfortunately, life is seldom so simple: lots of acronyms are conventionally lowercased, and some abbreviations are not only uppercased – as *R.S.V.P.* (*répondez, s'il vous plaît*) – but don't end in a period (except at the end of a sentence): the *AFL-CIO* is the ay-eff-of-ell-see-eye-oh and that's that. British English leaves the period off the end of Mr., Dr., etc.; in American English, however, the hard-and-fast rule is that lowercase abbreviations end in a period, period. Indeed, this rule has been so fanatically applied over the years that it has led to at least a couple of cases of punctuational overkill, viz., *oz.* and *viz.*

Viz. is an abbreviation of Latin *vidēlicet* ("evidently," and, by extension, "namely, to wit," from *vidēre* [to see] and *licet* [it is permitted], the same *licet* that underlies *license* and *licentious* and that appears in *scīlicet* [obviously, namely, to wit], the *sci-* part being from *scīre* [to know]). The *z* of *viz.* was originally a ligature of the Latin letters *et*, much like the ampersand (&). (*Ampersand* is a contraction of "and *per se* and," i.e., "and by itself and.") The ligature for *et* was first generalized to stand for the conjunction *-que* (and) that the Romans tacked onto the ends of words (as in "*Arma virumque canō,*" "[Of] arms and the man I sing," literally, "Arms the man-and I sing") and then got promoted to the status of official marker of the end of any abbreviation. When the people in orthographic administration decided that the period would replace the *z* at the end of abbreviations, *viz.* and *oz.* were apparently away from their desks and instead of getting rewritten as *vi.* and *o.*, they were merely issued a supernumerary termination.

The only problem with checking to see if a string of lowercase letters ends in a period and assuming that if it does, it's an abbreviation, and if it doesn't, then it's a regular, everyday word is that declarative sentences customarily end in a period and convention has it that you leave out the final period of an abbreviation when it comes at the end of a sentence: *E is for Etruscans*, etc. Not *E is for Etruscans*, *etc..* Whether it was to get around this problem or for some other reason, custom used to have it that abbreviations were to be italicized, so if the last string of letters in a declarative sentence appeared romanized, then the writer could be presumed to be not talking abbreviations but rather regular, everyday words.

Ah, but what if the last string of letters in a declarative sentence appeared in italics? Several possibilities, alas: the string could be an abbreviation, of course, as in "They always play the opening of Beethoven's Fifth *fortissimo,* i.e., *fff,*" or it could be a technical or foreign term, as in "They always play the opening of Beethoven's Fifth *fff,* i.e., *fortissimo,*" or it could be a matter of emphasis, as in "They always play the opening of Beethoven's Fifth really *loud,*" or it could be part of a title, as in "They always begin the program with the opening of Beethoven's *Fifth Symphony."* Or the whole sentence could have been in italics, as when a character in a novel is thinking: *They always play the opening of Beethoven's Fifth before playing the rest.* To be sure, there are some disambiguating conventions: a flip-flop rule says to romanize anything in an italic text that you would have italicized in a roman text: the hero thinks, *"They always play the opening of Beethoven's Fifth really* loud," the heroine thinks, "Zut alors," and so it goes. But the system tends to break down when you want to emphasize anything that would ordinarily appear in italics in a roman text – She thought " 'Zut alors'? *You've got to be* kidding."

Perhaps as a way of throwing up its hands, convention is changing in the direction of romanizing abbreviations: *i.e.* (for Latin *id est* [it is – i.e., that is]), *e.g.* (for Latin *exemplī grātiā* [by the grace of an example – i.e., for example]), *cf.* (for *confer* [compare, literally "bring together"]), and *viz.* are romanized more often than not nowadays. *Q.v.,* by contrast, is nearly always italicized, perhaps because if it weren't italicized as though for emphasis nobody would take the exhortation terribly seriously: *q.v.* stands for Latin *quod uidē* (which see). Various wags (*worthy American gentlemen?*) have proposed the adoption of *q.n.v. – quod nōn uidē* (which don't see) – for those references that the conscientious author feels obliged to cite but knows that the reader will find too tedious to have tried to chase down to have made it seem worth the effort.

But, then, there are those who would like to do away with anything with *uidē* in it altogether, thus giving the ax to such old standbys as *v.s.* (*uidē suprā*, see above), *v.inf.* (*uidē infrā*, see below), and just plain *v.* (*uidē*, see) in one fell swoop. One reason for wanting to do away with *uidē* is that its abbreviation, *v.*, is ambiguous: *v.* can stand for *volume*, *verb*, *verse*, *voce* (word), *uaria* (in *v.l.* – *uaria lectio* – variant reading), *uerso* (on the other side), and *uersus* (against). This last use of *v.* is restricted to Legalese, a language rich in abbreviatory devices. *Black's Law Dictionary* tells us that *T*

as an abbreviation . . . may stand for such terms as "term," "territory," "title," "table."

Every person who was convicted of a felony, short of murder, and admitted to the benefit of clergy, was at one time marked with this letter upon the brawn of the thumb. Abolished by 7 8 Geo. IV, C. 27.

By a law of the Province of Pennsylvania, A.D. 1698, it was provided that a convicted thief should wear a badge in the form of the letter "T.," upon his left sleeve, which badge should be at least four inches long and of a color different from that of his outer garment.

Medicalese is not to be outdone: *Rx* (*sic*) is short for *recipe* (receive, take), and a medication prescribed *a.c.* is to be taken *ante cibum* (before meal[s]), *p.c.* (*post cibum*) being for after a cozy meal with your personal computer. *Q.s.* – *quantum sufficit* – is as much as suffices, *q.p.* – *quantum placet* – is literally "as much as pleases," and *q.l.* – *quantum libet* – is "as much as you like" – there doesn't seem to be a medical prescription translating as "as much as it takes to make you utterly blotto." An *o.d.* is to be taken *omni diē* ([once] every day) – not to be confused with *O.D.* (overdose). *B.i.d.* is short for *bis in diē* (twice [in] a day), *t.i.d.*

(*ter in diē*) is "three times a day," and *q.i.d.* (*quater in diē*) is "four times a day" – no doctor, apparently, ever prescribing a five-a-day medication in Latin, since *quinque* (five) also begins with a *q* and you can't be too careful.

Indeed, the danger of abbreviation is twofold: not only may the reader not know what it is that's being abbreviated; misreading is easier, and ghastly mistakes can occur. It was not too long ago that a nurse in a hurry read *mg* (*milligrams*) for *μg* (*micrograms*), and a healthy malpractice suit was filed and won by the survivors of the unfortunate patient who O.D.'d by three orders of magnitude. This sort of difficulty, on a less dramatic scale, is bound to occur whenever a new abbreviation is minted: in the early days of government-issue products, during the Second World War (a.k.a., or aka, WWII), the story is told of medics and enlisted men arguing over what a *GI can* was, the medics holding that *GI* was short for *gastrointestinal* while the soldiers of the line (or at least those with experience in the sheet-metal trades) maintained that *GI* was *galvanized iron*. A compromise was finally reached: *GI* = *galvanized intestinal*.

And time takes its toll: most readers know who J.F.K., L.B.J., and F.D.R. were – one hopes – but how many people today can correctly name the various "alphabet soup" agencies of F.D.R.'s New Deal if given their abbreviations? A cantankerous Old Dealer used to like to say of the Works Progress Administration, "W.P.A.? Why, that stands for *Whistle, Piss* and *Argue!*" Q.E.D.

F

IS FOR *FEAST, FESTIVAL, FERIA, AND FES-toon*. Everybody likes a holiday, and the Romans were no exception. School children only got one day off every eight, a cruel irony considering that both of the common Latin words for school – *schola* and *lūdus* – originally referred to leisure time and its pursuits. The children's no-school day was termed *nōnus diēs* (ninth day), the Romans having customarily reckoned the passage of time inclusively. The same eight-day interval also determined when market-day (*nundinae*) would be. The days on which public business could be transacted were called *diēs fastī* and were liberally punctuated by days on which public business was forbidden (*diēs nefastī*) or partly so (*diēs nefastī partēs*), so that out of a possible 365 days, there were only about 230 on which all business was allowed. This compares favorably with our five-day work week with ten public holidays thrown in, which gives most of us 250 days a year to toil before we start earning time-and-a-half. (Slaves, of course, worked nearly all the time.) Another Roman term for *diēs fastī* was *diēs uacantēs* (empty days), i.e., days on which there was no official feast. By a bit of linguistic legerdemain, *diēs uacantēs* have become *vacation*, it now being the office rather than the calendar that is vacant. In British English, a vacation is a *holiday* (as in "I was on holiday when the embezzlement was discovered"), a more accurate rendering of the Roman *festum*.

Festum is the proximate source for English *feast*, which was spelled *fest* in Middle English and meant festival – as in the macaronic carol whose chorus is "*Mak we joye now in this fest/In quō Christus nātus est* [on which Christ was born]." *Feste* is the name of the clown in Shakespeare's *Twelfth Night*, a semi-allegorical figure like Puck who serves both as character in the action and as liaison with the audience. *Festum* and *fastī* are both from the root that, in its plainest form, appears as Latin *fās* (divine law, hence, "that which is lawful, right, permitted"). Our *fast* – as in "he fasted for forty days and forty nights and on the morning of the forty-first day ate a hearty breakfast" – does not apparently derive from *fastī* but rather from Old English *fœstan* (to hold fast, abstain from food), though from a sociological point of view, feasting and fasting are inextricably bound together, the excesses of the one being a mirror of the deprivation of the other.

Hunter-gatherer societies, being dependent on the availability of game and forage, are to this day committed to a feast-or-famine existence: when food is scarce, everybody hungers, and when there's a lot to go around, the tendency to tuck in liberally is understandably irresistible – especially in the absence of effective ways of preserving highly perishable sources of protein like raw meat and fresh fish. While the agrarian revolution of the late Neolithic times mitigated this fact to some extent, the nature of the seasons is such that there are times of the year when food is going to run a little lean, no matter what. If Lent didn't come in late winter, someone would have had to invent something like it to stretch the groceries until the first spring crops were in; and the pre-Lenten carnival – from *carnī* plus *ualē*, literally, farewell (*ualē*) to meat (*carnī*) – culminating in Shrove Tuesday – or *Mardi Gras* (Fat Tuesday) – would be common sense, even without the Church's blessing, in any society whose main sustenance came from the land rather than the supermarket. On a shorter schedule, compare "meatless Mondays" as a political metaphor for stretching the food budget, the notion underlying this volatile issue being that the only way to make sure that there will be meat for Sunday dinner is to start the week by doing without.

A second reason for festival feasting is a kind of sympathetic magic: by eating one's fill (in honor of the gods), we are in essence saying, "Thank the powers that be that we made it through another one, and if we demonstrate our gratitude, we also want to show the gods – while we have their attention – that this is the way we ought to be: happy and fed and full." In at least one primitive society, an appeal to the ancestral spirits in time of famine is made by gathering up all the goodies one can find and having a feast at their shrine; prayers are addressed to the forebears to the effect that the living are symbolically sharing what they have with the spirits now, but that that's all that's left and the living are in danger of extinction, and who will look after the ancestors then? This serves the ball effectively into the ancestors' court, and everybody belches and waddles home to wait for the spirits to make the next move, preferably one involving tying on the feed bag.

A third function served by feasts and festivals is a psychological one, namely, as "mental health days" – a concept only now being recognized in more enlightened types of labor relations, and known euphemistically as "personal days" or, on a smaller scale, as "being away from one's desk." In other words, a celebration gives you some temporary relief from the ordinary, and this is a good thing as long as you don't so thoroughly disgrace yourself at the annual Christmas office party that you wind up with a pink slip in your stocking – "temporary" is the operative word here with "relief" coming in a close second.

Just as people love a break from the ordinary, so everybody loves a parade, and the beauty of the Roman festivals was that so many of the *diēs fastī* – with the notable exception of the anniversary of Rome's defeat at the River Allia by the Gauls – were occasions dedicated to certain of the divinities whose priests got to put on a ritual public show. Thus, the *Lupercālia*, on February 15th, was the occasion for a general race by the priests of Lupercus (the Lycean Pan) during which the runners struck any women in the way with rawhide thongs. As this was supposed to promote fertility, women desirous of conceiving would line the race course so as to deliberately be in the way. Similarly, the *Saturnālia*, which began on December 11th, was a celebration of great merriment and license in honor of the god Saturnus, the great granddaddy of them all.

By contrast, some festivals were only for certain trades or

particular districts: in his *De Lingua Latina* (*On the Latin Language*), Varro mentions, among others, the *Pāgānālia* (Festival of the Boonies) that was celebrated only by the "rustic tribes" who lived in the outlying countryside (*pāgus*); and the *Diēs Septimontium*, a feast "so called from the *septem montēs* [seven hills] on which Rome is built, celebrated not by the general public, but only by those who lived on the hills." Probably the most exclusive festival was the *diēs ā deā Opeconsīua*, celebrated on July 23rd in honor of Saturnus's consort Ops, the goddess of abundance (whose name forms the basis of English *opulence*): because her shrine was so small, we are told, the participation in the ceremony was restricted to the Vestal Virgins and the public priest.

Varro lists only some of the *diēs fastī*, and then only for their etymological interest; happily, Ovid's *Fasti* goes through the first six months of the year day by day with extensive descriptions of the names, customs, and origins of the feast days, all in elegiac couplets. Thus, we learn why, at the Lupercalia, the priests ran around clad only in goatskin tunics: it seems that Lupercus/Faunus had his eye on a certain Lydian princess, but Hercules had come on the scene and was flirting with her, eventually persuading her to go off to a cave for a rest, after which they wound up in each other's clothes. When they had feasted and drunk their fill, they fell asleep. At this point, in came Faunus ("*very* horny," says Ovid), who grabbed for the figure in the filmy negligee. Hercules toppled Lupercus/Faunus to the ground with a crash, and the Lydian princess's attendants came rushing in with torches ablaze. Since then, "having once been fooled by clothes, Faunus prefers his worshipers to come to his rites without."

One of the chief festivals was the *Parīlia*, celebrated on April 21st. This shepherd's feast was thought to antedate the founding of the city of Rome, but was in any case taken as the official birthday of the city. It included sweeping out the winter stalls of the flocks and herds, the animals being officially turned out to pasture that day for the summer after fumigation with a mixture of burning sulfur, olivewood, laurel, and rosemary. Both beasts and human celebrants then jumped over a bonfire. The presiding deity was Pales, the protectress of cattle. The word *Parīlia* is a variant of *Palīlia* as the result of what linguists would term "progressive dissimilation" and what members of the medical profession might prefer to call "rhotacism," which *Dorland's Illustrated Medical Dictionary* defines as "the incorrect use or overuse of *r* sounds" – to which may be compared *lambdacism* "(1) the substitution of *l* for *r* in speaking. (2) the inability to utter the sound of *l* correctly" – though Latinists prefer to restrict the use of *rhotacism* to designating the change of intervocalic -s- to -r- that is evidenced in *fēriae* (holidays, days of rest, festivals), which comes from the same root as *fās, fastī,* and *festum. Fēria,* the singular of *fēriae,* is still with us as an ecclesiastical term meaning "weekday on which no feast is observed" and is the basis of *fair* in the sense of "regional event open to the public." England seems to have solved the pronunciation problem by quietly renaming the Parilia "Saint George's Day" and moving the date on which the celebrating takes place to April 23rd. The Parilia was briefly revived under its original name during the fascist regime of Benito Mussolini – *fascist* being no relation to *fastī* or *festum* (or their rhotacized cousin, *nefarious*) but rather a derivative of Latin *fascēs* (bundle of sticks with an ax, carried as an emblem of the highest magistrates' office), represented on the flip side of the American Mercury dime.

Another festival, the *Lemūria,* was celebrated on three days in May – the 9th, the 11th, and the 13th. The *lemurēs* were spirits of the dead who for one reason or another were supposed to be still at large, whether because of a dearth of kin or simple neglect on the part of their survivors to perform the proper funerary rites. The ceremony of propitiation was supposed to be carried out in each household at midnight by the paterfamilias. It began with the officiant making a fist with his thumb thrust between the fingers – still familiar as the "sign of the fig" in Mediterranean countries today as a charm to ward off evil influences. After washing his hands in spring water, the householder cast black beans over his shoulder, saying, "I cast these and with them redeem myself and my own," repeating this formula nine times. He then beat bronze pots together, calling out nine times, "Spirits of my forefathers, go forth!" Though many cultures in which respect for the dead is as much motivated by fear as by affection feature beans, loud noises, and the number nine in their rituals, Ovid derives the name of the observance from *Remūria*, saying that the original ritual was one performed by Romulus to lay to rest the shade of his brother *Remus* after he slew him; but this is what's known in the trade as a "folk etymology" – a derivation that makes sense from the point of view of semantics but falls on its face when it comes to a question of what actually happened historically, as with deriving "woodchuck" from "wood" plus "chuck" instead of from Cree *oček*, or "forlorn hope" from "forlorn" plus "hope" instead of from the Dutch *verloren hoop* (lost troops). Latin *lemur* is actually related to Greek *lámia* (witch, monster). The nocturnal prosimian of Madagascar with the nasty face and huge eyes was dubbed *lemur* by Linnaeus, whose flair for the metaphoric was proverbial even in his own day.

The public counterpart to the Lemuria was called the *Parentālia* (Feast of the Forebears), a ten-day festival which began on February 13th. During this period, families got together at the graves of their ancestors and offered wine, milk, honey, and oil, as well as flowers, such as were available at the time of year. The ceremony with which the Parentalia closed was called the *Cāristia*, from *cārus* (dear), and was in effect a reenactment of the funeral feast at which family quarrels were supposed to be made up or at least shelved for the nonce, and everybody was supposed to have a grand old time. The Chief Vestal Virgin performed a version of these rites on behalf of the common spirits of the departed.

The day after the Parentalia ended, along came the *Terminālia*, February 23rd being the end of the old Roman

year, and the date on which the boundary stones were cere-
monially rededicated, Terminus being the god of boundaries. An official boundary stone sat in a small atrium in the
temple of Iuppiter Capitolinus on the Capitoline Hill, and
it was from this point that all milestones were measured out
on the Roman highway network – a custom still surviving
among cartographers who plot local mileages using the
steps of City Hall as the point of reference.

In addition to these indigenous festivals, the Romans imported some others, the earliest being the feast of the Greek
wine-god Dionysus (probably of Thracian origin), known to
the Romans as *Bacchus* (originally a probably Lydian god of
vegetation and especially of the vine). His worship is attested in an inscription from Cumae, dating from the early
fifth century B.C., which prohibited anyone who was not a
devotee of the god from being interred in a cemetery set
aside for initiates of the cult. So riotous were the Bacchanalia held in the god's honor that they were outlawed in 186
B.C. – the first attested Roman law to be directed to the
Italian peninsula – though the expression *uīuere baccha-
nālia* (to live riotously) remained in the language, and even
today we speak of a particularly boisterous revel as a *bac-
chanal*.

But the banning of the Bacchanalia was no big loss, for
Bacchus became amalgamated with the native god Liber,
whose festival – the *Līberālia* – was celebrated on March
17th. Like the original Bacchus, Liber was a god of vegetation associated especially with the vine and its fruits. The
word *Līber* is probably the same as *līber* (free), *līberāre* (to
free – and the basis of *deliver*, but not *deliberate*, whose
-liber- is from *libra* [balances, scales], whence French *livre*
[pound] and the pound sign £), a *lībertīnus* being a freedman (later, a person so unrestrained as to give the libertine
a bad name), a *līberālis* being a person who behaved as a
free man should – namely, with generosity – and *līberī*
being (free) children.

The first *exclusively* nonnative god whose worship was
imported was Cybele, the Idean Mother. She was said to

reside in a meteorite that was carried from Phrygia as a sort of homeopathic response to a frightening shower of stones that fell from the sky in 204 B.C. At first, the divine stone was set up in the Temple of Victory on the Palatine Hill. Later (in 191 B.C.), Cybele got her own temple, also on the Palatine Hill, but for some time thereafter, Roman citizens were forbidden to serve as her priests or even to take part in her worship. In part, this was due to the ecstatic nature of her festival, the *Megale(n)sia* (from Greek *megálē* [*mḗtēr*] meaning "great [mother]"), which began on April 4th. Cybele's priests – the *Gallī* (named after the Phrygian river Gallus and no relation to the *Gallī* or Gauls) – were eunuchs, and the annual celebration included a symbolic reenactment of the death and resurrection of her lover, Attis (the Phrygian Adonis), the demonstrative mourning for whom required the Galli to slash their arms and legs with knives and play music on flutes, horns, and cymbals, all somewhat reminiscent of the carryings-on of the priests of Baal in their contest with Elijah. All of this was strictly supervised by the praetor, who had the unenviable job of keeping public order while permitting the worship appropriate to the goddess who had, after all, aided Rome in finally expelling Hannibal from Italian soil.

The worship of Cybele hung on and acquired great popularity, being at last raised to the respectability of a state-sponsored cult under the emperor Claudius. The dates were shifted around a bit to coincide more nearly with the vernal equinox, and the climax – the opening of the empty tomb and the proclamation of Attis's resurrection, on March 25th – was called the Festival of Joy, or *Hilaria*, whence English *hilarious*. Later on, as the expanding empire brought the Roman military and provincial government apparatus in contact with other exotic ecstatic cults, the veneration of Isis and Mithras would be brought back to Rome together with their festivals. Initially frowned upon or even rigorously suppressed by staid officialdom, but for that very reason attracting devotees even among the aristocracy, such cults, along with Christianity, offered the Roman mind a compelling alternative to the gray sobriety of stoicism or the quaint absurdities of pantheistic faith – a faith already stretched thin in the minds of many educated Romans by the time Plutarch (fl. 100 A.D.) wrote his dialogue "The Decline of the Oracles." Furthermore, in an age when one could go to the amphitheater and, for less than the price of a bath, see eighty pairs of gladiators hack each other to pieces in an afternoon, many a Roman contemplating a misty Hereafter wandering the Stygian plains found, through adoring Isis, Mithras, or Jesus, the hope of salvation and the promise of eternal life.

Ff

G

IS FOR GOVERNOR AND GUBERNATO-
rial, both ultimately from Latin *gubernātor* (helmsman) –
the verb *gubernāre* originally meant "to steer (a ship)"
though even in Roman times the word was widely used in
the extended senses of to direct, manage, rule. "Gubernatorial" is the more obviously Latinate of the pair: "gov-
ern(or)" was borrowed into English from Old French in the
thirteenth century, while "gubernatorial" wasn't Latin-to-
Englished until nearly five centuries later when, apparently,
it was agreed (at least in certain smoke-filled chambers) that
the need for a suitably dignified adjective to go with "governor" could not be met by simply appending to the word
one of the many native suffixes that might have applied for
the job but, instead, required a borrowing straight from
Latin itself. But, then, by the eighteenth century, English
had already grown quite accustomed to casting its linguistic
net in Latin waters when a posh new adjective was wanted
for a native noun (whether native Anglo-Saxon or native
borrowed from the Normans): *buccal, dental, nasal,* and
capital are definitely classier terms than "mouthy," "toothy,"
"nosy," and "heady," the distance between "gubernatorial"
and the Anglo-Saxon adjectives commonly applied to government and those in office being no less substantial even
in the best of times.

By the official fall of the (western) Roman empire in 476
A.D., when Odoacer and his rowdy crew took over and, in
so doing, once and for all abolished the title and the office
of emperor of the (western) Roman empire, most speakers
of Latin probably didn't have much nicer things to say
about government than most rational people do today.
What contemporary residents of the Eastern Roman Empire had to say about this as they strolled the streets of their

capital city of Constantinople – formerly the promising town of Byzantium, whither the upstart Flavius Valerius Aurelius Constantinus took his marbles on becoming Constantine the Great after beating out his Roman opposition in the early part of the fourth century A.D. – was, if perhaps less derogatory, largely in Greek: the Turks who eventually ousted the local form of government there even later having said, "Ha ha, we'll show you," or the like, renaming Byzantium/Constantinople *Istanbul*, from Greek *eis tèn pólin* (toward the city), as one of those bizarre but not infrequent left-handed compliments that seem to spring from the murky waters of a people's collective unconscious and are caught up in the language before they get away.

Odoacer – who had nothing to do with the original splitting up of the Roman empire into east is east and west is west and it's a tenuous meeting at best some years previously – was the son of a fellow named Aedico who served in the armed forces under Attila the Hun. Odoacer himself enlisted in the Roman army at about the age of thirty and rapidly worked his way up to a position of no little clout. The Roman army in which Odoacer got his start was actually a band of mercenaries of various linguistic persuasions whom Orestes had employed in his ultimately successful efforts to overthrow the (western) emperor Nepos and install his own son, Romulus Augustulus, in his place. When the successful troops demanded that Orestes divide a third of Italy among them for their trouble and he balked, Odoacer took charge and led his comrades-in-arms against Orestes, overthrowing him and giving Romulus Augustulus his pink slip.

Odoacer then installed himself as the man in charge (though he was at least nominally the vicar of the Eastern Empire's emperor), terming himself a "patrician," a clever way of harking back to the good days before the Romans had emperors. This was in 476 A.D. In 488–489, however, Odoacer's fortunes (and, arguably, those of Rome) took a turn for the worse with the invasion of the army of Theodoric, king of the Eastern Goths. Having spent much of his childhood as a hostage in Constantinople, Theodoric had developed survival skills that were apparently prodigious: in 493, he persuaded Odoacer that it would be best if they ceased fighting and, instead, ruled jointly, to which Odoacer agreed, only to be slain shortly thereafter by Theodoric at a banquet, after which Theodoric assumed the role of sole ruler of what was left of the western Roman empire until he was well into his seventies.

But this is the end of the story, the earlier chapters having involved a good thousand years during which Rome enjoyed at least a nominally republican system of government, and while, for half that time, supreme power had been in the hands of emperors, much of the day-to-day administrative work had continued to be carried on by civil servants who stood for election and were not merely a despot's culling of his cronies. It is hardly to be wondered, then, that democratic reformers of the Age of Reason, armed with a philosophy stipulating that, all other things being equal, people were capable of choosing their rulers wisely enough, should look to Roman government in its heyday for a paradigm when it came time to have done with kings and royal governors in favor of popularly elected assemblies. Prudence, indeed, drew the more conservative framers of the American Constitution to imitate the classical model of republican Rome – the word *republican* itself being from Latin *rēs publica* (the common weal), literally "thing belonging to the people," sometimes written *respublica* (commonwealth) – in preference to the free-for-all democracies of Greece – the word *democracy* being, appropriately enough, from Greek *dêmos* (common people) and *krátos* (power). Particularly attractive were those features of Roman government that allowed for a check on the many by the few, and on the few by each other, to prevent the extremes of tyranny on the one hand and mob rule on the other, with perhaps a preference for the former if it ever came down to an either/or situation.

Rome under the Tarquins already had some features of government that were quite possibly of Etruscan origin, the most notable being that the chief executives (next, of course, to the king) – the consuls – came in pairs, and continued to do so long after the office of king was cut from the bureaucratic starting lineup. (The origin of the word *consul*, which today designates not a governing magistrate but a government's resident representative in another country, is as obscure as the origin and original functions of the office itself, though Romans liked to derive the word from *consulere* [to gather together for deliberation], the basis of both English *counsel* and *consultation*.) Another possible borrowing from Etruria was the council of elders, or *senātus* – from the same root as Latin *senex* (old person) and its corresponding comparative form, *senior*. Americans in their ambivalence toward the elderly still call one of their two legislative branches the *Senate* (the other being the somewhat wordier Anglo-Latinate *House of Representatives*) without much thought about how old you have to be to be a senator – though, as it happens, the law says that you have to be at least thirty years old to be a senator (and twenty-five years old to be a member of the House of Representatives) – but *senior citizen* is a label with which only those with a penchant for irony are truly happy, and nobody but nobody wants to be called *senile*.

Otherwise, the Roman populace of the regal period was divided into the *patricii* (patricians – i.e., nobles – from *pater, patris* [father]) – sometimes known as the *quirītēs* (enfranchised citizens), a term of obscure origin but which the Romans linked either with Sabine *quiris* (spear) or with the Sabine city of *Cures*, the Sabines having been among the earliest to have thrown in their lot, willy-nilly, with the Latini as they began their clamber to the top of the heap – and the *plēbēs* (common folk – whence English *plebeian*) or *populus* (nonnoble people). The original distinction between the *plēbēs* and the *populī* – both of which, with *publicus* (of or pertaining to the people, public), probably come from the same root (of mysterious origin), and which eventually came to be used more or less interchangeably – seems to have involved the right to vote: the *populī* could and the *plēbēs* couldn't, though the Romans would have been neither the first nor last to experience some confusion at the polls, the word *poll* being of obscure Germanic origin and meaning, literally, "head," a *poll tax* being a tax on people rather than property and the *Gallup poll* being something of a head count, kindness of the statistician George Gallup.

The *plēbēs* could not own land with clear title, could not vote, could not contract strictly legal marriages, and were not eligible to serve in the army. The last Roman king but one, Servius Tullius, is credited with a number of reforms whereby in exchange for being made subject to the *tribūtum* – basically a war tax – the *plēbēs* were given representation in the new assembly, the *Comitia Centuriata*, made up of both patricians and members of the nonnoble populace. (The *Comitia Centuriata* was, literally, "the going-together [*comitia*] in the manner of a military division of a hundred men [*centuria*]" – no relation to the putting-together that gives us *committee* from Latin *committere*.) The powers of the *Comitia Centuriata* grew rapidly: though originally it could be called together only by the order of one or the other of the current two consuls, it became, with the passage of the Lex Valeria, the body to which anyone could appeal a sentence of whipping or *poena capitis*. This law, significantly enough, was said to have been passed in 509 B.C. at about the time that Rome expelled the last of the Etruscan Tarquin kings. Sixty years later, it was the *Comitia Centuriata* that ratified the Laws of the Twelve Tables, the first written-down legal code that Rome had ever seen, after plebeian agitation against a system of law that seemed (a) opaque and (b) by and for the exclusive benefit of the patrician class.

A second assembly, the *Concilium Plebis*, had been created around 470 B.C. – *concilium*, the basis of English *council*, being a literal "calling together," from *cum/com* (with, together) and the verb *cālāre* (to call, summon). One of the functions of the *Concilium Plebis* was the election of tribunes, who served as advocates for the plebeians with a certain amount of veto power over patrician legislation.

The persons of the tribunes were sacrosanct during their term of office – a year – which meant that if they annoyed even patricians and were struck, let alone killed, the striker or killer was in very hot water indeed. Moreover, votes taken in the *Concilium Plebis* – the *plēbiscītum* (whence our *plebiscite*) – were binding on all plebeians, and, by 450 B.C., on all patricians as well.

How, one might wonder, did the plebeians manage to wring these concessions, and the others that followed, from an unwilling oligarchy? In the first place, the common folk could pack up and leave for greener pastures, usually one of the other hills of Rome, and, with nobody else handy to tote those barges and lift those bales, wait until the patricians gave in. This they did on several occasions. Second, with the passage of the Canuleian Law in the fifth century B.C., the prohibition against patrician–plebeian intermarriage was removed, and consequently plebeians often found support from liberal patricians who were allied to their class by kinship ties.

In practice, then, Rome, which in the sixth century B.C. might have ended up as two separate communities like the Spartans and their Helot serfs of the same era, was, by the end of the following century, one people governed by one set of laws. This is not to say that inequity and class struggle were eliminated: indeed, up to the end of the Republic, there was considerable seesawing as now and again plebeian or patrician interests got the upper hand. What kept the system operating as well as it did was that the mechanism for class struggle was, so to speak, subdued and made part of the rationale of government: the consuls had a great deal of executive power, and they were almost invariably senators and members by birth of the property class that was a prerequisite for a senate seat; but the tribunes had an absolute power to interfere in actions involving anyone from consul right on down against a plebeian whom they thought was being unfairly treated. The senate could propose its legislation, but a plebescite in the *Concilium Plebis* was binding on everyone from senator to the lowliest freedman.

Furthermore, because consuls came in twos, the danger of a strongman seizing power was always checked by the fact that he had an equally powerful colleague to reckon with – and everybody knew that, as a last resort, the *plēbēs* could, after all, simply leave town: it had happened before. Small wonder, then, that the representatives of the new United States found the old Roman model attractive: fresh from what they considered to have been the tyranny of a king and parliament across the Atlantic, they felt they could do worse than base their own constitutional system of checks and balances on the Republic that was Rome.

A Roman setting out on a career in government followed what was called the *cursus honōrum* – *cursus* (from which English *course* is derived) comes from the verb *currere* (to run, race) – which involved the holding of a series of offices in turn. The *cursus honōrum* was basically a tenure track with something like a fast lane, a slow lane, and, in later times, a breakdown lane. The fast lane was the senatorial *cursus honōrum* traveled, for the most part, only by the more noblesse-obliging or power-hungry members of the nobility. The slow lane was the equestrian *cursus*, in which the well-to-do (or nouveau noble) *eques* (knight; literally, horseman) jockeyed for position with the possibility of slipping into the senatorial lane. The breakdown lane was modeled on the senatorial and equestrian tracks and seems to have been invented to make petty functionaries feel that they were at least on the road and going somewhere.

Square one for runners in both the senatorial and equestrian courses was military service, at least officially – there were get-arounds (alternative civil service) for those whose family history had given them a handicap in the senatorial race. For those in the equestrian order with political ambitions, there was the possibility of finessing one's assignments, *equitēs* being obliged to serve in no more than ten campaigns (making the most of booty-grabbing opportunities while preserving one's physical health being, if not prerequisites for promotion, at least bold lines on one's résumé).

The next step was a quaestorship, an army post carrying responsibility for financial affairs. After a year or so as a *quaestor*, the budding politico might become an aedile (*aedīlis*) or a tribune (*tribūnus*), assuming that he hadn't been caught with his hand in the till or otherwise disgraced himself. An *aedīlis* was essentially a glorified commissioner of public works (cf. *aedēs* [edifice]), the position having been open to plebeians as early as the fourth century B.C. The ediles (sometimes known as "curulian aediles" because they were allowed to sit on a *sella curūlis*, a fancy chair that magistrates got as a sign of office) came to have a number of functions, including administering the public games (at some personal expense).

A *tribūnus* was literally "one of the tribe," i.e., "one representing or in charge of the tribe." Tribunes came in both civilian and military flavors, the *tribūnus plēbis* being, originally, a civilian magistrate appointed to look out for patrician abuses of the plebeians, the *tribūnus aerārius* being the bagman, basically, for the military (his chief duties being collecting the war tax and doling out the soldiers' pay), and the *tribūnus lāticlāuius* (literally, "wide-striped tribune," after the senatorial stripe that was part of the uniform of the up-and-coming officer) being a senior officer on the move.

After the quaestorship and the optional stint as aedile or tribune, the next stop in the senatorial *cursus* was the praetorship, *praetōrēs* having considerable authority in their courts to say how their predecessors' annual edicts and the Laws of the Twelve Tables were to be interpreted. The corresponding move for an *eques* would have been to a procuratorship, a post involving any of a variety of administrative duties in civilian government, the literal meaning of *prōcūrātor* being "one who takes care (of something)." After this, an *eques* might go on to hold one or another of the *praefectūrae*, administrative offices ranging from military commander to lieutenant governor to governor of one of the provinces.

At this point, since the census every five years allowed one to be enrolled in the ranks of the *equitēs* or senators if one met the property qualifications and was not of patently immoral character (conversely, *not* fulfilling these conditions could get one drummed out, though this was rare), there was a good chance of sitting in the senate, with the consulship as the final plum for those who had completed the senatorial *cursus:* aside from the civilian authority the consuls had, each also commanded a consular army.

In theory, this meant that a reasonably prosperous "new man" (*nouus homō*) might slip through the old-boy network and rise from relative obscurity to Rome's highly visible top post in a period of twenty to twenty-five years of public service. In practice, however, it became increasingly more difficult to do so as time went on: Cicero was the first "new man" in nearly a century, and he possessed exceptional gifts. The patricians naturally tended to back their own, and even the populace at large tended to vote for a member of one of the established aristocratic families – the Claudii, the Fabii, or the Valerii, say – against a relative newcomer, and it would not be until the days of the empire that freedmen would sit in the senate, facts of political life that are still with us today.

What went sour for the Republic was not so much the system of government itself but other factors beyond its control. A source of friction that got out of hand was the decline of the small farmer against the large landowner working his estates with slave labor: many displaced farmers moved to Rome, when their holdings were swallowed up by the competition, to become protégés of rich urban patrons or, more often, disaffected urban proletarians subsisting on public doles or whatever else they could hustle, unless they went into the army.

A second fly in the ointment was, ironically, Rome's success as a world power: having subdued southern Italy and then Carthage, and embroiled itself in the wars among the Greek city-states at the beginning of the second century B.C., Rome found itself with a great deal more turf to manage than it quite knew what to do with, the turf coming, naturally, with great numbers of residents with whom the government had to deal in one way or another. While the new provinces were a splendid place to learn a trade and earn a fortune, they also became pawns to fight over, and the alternating dictatorships of the consuls Sulla and Marius in the early years of the first century B.C. left a lot of people dead in the struggle for power, civil strife which the regular governmental apparatus of the Republic found itself powerless to restrain.

In 52 B.C., Pompey was consul without a colleague, an unprecedented thing, though somewhat short of a dictatorship. So had been the triumvirate of Pompey, Julius Caesar, and Crassus, but in this case catastrophe was averted for the time being when Caesar got command of an army and busied himself with the conquest of Gaul while Crassus set off to be beaten and killed trying to go him one better in an attempt to subdue Parthia. With Crassus out of the way, Pompey and Caesar squared off in 49 B.C. when Caesar crossed the Rubicon (the official border between the Roman state and Gaul, apparently a tiny stream whose historical location is unknown today) under arms in defiance of a senatorial order to relinquish his command, and Pompey marched forth with the senate's backing to try to stop him. Caesar's victory, so bitingly described in Lucan's epic *Pharsalia*, left Pompey dead and Caesar dictator for life – that is, through the fifteenth of March, 44 B.C. The conspirators – or, as they called themselves, the "liberators" – who did Caesar in were promptly dispatched by the Second Triumvirate, consisting of Marc Antony, Octavian (afterward Augustus), and Lepidus.

By this time, it was pretty clear that the Republic had had it, and despite the fact that the Second Triumvirate took pains to see to it that their extraordinary powers were ratified by the popular assembly, infighting among them left Antony dead and Lepidus in permanent exile. Suetonius says that Octavian considered restoring the republican form of government once Antony was out of the way, but decided against it on the credible grounds that all that would have come of it was yet another civil war: he preferred, he said, "to build solid and permanent foundations for the government of the country." So when the doors of the temple of Janus closed – this was done only in the rare outbreaks of peace that punctuated the usual Roman state of war – they closed on the last chance for the Republic too, Octavian having realized that the empire he ruled had outgrown the republican system that had made possible the winning of it.

This is not to say that the underpinnings of the Republic did not hold – the aedileships and quaestorships and all the rest. But the senate came to have little power after the periodic purges of Tiberius, Caligula, and Nero and in the civil wars of the Year of the Four Emperors (69 A.D.); and the reign of Vespasian, his sons Domitian and Titus, and the succeeding Five Good Emperors was founded on capable autocracy and an effective bureaucratic machine. In the correspondence between the emperor Trajan and his governor of Bithynia, Pliny the Younger, we see at once the strength and weakness of the new order: as long as a capable ruler was at the helm of the ship of state and authority was delegated only to the reasonably competent, a huge empire could be administered with comparative smoothness, even in the face of novel problems at home and abroad (e.g., Pliny's famous query to Trajan about what to do with accused Christians who refused to sacrifice to Roman gods). In the centuries that followed, it became clear that this system was the exception rather than the rule, and the last of the Five Good Emperors, Marcus Aurelius, experimented briefly with a co-regent. Later, co-regency would again become the rule: two emperors would reign, one over the eastern empire and the other over the western empire, each with the title of Augustus, each with an understudy called Caesar.

Nevertheless, some of the language of the Republic would persist, lip-service to a state of affairs long gone, and the governmental doublespeak of today especially in times of war and civil strife – "build-down" for rearmament, "peacekeeping force" for head-beaters, "selective ordnance" for napalm, "pacification program" for genocide, and "frank disclosure" for lies – has its precedent in the last days of the empire when Odoacer dubbed himself a patrician when what he actually meant was Big Brother, anticipating George Orwell's observation that, when it comes to official-dom's trying to pull the wool over people's eyes, "a mass of Latin words fall upon the facts like light snow."

Gg

H

IS FOR *HANNIBAL, HASDRUBAL, HAMIL-car,* and *Hanno,* Carthaginians all. *Carthage* (Latin *Carthāgō,* Phoenician *qrt-hdsht* [New Town]) was founded as an offshoot either of Utica or of its parent city, Tyre, in Phoenicia. Starting in about 500 B.C. and for some 350 years thereafter, the Carthaginians were the major maritime power in the western Mediterranean until the Romans finally burned their city to the ground at the close of the third Punic War. (*Punic* is cognate with *Phoenician,* though the Romans used the term to refer specifically to the Carthaginian branch of the Phoenician family.) So thorough was the Roman destruction of Carthage that archaeologists are uncertain as to precisely where the ancient city stood on the peninsula just north of what is today the Bay of Tunis.

Phoenicia was a strip of land barely thirty-five miles wide but over two hundred miles long, extending from the south coast of Asia Minor all the way down to Gaza – the western coastline of present-day Syria, Lebanon, and Israel. It was a loose confederation of cities rather than a unified kingdom, the principal settlements being Tyre and Sidon, Berytus (modern Beirut) being somewhat obscure until Roman imperial times, when it came to house one of the foremost law schools of the empire. From about 1600 B.C. to 1100 B.C., Sidon was the chief city; Tyre later eclipsed it. In the middle of the ninth century B.C., Phoenicia was conquered by the expanding Assyrians. Held briefly by the Egyptians in around 600 B.C., it was absorbed into the Babylonian empire and, under Cyrus, became a province of Persia. Alexander the Great destroyed Tyre in 332 B.C. At his death, Phoenicia became part of the Seleucid kingdom of Syria, which was in turn annexed by the Romans under Pompey in 64 B.C.

The Greeks said that Phoenicia was named after *Phoinix*, brother of Europa and Kadmos – the same Kadmos who, according to legend, brought the alphabet to Boeotia. (That the Phoenician alphabet was the precursor of all the other alphabetic scripts known to the world today is certain: an early form of the alphabet is reported from Ugarit at Phoenicia's northern end from as early as 1200 B.C.) The Greeks also suggested a connection between *Phoenician* and *phoinós* (blood red), whether as a reference to the famous purple-red dye that the Phoenicians made from crushed snail shells, used to color their distinctive naval uniforms, and exported all over the Mediterranean, or as a reference to the color of the Phoenicians' skin (much as the *Picts* – Latin *Pictī* [Painted Ones] – were so called because of their practice of painting their bodies before charging naked into battle). In either case, it is doubtful that the Greeks recalled the original sense of the root from which *phoinós* is descended, namely, "smite, kill," whence the *-fend* of *offend* and *defend* and, via Norse, the word *gun*. And as if this were not enough, the Greeks saw a further connection between *Phoenicia* and the fabulous bird called the *phoenix*, which lives five hundred years, consumes itself in its funeral pyre, and leaves behind an egg which hatches to become the next phoenix. This creature was supposed to be indigenous to Egypt. The Egyptians, for what it's worth, called the Phoenicians *Punti*. As for the Phoenicians, they thought of themselves as Canaanites.

Phoenicia produced cedar lumber (from the famed cedars of Lebanon mentioned in the Bible and depicted on the modern-day Lebanese flag), paper (from the port city of Byblos, north of Tyre and Sidon, and so celebrated that its name was borrowed by the Greeks as their word for book – *biblíon* – whence our *Bible*), the dye known as *Tyrean purple*, glass (fused from the silica sands of Phoenicia's generous coastline), and ships, sometimes over a hundred feet long, in which the Phoenicians made trading voyages all over the Mediterranean. Many of the trading posts that they established became respectable colonies in their own right; and the greatest of these was Carthage.

Latin and Greek writers of antiquity generally agreed that Carthage was founded by Queen Elissa, who was also called Dido (an epithet of the goddess Astarte – Ishtar, the moon goddess of the Babylonian pantheon, later identified with Greek Artemis, whose great shrine was at Ephesus). Dido left Phoenicia as the result of a dispute with her brother, Pygmalion – not the Pygmalion of Greco-Roman myth who carved a statue so beautiful that he fell in love with it and whose prayers were answered by the gods when they changed it into the real live maiden Galatea, the inspiration of George Bernard Shaw's play ultimately metamorphosed into the Broadway musical *My Fair Lady*. The Phoenician Pygmalion was the king of Tyre (and the nephew of the biblical Queen Jezebel) who murdered Dido's husband Sychaeus for his wealth. Dido, fearing for her own life, fled to North Africa where she made a deal with the local inhabitants to buy from them, for a certain price, as much land as could be contained by a bull's hide. She then diddled them by cutting the hide into thin strips and so encompassed the better part of the point of land north of present-day Tunis and south of the *stagnum marīnum* (literally "sea swamp," or what we might better call Back Bay) which would later serve as Carthage's military harbor. The area measured out was known as the Byrsa (from Greek *býrsa* [hide] which appears in Latin as *bursa* [sack, pouch] which, in turn, survives in medicalese as *bursa* [saclike cavity between joints or points of friction], the inflammation of which is called *bursitis*; in English as *purse*, the *purs-* of *purser*, and the *burs-* of *bursar*; and in French as *Bourse/ bourse*, the lowercase version being a bag or purse, and, by extension, a grant, and the uppercase version being the Gallic Stock Exchange, the original having been a hotel in Bruges run by a family named Van der Burse – Italian *della Borsa* – catering to Venetian businessmen). The Byrsa contained the citadel of Carthage, an acropolis with its own walls and approached by a flight of sixty steps. Surrounding the Byrsa was a triple wall within whose bounds was shelter for three hundred elephants and four thousand horses. South of the Byrsa was a suburb called Magalia (modern-day Mara) and the harbor for commercial vessels which had access to the Bay of Tunis.

Dido is also credited with having entertained Aeneas on his flight from fallen Troy and is said to have killed herself when he abandoned her to follow his destiny to the shores of Italy, all of which Vergil describes in the *Aeneid* in great hexametrical detail. Another tradition has it that Dido died by her own hand rather than be forced to marry a neighboring king named Iarbas. Aeneas's shipboard view of the smoke from Dido's pyre as he sailed away was probably invented by Vergil to tie in with the much later burning of Carthage by his countrymen. Seventeen hundred years later, Nahum Tate, whose libretto Henry Purcell used for the opera *Dido and Aeneas*, would rewrite Vergil in turn, making the messenger calling Aeneas away not Mercury but a false spirit concocted by three witches with a grudge against "the Queen of Carthage, whom we hate/As we do all in prosp'rous state." At the end of the three witches' scene, the chorus sings:

> *Destruction's our delight,*
> *Delight, our greatest sorrow:*
> *Elissa bleeds tonight*
> *And Carthage flames tomorrow!*

Fire did, in fact, play an important part in Carthaginian religion: although Dido is said to have made Astarte the tutelary deity of the new city, by the time of the Punic wars at least as much attention was being paid to Moloch, whom we also know from biblical references, mainly those prohibiting child-immolation in the fires of the god's worship. (While, in all likelihood, the sacrificial victims tended to be drawn from the ranks of prisoners of war, it is claimed that in extreme circumstances the Carthaginians were not above sacrificing their own children, it being said that no fewer than two hundred aristocratic babies were offered to Moloch when the Carthaginians were besieged in 310 B.C. by Agathocles, tyrant of Syracuse.) Baal – familiar from Elijah's contest with the two altars, as set forth in II Kings (1:10 ff.) – also had a considerable following at Carthage: the Punic names *Hannibal* and *Hasdrubal* meant "Mercy of Baal" and "He Whose Help Is Baal" respectively. That the Carthaginians also sacrificed to Greek gods for good measure is suggested by the story that Hamilcar Barca had made the nine-year-old Hannibal swear eternal enmity to Rome on an altar dedicated to Zeus. Greek and Roman writers report that the Carthaginians' religious practices included obscene rites, but the extant Punic inscriptions and bas-reliefs fail to substantiate this, and some of the grosser allegations, such as that the Phoenicians regularly copulated with animals, are pretty clearly biblical invective against the Canaanites, whom the Jews were vigorously trying to make go away. Aristotle, in the *Oeconomica* i.5, says that the morality of the Carthaginians was if anything a little on the straitlaced side. The Romans, on the other hand, ascribed to Carthage all the wiles of an Odysseus, and even the Greek Polybius describes as "a typical Punic trick" Hannibal's wearing several different wigs in order to make it hard for the Celts of Cisalpine Gaul to recognize him from one day to the next, as he did not trust his brand-new allies overmuch and thought it prudent to guard against an assassination.

It was inevitable that the expanding spheres of influence of Rome and Carthage should collide. The only reason that they did not do so sooner was that Greek colonies lay in the paths of both. While Rome was still forging alliances with neighboring city-states and kicking out the last of the Tarquins, the Greeks and the Phoenicians between them had sewn up much of the coastline of the Mediterranean Sea: Greeks controlled the southern coast of Italy and what is now the French Riviera, with important colonies at Tarraco, Massilia, and Nicaea; the Phoenicians for their part held sway all along the North African coast from the Gulf of Sidra to the Straits of Gibraltar, as well as the entire southern coast of Spain. In addition, they controlled the western tip of Sicily – Greeks had colonized the rest – as well as the perennially strategic islands of Majorca and Minorca off

Spain, Melita (now Malta) off the southern corner of Sicily, and much of Sardinia. The Phoenicians also had a toe-hold in Etruria, and it was a combined force of Carthaginians and Etruscans who fought against Phocaean colonists from Asia Minor in 536 B.C. for possession of Corsica, a struggle that the latter lost after inflicting such awful casualties that the Etruscans thought better of trying to hold the island and withdrew to the mainland instead.

The first treaty between Rome and Carthage dates from 509 B.C., shortly after the expulsion of Tarquin the Proud and the Etruscan ruling class. The Romans agreed not to sail south of "the Fair Promontory" (probably Cape Bon) and, if blown off course, not to remain longer than five days for repairs and provisioning, all of which amounted to the Romans' conceding Carthaginian hegemony in North Africa, and (elsewhere in the treaty) in Sardinia as well. Each agreed not to attack the other's allies in Sicily. Nevertheless, the Carthaginians a scant thirty years later mounted an assault on the Greek cities in Sicily, timed apparently to coincide with the Persian invasion of Attica under Xerxes. A Punic commander named Hamilcar – not the Hamilcar Barca who was the father of Hannibal, neither of whom would be born for another two hundred years or so – suffered a crushing defeat of his force of three thousand ships and a hundred times as many troops (including not only Carthaginians but Spaniards, Corsicans, Sardinians, and possibly Volscians from mainland Italy) almost simultaneously with the Persian disaster at Salamis, which had a decidedly quieting effect on any talk of Carthaginian pugilistics in Sicily for the next seventy years.

Besides, the Carthaginians had business elsewhere, since the expeditions of Hanno and Himilco around 500 B.C. had opened up the northern Atlantic coast of Africa – which Hanno seems to have explored as far south as Senegal, founding en route the town which became present-day Tangier – and the tin deposits of Cornwall to Punic exploitation. But Carthage could not resist the temptation to take Sicily under its protective wing and so spent much of the period from 411 B.C. (when Syracuse drove the Athenians out) to 264 B.C. (the outbreak of hostilities with Rome) attempting to do just that. The first Punic War lasted nearly twenty-five years and made the reputation of Hamilcar Barca (*Barca* being the Latin rendering of Phoenician *brq* [lightning]), who was, however, empowered – enjoined, really – to sue for peace when things got hopeless and acceded to Roman demands for indemnities of 3,200 talents of silver to be paid over ten years, and the permanent withdrawal of the Carthaginians from Sicily. Civil war ensued at Carthage, together with the revolt of the Libyans and Numidians at home and the loss of Sardinia abroad: the Carthaginians managed with difficulty to subdue their immediate neighbors, but the Romans moved into the power gap in Sardinia without so much as a by-your-leave. Hamilcar was sent to Spain and spent the next ten years consolidating Punic power there, his sons Hannibal, Hasdrubal, and Mago learning the family trade at their father's knee and succeeding him when Hamilcar drowned while withdrawing from a siege.

In 218 B.C., Hannibal, acting on assurances of help from the Italian Celts of Cisalpine Gaul, set out from New Carthage in Spain (nowadays known as Cartagena). Marching up the coast through southern Gaul, he won over the Greek towns and Roman allies along the way, whether by force or by promises of the greater benefits to be gained from alliance with Carthage. His famous crossing of the Alps, elephants and all, was accomplished with heavy casualties – some say as high as fifty percent – but the element of surprise more than made up for it when he arrived in Cisalpine Gaul, probably via the Col de la Traversette, upstream from Turin. (The *cis-* of *Cisalpine Gaul*, by the way, is a nifty Latin preposition meaning "this side of," Cisalpine Gaul being the part of Gaul, from the Roman perspective, on this side of the Alps. *Cisvestitism*, first cousin to *transvestitism*, refers to the practice of dressing up in clothes appropriate to one's sex but inappropriate to one's station in life, as when a policewoman dresses up as a prostitute or a king dresses up as

a priest.) The inhabitants of northern Italy had doubtless never seen an elephant – or, for that matter, a black African: a coin of the period, apparently struck by the Carthaginians as part of an issue to pay off their Italian allies, depicts an elephant driven by a black mahout. (Some of the drivers may have been from India, as is the word *mahout* – from Sanskrit *mahāmātra*, an honorific title whose literal meaning is great [*mahā*] measure [*mātra*] – but this, like so much else in life, is not so certain as it might be.) It is possible that Hannibal had camels along as well. Who knows? In any case, it was an outstandlandish cast of Celts, Moors, Spaniards, Carthaginian regulars, and weird animals that the Romans faced on their first blind date with Hannibal at the River Trebia, and, though commanded by the able Publius Cornelius Scipio (the Elder), the Romans were soundly trounced.

Once south of the Alps, Hannibal pressed on down the west coast of Italy, simultaneously cajoling Rome's Italian allies over to his side and destroying farms and villages when the locals refused to come along nicely. Hannibal lost an eye to what appears to have been ophthalmia that wet winter, and his troops were generally miserable, being sometimes obliged to bivouac, it is said, on the piled-up bodies of drowned pack animals, the only dry spot around. But in spite of their privations, the Carthaginians inflicted on the Romans their most ghastly defeat since the Gallic victory at the River Allia in 390 B.C.: fifteen thousand Romans and their allies were cut to pieces in the mists of the Etrurian shore of Lake Trasimene.

In dire emergencies, the Romans would suspend their usual consular form of government and appoint a dictator whose term was limited to six months; and this is what the Romans did now. Quintus Fabius, realizing that the Carthaginians could probably destroy the Roman army in open combat, avoided getting blown away by going for on-going harrying actions, which earned him the agnomen *Cunctātor* (Delayer). When his term of command was up, however, his superior, the consul Varro, determined on taking Hannibal's bull by the horns and, joining forces with his more cautious colleague, Paullus, led both armies out against the invaders at Cannae. This time, the losses were far greater even than at Lake Trasimene: the Romans and their allies lost between fifty and seventy thousand soldiers, and had Hannibal not been less headstrong than his cavalry commander Maharbal, who was all for making an immediate dash on Rome itself, modern Europe might be speaking some northern dialect of Phoenician today. As it was, scarcely seventy souls escaped the battlefield with Varro, while Paullus and his army – save for a contingent left in camp – were totally wiped out.

The terrible news of Cannae threw Rome into near panic, partly because the military scene wasn't at all bright and partly because some evil portents happened to portend themselves at the time as a sort of negative lagniappe: an earthquake did its thing, and it was discovered that one of the Vestal Virgins wasn't. The Romans did what they could: an envoy (Fabius Pictor) was dispatched to the oracle at Delphi, while the younger Scipio (who had fought alongside his father of the same name at Trebia and received a wound from which he was barely recovered) was put in charge of the remains of Paullus's army, and Appius Claudius Pulcher (the Fair) was made a naval commander and set to work building up the Roman fleet, which he remodeled largely on the Carthaginian vessels captured earlier in the war. Troops were posted for the immediate defense of the city, but Hannibal contented himself for the moment with trying to subvert Campania, without much success, and sending back to Carthage the spoils of war (including a huge pile of rings stripped from Roman casualties of equestrian rank) with a request for more troops. Back in Carthage, however, Hanno – the leader of the anti-Barca faction in city politics – opposed sending Hannibal any further aid, and what little was sent (mostly cavalry) was slow in coming, as much from bureaucratic red tape as from coolness on the part of the folks back home. It could be argued that at this point Hannibal's fortunes began to falter as the Romans' began to rise.

In spite of these setbacks, however, Hannibal continued

his policy of laying waste the Italian countryside and subverting the Italian allies – from which southern Italy, says Toynbee, has never recovered to this day – carrying on for another thirteen years though never doing anything like the damage he had done in the first three. Eventually, his failure to bring the war to a quick end after Cannae caught up with him: the successes of Scipio in Spain together with the reconquest of Sicily left Hannibal without support from allies in either place after 210 B.C., and there was increasing opposition back home in Carthage. Hannibal's attempts to enlist help from Greece were countered by Roman expeditionary forces whose involvement in Greek affairs of state was to set in motion the process by which most of Greece would later become a Roman province. Hannibal's brother Hasdrubal was slain at the battle of Metaurus River in 207 B.C. while on his way with relief forces; and Hannibal himself was defeated at Crotona four years later and forced to withdraw to Africa. In 202 B.C., Hannibal was beaten for good at Zama, south of Carthage, by Scipio's army (with the aid of cavalry supplied by King Massanissa of Numidia).

This time, the Romans demanded reparations of 10,000 talents to be paid back over the next fifty years. No particular restrictions were placed on future Carthaginian merchant voyages, but the war fleet was reduced to a mere ten triremes, and Carthage had to promise not to make war on anyone, inside or outside of Africa, without permission from the Roman senate. One hundred hostages were sent to Rome to secure the peace. One might have expected another civil war in Carthage in the wake of this humiliating peace, but Hannibal's faction held the upper hand and ruled the city for another six years with Hannibal himself holding a magistracy from which he strengthened the collective hand of the magistrates (*suffetēs*, or, in Punic, *suffetim*) against the aristocratic party which, through its five-man commissions, the *pentarchies*, had for some time been nibbling away at the power of the suffetes and the Carthaginian senate. Revenge, however, seems not to have been far from Hannibal's mind, and when his party was overthrown and he was forced out of Carthage, he fled to Antiochus, the king of Syria, who viewed with understandable alarm the Roman interventions in the quarrels among the Greek city-states. The Romans eventually put pressure on Antiochus to surrender Hannibal who, seeing no way out this time, poisoned himself rather than risk the ignominy in being the main attraction in someone else's triumphal march before being strangled in prison.

Ironically, it was the ease with which the Carthaginians paid off the Roman reparations debt that gave the excuse for the third Punic War. Although Carthage's army had its teeth drawn, the city continued to fare very well in trade, and it was Roman envy, coupled with the constant harping upon the same string by the senator Cato the Elder – he would end every speech, on whatever subject, by saying that, by the bye, Carthage ought to be destroyed (*Carthāgō dēlenda est*) – that resulted in Rome's declaring war on Carthage once again on the flimsiest of pretexts and obliterating the place in 146 B.C. The city burned for seventeen days and nights and was then plowed under and sown with salt. What was left of it was used as a quarry both by the builders of the Roman colonies sent out in 122 B.C. (to Iunonia, which did not prosper) and in 46 B.C. (to *Colōnia Carthāgō*, which did just fine, rising to rival Alexandria as the second most important city in the empire, the Carthage of Saint Augustine's young manhood), and by the merchants of Genoa when they crossed the sea to trade with Tunis during the Middle Ages. Ironically, some of the latest work of destruction was carried out by the builders of the Tunisian Railway at the beginning of this century. Virtually all that remains of this once great city are the ruins of an aqueduct of some fifty miles' length which supplied the locals with water in its heyday.

The emperor Claudius, an amateur philologist and historian of no mean accomplishment, is said by Suetonius to have written a history of Carthage in eight books – now lamentably lost. Considering their long if less than peaceful coexistence, it is a little surprising that so little of the Phoenician language found its way into Latin. One survival is the word *cucumber:* the Latin version was *cucumis, cucumeris* and seems to have been a borrowing of Punic *cumsisezar.* Another notable steal is the salutation Auē (hello, hi there). Although the imperial Romans construed a verb *auēre* to account for *auē,* this appears to have been something of an afterthought built on the analogy of *ualēre* and *saluēre,* whose imperatives – *ualē* (goodbye) and *saluē* (howdy) – were standard forms of greeting. Auē is unattested prior to the late Republican period. The playwright Plautus, who flourished at the end of the second Punic War and whose *Pseudolus* is still alive and well, its latest incarnation being as the musical comedy A *Funny Thing Happened on the Way to the Forum,* used *auō* as a singular and plural imperative form, suggesting a vagueness as to the actual grammatical status of the word. (Plautus may or may not have known some Punic: his *Poenulus* [*The Little Carthaginian*] has some twenty lines of what is generally thought to be Phoenician in it – scholars are still slugging it out over the translation of the fragment. Terence, the Roman comedian who forms a boxed set with Plautus, hailed, it is said, from Carthage but seems never to have written anything in the lingo for popular consumption.) Formulaic salutations are often passed from one language to another even among unfriendly speakers: Italian *ciao* is used in France and in Austria, where it's spelled *tschau,* a greeting apparently derived from Latin *sclāuus* (slave, Slav) through Italian *sciavo* ([your] servant), and brought back by Austrian troops who had served in the armies of Venice; German-speaking Swiss say *salut* (health); Dalmatian Croats say *addio* (which they accent on the first syllable), and Americans, depending on how pretentious they feel like being at the time, say *adieu, adiós, ciao,* or *see you down on the farm, sport.*

I · J

IS FOR *INDO-EUROPEAN* – *AND FOR JOKE*.
(It's also for *Incitatus*, the only horse ever to be proposed –
by the mad emperor Caligula – for a consulship.) The Indo-
Europeans were nomads who seem to have originally lived
just north of the Caucasus mountains some six thousand
years ago, whence they migrated outward in several waves,
some to India, others to Asia Minor and to Europe. We
may be certain that such a people existed from, among
other things, the evidence provided by historical linguistics,
and can postulate with reasonable confidence a common
language which these people spoke – Proto-Indo-European (PIE for short) – and from which the Balto-Slavic,
Celtic, and Germanic languages are descended, as are Sanskrit, Old Persian, Hittite, Greek, and Latin.

The assumption is, basically, that when different languages have systematically similar words for the same lexi-
cal item throughout their whole vocabulary, the similarities
are more likely to betoken a shared linguistic ancestor than
rampant borrowing between linguistic strangers. A further
assumption is that certain kinds of vocabulary are more
likely to be inheritances than the result of a cultural swap:
basic kinship terms, the words for the numbers from one to
ten, the words for the basic parts of the body, and so on,
aren't quite so apt to be passed around as are the words for
new technological goodies or exotic foods. So, when it
turns out that Latin *duo*, Greek *dúo*, Sanskrit *dvāu*, English
two, Latvian *dīv*, and Irish Gaelic *dó* all mean "two"; Greek
pénte, Sanskrit *pañca*, Welsh *pimp*, English *five*, and Latin
quinque all mean "five"; Sanskrit *pita*, Latin *pater*, Greek
patēr, English *father*, and Old Norse *fadhir* all mean "father," we begin to suspect the presence of a trout in the milk
and begin to round up all of the suspects that look like Indo-
Europeans.

The *Indo-* of *Indo-European* comes through Latin from Greek *Indós* (Indian), Indians being so called by association with the Indus River – *Indós* – the name for which the Greeks borrowed from Old Persian in which *Hindu*, like its Sanskrit cognate *sindhu*, meant "river, especially the Indus." The lowercase version of the *Indo-* prefix, as found in such chemical terms as *indoaniline* and *indophenol*, is derived from English *indigo*, itself derived from Greek (*phármakon*) *indikón* (Indian remedy), specifically, dye from Indian plants of the genus *Indigofera*. The Romans, however, did not have to worry about the distinction between upper- and lowercase, since originally there wasn't any: one set of quasi-block capitals was apparently sufficient unto the day. (*Uppercase* and *lowercase* as items of vocabulary, superseding *majuscule* and *minuscule* for capital and small letters respectively, come from the days of cold type in which the compositor sat at a bench facing two wooden type cases from which the type was extracted letter by letter and set in racks called galleys; the lower – and closer – type case held the small letters, and the upper case held the capitals. With the advent of computer typesetting, the type case of today is more often than not an interior decorator's prop for storing spices or knickknacks in somebody's upscale home.)

As a result of the lack of differentiation between minuscule/lowercase and majuscule/uppercase in Roman times, speaker-writers of Latin may not have had as fancy spice racks as we have today, but they also didn't have to bother dotting their *i*'s. For the Romans, who after all had borrowed the nuts and bolts of writing from the non–Indo-European Etruscans (who ultimately had to thank the equally non–Indo-European Phoenicians for their alphabet), the nondotted letter *i* did quite a bit of work: it represented both the short and long *i* of the language – contrast *pĭlus* (hair) with *pīlus* (spear), two quite distinct words for the Romans – and the semiconsonantal *y* sound of, say, *Iugurtha* (the African monarch defeated by Marius – later dictator – around the beginning of the first century B.C. and subsequently strangled in a Roman prison). The earliest

Roman users of the alphabet presumably figured that it wasn't worth the bother of inventing new orthographic symbols to distinguish among short, long, and semiconsonantal *i* (though in India, the refiners of Sanskrit's Devanagari script did just that and then some) because nobody's perfect and, besides, semiconsonantal *i* only showed up before a vowel, while long and short *i* generally showed up elsewhere, or close enough to avoid any unpleasant confusion, so why muddy the water?

In the uncial period, when Romanesque writing got fancier, scribes took to adding a little tail on the bottom of the still-dotless *I*. Later, somebody – or a number of somebodies – got the bright idea of writing *I*-with-a-tail – *J* – exclusively for semiconsonantal *i*, as in *major* for *maior* (the greater), *Juppiter* for *Iuppiter* (Jupiter), *jocus* for *iocus* (jest, joke), and the like. Subsequently, *J* also came to be written for any *I* in word-final position: *filij* was written in place of *filii* (sons), and *IIJ* replaced *III*, the Roman numeral for three. It is from this latter practice that *IJ*, the new version of the Roman numeral *II*, came to be written under or after an item to be repeated, eventually becoming identical with the regular double quotation mark (which evolved, however, from a quite different source, as will be explained below). The use of the letter *y* at the end of English words like *family* and *fray* is a confused borrowing of the uncial use of final *J* in place of *I*: we are taught to change the *y* to *i* and add *-es* when making the plural of *family* and the like, but actually it would be more accurate to say that the way you make the singular of *families* is to drop the *es* and change the *i* to *y*. *Fray* and other words ending in vowel plus a *y* sound are conveniently ignored, as are proper nouns: the plural of *Harry* isn't ordinarily *Harries* but *Harrys* (which the shaky in their spelling are known to spell *Harry's*, hoping that nobody will notice). Our practice of capitalizing the first person singular pronoun – *I* – is also bizarrely tied in with the badly understood conventions of when to write Roman *I* with a tail and when to leave well enough alone.

In the latter days of the Middle Ages, minuscule (lowercase) *i* and *j* both got dots, presumably so that they wouldn't be confused with minuscule (lowercase) *l*. Meanwhile, Latin's *y* sound got palatalized in Old French to [ǰ], as did Latin's *g* before *i* and *e*, changes preserved in such English borrowings from French as *judge* (from Latin *iūdicāre*) and *German* (from Latin *Germānus*). To complicate matters, Old English [g] became a spirant in some environments – compare *yard* (Old English *geard*) with its cognate *garden* – where it was written with the Middle English character *yogh* (ȝ). *Yogh* eventually got replaced with the letter *y*, originally borrowed for other purposes, and *j* and *g* got used hit or miss for the [ǰ] of *gist* (from Latin *iacere* [to throw]) and *jest* (from Latin *gesta*).

Gesta was originally the neuter plural form of the past participle of the Latin verb *gerere* (to make, do, act), as in *bellum gerere* (to wage war, whence *belligerent*). *Gesta* literally meant "things done, deeds." A book entitled *Gesta Romanorum* (Things That the Romans Did) was compiled at the turn of the fourteenth century A.D., apparently for the use of clergymen, containing as it did tales to enliven otherwise soporific sermons. The stories in it were largely apocryphal, not about actual Romans at all – many are of Oriental origin, borrowed either through Greek or, one suspects, from Arabic sources. Chaucer, Shakespeare, and a host of other English writers used the plots of the stories in this book, sometimes at second or third hand. *Gesta* comes down to us in English through French *geste:* of the various so-called *chansons de geste* in which the French recounted the stories of their favorite heroes and heroines in verse, perhaps the most familiar to modern readers is the *Song of Roland*, which tells how Charlemagne's young kinsman and his companions were slaughtered at Roncesvalles in a rear-guard action during a campaign against the Muslim-held citadel of Saragossa. *Jest*, then, originally meant deed, then, "tale about a deed," and, eventually, innocent fiction or funny story.

Iocus (funny story, pleasantry, play on words, whence French *jeu* [game, play] as in *jeu de cartes* [card game] and *jeu de mots* [play on words]) was originally used in opposition to *sērium* (something serious), on the one hand, and *lūdus* (physical game, play, whence English *ludicrous*). In his primer for aspiring members of the legal trade, the *Institutio Orationis*, Quintilian (who flourished under the Flavian emperors in the first century A.D.) discourses at some length on the use of humor in the courtroom – "a power which," he says, "by moving a judge to laugh, often turns him aside from the thrust of the facts, and now and then can be used to rescue him from feeling tired and fed up with the proceedings." Quintilian had a marked preference for jokes which turned on the meanings of words, and much of the humor which has been handed down to us from the Romans is of this sort. Quintilian's younger contemporary, Suetonius (on whose *Twelve Caesars* Robert Graves's *I, Claudius* is based), repeats a number of mots of the emperor Vespasian, first of the Flavians, ranging from the catty to the erudite: when, for example, a perfumed young man came to the emperor to thank him for a promotion, Vespasian, revolted, rescinded the order, saying that he wouldn't have minded the smell half as much if it had been garlic. (Julius Caesar, says Suetonius, used to maintain that his men fought just as well stinking of perfume as not – if it was someone else's at least.) Again, when Mestrius Florus criticized Vespasian for pronouncing *plaustra* as though it were *plostra* (as a Bostonian might poke fun at a Midwesterner for pronouncing *Mary* and *merry* the same), Vespasian twitted the pedant the next day by addressing him as "Mestrius *Flaurus*." A further story is told that Vespasian, whose somewhat priggish son Titus (the future emperor) took him to task for putting a tax on the contents of the municipal privies (for urine was part of the recipe used by the fullers to clean togas and, therefore, a valuable commodity), waited until the first day's proceeds were in; then, taking one of the coins, he brought it to Titus, asking, "Say, does this smell bad to you?" Titus, suspecting nothing, said, "No," to which his father gleefully responded, "Funny. It came straight from the pisspots!" Vespasian's fi-

IJ

99

nal attempt at boffo humor came on his deathbed when, in ridicule of the current practice of deifying emperors once they shuffled off this mortal coil, he remarked "Good Lord! I must be turning into a god!"

The Cicero to whom one is introduced in high school or college Latin courses as some minor Roman deity, and who seems a very dry and pedantic fellow, actually had a sense of humor too, believe it or not. Suetonius again reports that Julius Caesar had debauched Tertia, the daughter of Servilia (and sister of Marcus Brutus, who eventually had a hand in doing him in). Servilia is said to have facilitated the contretemps between Tertia and Caesar, and surely they were good friends. When Caesar subsequently sold Servilia some of his estates at an astonishingly low price, Cicero remarked that "it was even cheaper than you might think, for it was discounted by a third (*tertiā*)." Quintilian further notes that when one Fabia Dolobella gave it out that she was thirty years old, Cicero rejoined that this must be true because "I've heard this said for the past twenty years."

Caesar Augustus, although solicitous to a fault of the moral climate at Rome, was himself by no means a humorless man. To a timid petitioner he once said, "Come on: don't hold it out as though you were giving a penny to an elephant!" And when he decided that the great tragedy that he had been writing – *Ajax* – wasn't worth completing, Augustus answered queries as to how the work was going by saying, "My Ajax, rather than falling on his sword, has rubbed himself out with my sponge." It is perhaps an even greater tribute to Augustus's sense of humor that he was willing to tolerate one of his knights' getting the verbal better of him within earshot of at least one historian: Augustus reproved the fellow for drinking openly in the theater, saying, "*I* dine at home," to which the knight replied, "*You* don't have to worry about losing your seat."

Roman humor was by no means confined to the courtroom or the court, as the plays of dramatists Plautus (254?–184 B.C.) and Terence (190?–159 B.C.) happily attest. Latin plays drew originally on Greek models, and it is perhaps no surprise that much of Plautus and Terence is adapted from the Greek comic playwrights of a few generations before, particularly Menander (fl. 300 B.C.). A favorite theme of Plautus's is the mistaken identity – whether through the appearance of the long-lost twin (in the *Menaechmi*) or through impersonation by the gods (in *Amphitron*). From the point of view of stagecraft, of course, this involved the same actor merely going out one door and reappearing through another, perhaps with a quick change of clothes behind the scene, but comics – and comic writers, notably Shakespeare – have been ringing changes on this routine ever since and will probably continue to do so for as many years to come. Comic patter-songs, a staple of the Greeks, were equally popular among the Romans, and certain stock characters – the slave who could "fix" everything, the pompous old father, the young starry-eyed lovers – were always good for a laugh as, indeed, they would continue to be in the late medieval *commedia dell'arte*, which was Roman comedy's rightful heir and the training field for – among others – the French master Molière.

Another standard vehicle for Roman humor was the epigram, of which the masters were Catullus, who flourished in the last days of the Republic, and Martial, a friend of Quintilian's and Pliny the Younger's. Catullus burned out at an early age – he was barely thirty when he died in 54 B.C. – but left for posterity over a hundred poems, of which some, like the elegy for his brother (which ends with the line *"frāter, auē atque ualē"* ["brother, hail and farewell"]) and his love lyrics to "Lesbia" (Clodia, wife to Metellus Celer and lover to a host of others) became instant classics.

Martial, who greatly admired Catullus's work and in a few instances reworked it as his own, came to Rome in 64 A.D. or so and befriended his fellow Spaniards Quintilian, Seneca, and the poet Lucan. When Nero ordered the latter two to commit suicide for their complicity in Calpurnius Piso's assassination plot, Martial fortunately escaped harm and seems to have kept a low profile through the succession of struggles of the Year of the Four Emperors which eventually landed the Flavians on the throne. Martial's first book of poems, the *Liber Spectaculorum*, was published in 80 A.D., when Martial was about forty, to celebrate the inauguration, under Titus, of the Colosseum (built over Nero's fishpond, as a rebuke to him). By 85 A.D., Martial was an established – and often plagiarized – poet, and he remained at Rome for another fifteen years, issuing new books of epigrams at the rate of one every eighteen months.

Martial had a wonderful sense of irony, and he did not mince words. Indeed, until recently, English translations of his work often balked at printing some of the racier bits in anything more intelligible than Italian, which at least tipped the reader off to where the really good stuff was. One of the milder of these runs:

Such a huge penis you have, Papylus, and such a great nose, too.
Whenever you take a piss, you can sniff it as well.

The epigram immediately preceding this one is much cleaner, as befits the courtroom, where a speaker was timed by the standard twenty-minute water clock (*clepsydra*):

Strident Caecilianus, demanding time for your pleading;
Seven clepsydras the judge grudgingly grants to you;
But you say much, and too long, and with your head
tilted backward
Guzzle water, lukewarm, draining glass after glass.
Here's how to slake your thirst, and with it your thirst for
declaiming:
Caecilianus, we pray, drink the clepsydra instead.

Martial was considered the epigrammatist par excellence in Tudor England, where the epigram was a popular form of court poetry. Here is a partial translation by the witty Sir John Harington (whose monumental *Metamorphosis of Ajax* appeared in 1596) of one of Martial's poems about a poet with a passion for reading from his own work:

Alas my head with thy long reading aches,
  Standing or sitting, thou read'st everywhere.
If I should walk, if I would go t'a Jakes,
  If to the bath, thou still art in mine ear.

Of his own fame, Martial wrote:

I, with my elegaics and eleven-
Syllabled lines aflow, not forward, salty
Of wit, am Martial – known to all the nations
And to all Rome. Why envy me? I'm no more
A household word than is that horse, Andraemon.

– evidently the Incitatus of Martial's generation; but Andrae-mon is forgotten today, while Martial is remembered, so there is perhaps some justice after all.

Roman humor on a grand scale is nowhere better represented than in the *satire*, a form which the Romans could rightly claim to have invented. The word *satura* designated, among other things, a dish containing a variety of ingredients, a hodgepodge, hence, a literary *mélange*. The first satirist of note to write that blend of poetry and invective in Latin was probably Lucilius. Though earlier so-called satires exist at least in fragmentary form by Naevius and Ennius, Lucilius was the first to write satire exclusively – and to get away with it (in large measure because he had influential friends, notably among the Scipio family, as powerful in Roman politics after the second Punic War as were their opposite numbers among the Barca family in Carthage).

It is through satire that we get a really good glimpse of the underbelly of Roman life, a seamy side invisible to readers of a decorous poem like the *Aeneid* or of official correspondence such as the letters of Pliny the Younger. Roman satire took several forms: straight prose (Apuleius's *The Golden Ass*), mixed prose and verse (Seneca's *Pumpkinification of the Deified Claudius*, Petronius's *Satyricon*), and unadulterated poetry (Lucilius, Horace, Persius, Juvenal, et al.).

Juvenal is for many readers *the* Roman satirist: bitter and merciless, with a keen eye and a quick turn of phrase. What little we know of his life is pieced together almost entirely from the internal evidence of his works: probably a Spaniard by birth, possibly the son of a freedman, Juvenal seems to have served in the army as a commander of Dalmatian auxiliaries in Agricola's British campaign, returning to Spain in 80 A.D. to be made co-mayor of Aquinum. Two inscriptions – recorded at modern Aquino but now lost – note that he was given a vote of thanks by the people of the district and promised a statue at public expense, and that he dedicated a shrine to Ceres. He seems to have been made a priest of the deified(!) Vespasian and to have commuted between Aquinum and Rome, hoping to advance his career still further, which, now that Domitian was emperor, rested less on merit than on the cultivation of favor at court. How successful Juvenal was at this game is not known, though he did meet Martial and other Spanish-born intellectuals at Rome; but it is definite that his career was abruptly put on hold when Domitian exiled him (about 93 A.D.) to Syene in upper Egypt, perhaps under the guise of a promotion, a typical trick of Domitian's, rather like the British practice of posting a man under a cloud to be governor of New South Wales, Australia, at the close of the last century.

Fortunately, Domitian was not immortal, and when Nerva came to power in 96 A.D., Juvenal was allowed to return to Rome, where he spent the next ten years teaching declamation and polishing his first three books of satires for publication. These are the bitterest of the lot, and while it could be said (as Deems Taylor would write of W. S. Gilbert) that Juvenal combined "a gift for saying cutting things with a complete inability to refrain from saying them," it must also be said in his defense that he had a good deal about which to say cutting things. But in any case, by 115 A.D., Juvenal's fortunes had risen sufficiently that he owned three slaves and a small farm at Tibur (upstream from Rome, the modern Tivoli), probably thanks to the munificence of Hadrian who, while not altogether discriminating in his own artistic taste, nevertheless did believe in state support of the arts. Juvenal's later satires, then, are rather gentler than the early ones, which is to say that their subjects were merely scalded rather than flayed alive.

Consider Satire VI, Juvenal's famous attack on the degeneracy of Roman womanhood. It begins:

Back in Saturn's golden age, when chastity lingered
Yet awhile, I believe, in drafty, badly lit caverns –
These were the only homes people knew, with household and
*   hearth-fire,*
Family, cattle, and gods, in the shadows all crowded together –
Women were different then . . .

Here lies the thesis implicit in all of Juvenal's work (and, by extension, perhaps in all satire): in the good old days, things were not come to the pretty pass they have today – troops were brave, wives were chaste, courtiers did not fawn, perverts didn't have the ear of the Censor of Public Morals, the arts were rewarded, the wicked got their just deserts, and the Greeks didn't dictate literary taste. If Quintilian's ideal was Cicero, Juvenal's was Cato the Censor, that austere figure who was said to have claimed that he never embraced his wife standing up save once when she fled to his arms during a thunderstorm (a pronouncement that moved one wag to suggest that she probably prayed to Iuppiter Fulminans to make more thunder again as soon as possible) and whom Augustus Caesar no doubt had in mind when he said, as he often did, "Let us content ourselves with *this* Cato," meaning the Censor's grandson, a staunch if unsuccessful defender of the Republic in its last days, and a distinct thorn in the side of Julius Caesar. To be sure, Juvenal himself stops far short of republicanism – a lost cause for at least two generations; but he pillories bad imperialism, and it is significant that of all the authors he parodies, it is Vergil who gets it the worst and the most frequently.

Apuleius, an African provincial, wrote *The Golden Ass* around 150 A.D. while a young lawyer at Rome. This satire in prose was probably published anonymously at first; it would not appear under his own name until 169 A.D. – a fortunate thing, as Apuleius was put on trial for sorcery back home in Madura in 158 A.D., and the goings-on described in the book might have been adduced as evidence to support such a charge. As it was, Apuleius defended himself so brilliantly that the case was dismissed as frivolous.

The Golden Ass – entitled *Metamorphoses* by its author, no doubt intentionally to echo Ovid – is about a young man who gets into a number of misadventures during the course of which he is turned into a donkey – he gets changed back at the end by the intercession of the goddess Isis and becomes a priest of her cult. What happens to him in between is a string of fanciful tales, some no doubt of Eastern origin – how a clever thief disguises himself as a bear, but is then set upon by dogs and spearsmen and is killed for his meat and hide; how a woman, whose husband comes home unexpectedly while she is in the process of cuckolding him, hides her lover in an old wooden tub and not only gets away with it but takes the ruse a step further; the tale told of Cupid and Psyche; tales of poisoners; tales of witches; and so on. *The Golden Ass* has rightly been called a picaresque novel, but it is legitimate satire too in the way in which it sends up the provincial middle class of the day about whom tales are retold from the perspective of the man-turned-ass. In this instance, the lost innocence and purity with which Apuleius contrasts present wickedness is not a Saturnian Golden Age but rather the bliss of the devotees of Isis and Osiris, and the book is of particular interest because of the unusual detail with which it describes initiation rites into this popular cult of the period – a detail found nowhere else in classical authors.

Petronius's *Satyricon* belongs to the class of satires called *Menippean* (after Menippus of Gadara who first developed this mixture of prose and verse as a literary genre). Petronius seems to have led the life of a refined hedonist, to all appearances, but served as governor of Bithynia and later as consul, discharging both offices, says Tacitus, with "capability and energy." Nero made him an unofficial court authority on matters of taste and luxuriousness – his official title was *Arbiter Elegantiae* – which ultimately led to Petronius's downfall, for he excited the envy of Nero's minion Tigellinus, who had him accused of complicity in a conspiracy against the emperor. Nero then condemned Petronius to death by suicide. Displaying the panache for which he was so justly famous, Petronius held a party and, having had a surgeon sever the veins in his wrists, bound them up again and so spent several days bleeding to death in his own good time, during which he conversed about "light and frivolous poetry" (according to Tacitus), rewarded some of his household servants and punished others, wrote out a catalogue of Nero's various misdeeds (listing all of the emperor's sexual partners, both male and female), sending the document under seal to Nero instead of the customary will leaving one's property to the Privy Purse, and destroyed his signet ring thereafter so that nobody could use it after his death to forge documents incriminating any of his friends. We know little else of him or of his family, save that Suetonius mentions that Petronius's daughter was married to Vitellius, who was emperor for a little over eight months in 69–70 A.D. and who outlived both her and their son Petronianus, whom he was commonly suspected of having poisoned.

The Satyricon comes down to us in a hopelessly fragmentary form, and if one is to believe a note appended to the manuscript – discovered in Dalmatia in 1663 – what has come down to us is only part of Books XV and XVI, though this assertion seems a bit grandiose to say the least. In any case, what we do have is, like the later *Golden Ass*, somewhat of a picaresque novel: set in the more down-to-earth sections of Naples, Crotona, and (perhaps) Massilia, the story, such as it is, centers on the love of the narrator, Encolpius, for Giton, a young boy already wise beyond his years who plays Encolpius off against their companion, Ascyltus, who also covets the boy. Encolpius, as the result of having blundered into the all-female rites sacred to the god

Priapus (the garden god, customarily represented as having an immense phallus, who gives his name to the medical condition known as *priapism*), is rendered impotent and spends most of the book trying to get cured.

The *Satyricon's* longest unified passage – roughly a fifth of the extant work – is taken up with the *cēna Trimalchiōnis* (Trimalchio's dinner party), whither the three protagonists go to wangle a free meal. The festivities soon prove much more than they had bargained for: Trimalchio is a wealthy but unbelievably boorish freedman who delights in ludicrous, tasteless ostentation to the brink of nausea. Indeed, it is the manipulation of the protagonists' – and the reader's – sense of queasiness in this extended passage that shows Petronius off for the master satirist that he is. The wine is disgustingly bad; the food is revolting in appearance (a sow is slit open to reveal itself stuffed with sausages; cakes, when touched, squirt saffron at you); and the behavior of the host and hostess is downright piggish. Even the color scheme is offensive: all of the senses are assaulted. The only thing that keeps the narrator (or the reader) from becoming actively ill is the not quite dizzying pace at which the "entertainments" switch from one unpleasant episode to another. The uproar with which the party ends – or at least allows Encolpius, Giton, and Ascyltus to make their escape – can be interpreted as the social equivalent of a definitive, orgasmic throwing-up.

Federico Fellini's movie *Satyricon* is drawn from Petronius's book and is remarkably faithful to the original: the abrupt breaks in the manuscript lend themselves well to the cutaway and fade of cinematography, and the surreal quality of a fragmentary text is right up Fellini's alley. The best satires last long after the age they satirize, no doubt because the follies of human frailty – greed, lust, envy, foppishness, jealousy, bad taste, and the rest – are by no means the monopoly of any particular civilization but are familiar in whatever clothing they appear on whatever stage. Like Juvenal and, to a slightly different extent, Apuleius, Petronius invites implicit comparison of the sordid side of life that he shows us with whatever our notion of a better world might be. It is the essence of satire, however, that the good be implicit rather than explicit: C. S. Lewis, in the foreword to his most brilliant satire, *The Screwtape Letters*, answered a critic who asked why there was not a parallel series of letters from On High to the subject's guardian angel by saying that while it is relatively easy, if uncomfortable, to put oneself in the mind-set of a thoroughly nasty being, it is extremely difficult to envision how a creature might think who is several orders of magnitude more virtuous than oneself. Nor was Lewis mistaken: the serious flaw in his *Great Divorce* is that the devils are magnificent while the saints are simply unbelievable. It is to Petronius's credit that he doesn't ask us to believe in his saints, for in what we have of *The Satyricon*, there aren't any.

IJ

K

IS FOR *KALENDS*, THE FIRST DAY OF THE
Roman month. The word is remarkable on a number of
counts, not the least of which being the fact that *kalends* is
one of the very few Latin words routinely spelled with a K.
When the early speakers of Latin borrowed the alphabet
from the Etruscans, they got three letters with which to represent the sound [k]: K (= Greek *káppa*), C (= Greek
gámma – the Etruscans apparently did not distinguish between phonetic [k] and [g]), and ʔ (Old Greek *kóppa*, a
letter with which the Greeks eventually dispensed except in
mathematical notation). Etruscan practice seems to have
leaned heavily toward using K before A, ʔ before U, and
C elsewhere. Speaker-writers of Latin twiddled with this
system in a couple of ways. They by and large did away with
the letter K – except in the word *kalends* and, half-
heartedly, a few others – and used C instead – except before
U, where they continued to use *kóppa* (whence the letter
Q). Because Latin speakers did distinguish between [k] and
[g], they figured that it might not be a bad idea to have a
separate letter for the latter sound and so modified C to
make G.

Early English practice, incidentally, went the Romans
one better: C was used to represent phonetic [k] pretty con-
sistently, while the letters K and Q were largely relegated to
the dustbin, though all of this changed with the arrival of
the Normans in 1066. The English continued to prefer
using C to represent their [k] sound, but grudgingly adopted
the French practice of using Q before semiconsonantal U –
phonetic [w] – and also took K out of mothballs for use
before E and I (and, more or less randomly, a few other
places) because French C before E and I didn't represent [k]
anymore (because [k] before [e] and [i] had become a sibi-

lant in French). So Old English *cwicu* (alive) shows up as *quick*; and *cyning*, after a bit of phonetic fumbling, shows up as *king*, while a *cū* is still a *cow*.

But back to Latin *kalends*, which has more to offer than merely the fact that it begins with K. Its etymology is obscure, though the Romans were in general agreement that the word probably came from the verb *calāre* (to announce, call out) because it was on the *kalends*, i.e., the first day of the month, that the priests formally declared whether this was going to be a month in which the *nōnae* (nones, nine days before the ides) would fall on the fifth or the seventh day of the month and, as a corollary, whether the ides were going to fall on the thirteenth or the fifteenth, since the Romans reckoned the number of days, weeks, years, etc., inclusively, counting both the days in between and the days at either end. (This method survives in French in which *huit jours* – literally, eight days – and *quinze jours* – literally, fifteen days – designate a week and two weeks respectively. Contrast English *sennight*, which nobody but a confirmed pedant or a time-traveler from a previous century would use today, and *fortnight*, which only a confirmed Englishman would use.) The Roman pontiffs, according to Varro, would gather in Announcement Hall on the Capitoline Hill and the proclamation would take the form "*Iuno Couella* [Juno of the Crescent Moon], I announce thee on the fifth [or seventh] day." (A tradition that the pontiffs repeated this formula five or seven times has now been largely discredited, it being now assumed that Macrobius – who recorded this practice – was working from a botched text of Varro, who really said no such thing.)

The *ides*, while we're about it, are said by Varro to come from an Etruscan word meaning "divide," the ides coming midway through the month. Maybe so. In any event, the days immediately following the ides – and the kalends and the nones – were considered *nefasti* (ill-omened) and so it was forbidden to transact any business on them. (The Romans had no weekends, so these had to do.) The O.K. days were called *fasti*, which Ovid took as the title of a delightful treatise in which he describes the feast days of the Roman year in chronological order, and there was an intermediate category of days on which it was all right to transact some kinds of business but not others. Which brings us to another noteworthy aspect of the word *kalends*: not only was the *kalends* the day on which the Roman people – who didn't have a mnemonic like "thirty days hath September,/April, June, and November" – would be reminded about the structure of the coming month: it was also the day on which the interest on loans was due. It is from this sense of the word that *kalendārius* (account book, ledger) is derived. *Kalendārius* gives us *calendar*.

So, what about the calendar? In attempting to reconcile the twenty-nine-day period of the lunar month with the solar year, the early Romans settled on a twelve-month, 355-day year, with an extra month added every two years (between February and March) to make up the difference. Originally, the Roman year was ten months, with an undifferentiated winter spell before the regular calendar took up again in March, an oscillation between "real" and "winter" time reminiscent of our own society's switch between standard and daylight saving times and the alternation of "real" time and "sacred" time so eloquently described by Edmund Leach in his "Symbolic Representation of Time – Time and False Noses." The fifth Etruscan king of Rome, Tarquinius Priscius, has been credited with introducing the other two months and with trying to get the year reckoned from January onward in honor of his favorite god, but the latter reform was abandoned when the Romans kicked out his heir, Tarquinius Superbus (Tarquin the Proud), the last of the kings, in 510 B.C., and the Romans went back to starting their year in March, thank you just the same. It is tempting to derive the March town meeting in many New England villages from the Roman practice of reckoning the year from March to March, but the true story, not much different, is that the English reckoned the year (from the fourteenth century up to the adoption of the Gregorian calendar) from March twenty-fifth to March twenty-fourth, i.e., vernal equinox to vernal equinox, give or take. The Romans, on the other hand, began installing their consuls in January, starting in 153 B.C., and January won out, for a time at least, as the official beginning of the year, much as July has won out in the U.S.A. as the official start of the fiscal year, September has won out as the beginning of the school year, and your taxes are due by April 15.

The Roman months were as follows:

Iānuārius, from *Iānus*, a native Italic god whose two faces face, in this case, toward the new and old years, respectively.

Februārius, from the Sabine god *Februus*, the Purifier, or else from *febris* (fever), this being the worst month for them. The Romans held a festival of purification on the fifteenth of this month. It seems that when January and February were added to the old ten-month Roman calendar, February was first used as the last month of the year, coming before January. Note that if the year is reckoned, as it once was, with March as the first month, February still comes last. In Old English, by the way, the word for this month was *solmonath* (mudmonth).

Martius gets its name from the native Italic god *Mars*, who was originally associated with agriculture and only later fell in with bad company and became associated with Ares, the Greek god of war. It is with his war hat on that Mars gave his name to the planet and to the day following Monday in the Romance languages.

Aprilis might come through Etruscan from the Greek goddess *Aphrodite*, or it might come from Etruscan *Aplu* (Apollo), or not.

Māius is from *Māia*, another native Italic goddess, the daughter of Fauna and Vulcan.

Iūnius is from *Iūnō*, yet another native Italic goddess, later identified with Hera when it became fashionable to pretend that the Roman gods were just like the classier Greek ones.

Quintilis basically means "fifth" and, if you number from the beginning of March, this was the fifth Roman month. Apparently the Romans got tired of naming months after gods as it came time for summer vacation and so resorted to doing it by the numbers. This month was later renamed *Iūlius* for Julius Caesar shortly after his death and apotheosis.

Sextilis (sixth) was subsequently renamed *Augustus* for Augustus Caesar, Julius's successor. Both Caesars, it is only fair to say, were active in calendrical reform.

September, October, November, and *December* are from *septem* (seven, whence also *septimāna* [week], the basis of French *semaine* and Spanish *semana* [week]), *octō* (eight), *nouem* (nine), and *decem* (ten).

In typically Roman fashion, Julius Caesar, having determined that the calendar needed reforming, engaged a Greek to do it. Sosigenes, an astronomer living in Alexandria, suggested that the only way out was to abandon the lunar calendar altogether, since the solar and lunar cycles only coincide every thirty-two years, i.e., every 403 lunar months. Moreover, he suggested that a year of 365.25 days be used, introducing an extra day every four years to make it neater. This extra day was to come between the twenty-third and twenty-fourth of February, the usual month for intercalary adjustments. Caesar called the new day *punctum temporis* (point of time) in his edict on the subject but, because it repeated day "six" before the kalends, it was called *bis-sextō-kalendae*, which survives as the word *bissextile* (leap year). (The "leap" of leap year, as it happens, comes directly from Old Norse *hlaupa*, presumably because fixed dates after February in leap years do not merely fall on the next day of the week from last year but leap ahead two, prompting Walt Kelly's famous observation that "Friday the thirteenth come on a Wednesday this month.") If you were born on the extra day, you were assigned February 23rd as your "official" birthday.

Having, he thought, provided for calendrical reliability for the future, Julius Caesar brought the year and the calendar back onto alignment by causing an extra sixty-seven days – plus a twenty-three-day intercalary month which was due anyway – to be inserted at the end of 46 B.C., since the solar year and the Roman calendar were a whole season off by the time he brought Sosigenes in to set things right.

All, one might think, would have been well (with a bit of grumbling) had the pontiffs not misinterpreted the edict as meaning "every fourth year (including this one)" – inclusive numbering again – with the result that the extra day was inserted every three years instead of every four. This was, however, so minor an error compared to the egregious misalignment preceding the Julian reform that nobody much noticed for another thirty-five years, at which time Augustus Caesar made an ad hoc correction by eliminating leap year from 8 B.C. to 4 A.D. and got the priests straightened out on how often they should insert it henceforth. Rome now had a calendar on which official administrative days could be fixed and that wouldn't drift quickly and inexorably out of whack with the solar year. This system worked pretty well for the next twelve centuries.

Since the Roman month was subdivided somewhat by the kalends, the nones, and the ides – and the *nefastī* that followed them – the concept of the week was unknown and unnecessary. The modern seven-day week derives instead from the Jewish calendar with its Sabbath every seven days. This calendar has thirteen months with an intercalary month added every few years. Inserted after the month of Adar, this extra month is called, sensibly enough, Second Adar. Like that catch-all, February, Adar comes in midwinter. All the holidays that regularly come in Adar are simply pushed ahead to the corresponding date in Second Adar –

most notably Purim, the Feast of Lots, which is celebrated on the fifteenth of Adar and commemorates Esther and Mordecai's deliverance of the Jews from the genocidal scheming of Haman at the court of Ahasuerus, i.e., Xerxes, possibly the same Xerxes of the Persian wars. The names of the Jewish months are, with one exception (Tammuz), nearly identical with the Babylonian ones – during the Babylonian Captivity, the Jews borrowed not only the Babylonian calendar but also the notion of dividing the day up into twenty-four hours of equal length. (The Romans designated a unit of time the *hōra* – whence *hour* – but this was not of uniform duration.) The week was introduced into Rome by the Christian emperor Constantine I in the fourth century A.D.

The Muslim calendar has twelve months of twenty-nine or thirty days each, with an occasional extra day in the last month of the year. The year is thus ten days off and simply regresses through the seasons until it comes back in line with the same (solar) date every thirty-two and a half years. This keeps the year in line with the moon, and the seasons be damned. The French revolutionaries, on the other hand, instituted a Revolutionary calendar in 1793 that was divided into twelve months of thirty days each, with five intercalary days – a reckoning nearly identical with the Egyptian calendar of about 5000 B.C., although the resemblance seems to have been coincidental. The French months were named with an eye to being seasonally descriptive: *Vendémaire* (vintage), *Brumaire* (misty), *Frimaire* (frosty), *Nivôse* (snowy), *Pluvôse* (rainy), *Ventôse* (windy), *Germinal* (seedy), *Floréal* (flowery), *Prairial* (meadowy), *Messidor* (harvest), *Thermidor* (hot), and *Fructidor* (fruity). The week was replaced by the ten-day *décade* with a day of general rest at its end. The five intercalary days were holidays: the festivals of Virtue, Genius, Labor, Opinion, and Rewards, with a sixth thrown in for good measure – the Feast of the Revolution – every four years. The intercalary days came at the end of *Fructidor* – the year began with 1 *Vendémaire*, which replaced old September 22nd, the anniversary of the proclamation of the

Republic. The French used this system for a dozen years and then abandoned it under Napoleon I, reverting to the Gregorian calendar.

The Gregorian calendar was an update of the Julian one whose leap day every four years cut the difference between the solar and calendrical years to an error of about twelve minutes a year – or about seven days every thousand years. By the mid-1500's the error was up to some ten days, producing a crisis in astronomy, for astronomers and mathematicians (as Copernicus was to complain in 1543) were in general disagreement over when Easter "really" was (and thus all the movable feasts keyed to it). Pope Gregory XIII, on his election, found several proposals for calendar reform on his desk. He chose the one drawn up by the astronomers Aloysius Lilius and Christopher Clavus which (a) took ten days out of October 1582, and (b) provided that every hundred years the usual leap day should be deleted except for centuries divisible by 400: 1600, 2000, and so on. (It is this curious exception that made 1900 a non–leap year, thus extending Frederick's period of indenture with the Pirates of Penzance to 1944. The Romans would simply have registered him as having been born on February 23 and let it go at that.) Catholic countries quickly adopted Pope Gregory's new calendar, Protestant countries not so quickly – England held out until 1752 – and Eastern Orthodox countries still less so: Russia adopted the New Style in 1918, trimming what were by then thirteen extra days from – naturally – February. (In 1929, a Russian Revolutionary calendar was proposed but never adopted.)

Less sophisticated methods for bringing the solar and lunar years more or less into line seem to have served well enough elsewhere in the world: the Yami fisherfolk who live off the coast of Taiwan use phases of the moon to determine when to go out on the first fishing expedition of the spring. They take lighted flares along and, if the flying fish rise to the light, the fishing season is declared open. If the fish are otherwise occupied and don't rise to the light, the Yami pack it in and sail home to give it another go next month. (This is somewhat reminiscent of the Northeasterners who set out along a country road with their shotguns only to encounter a sign saying "Bear Left," so they went home.) Hesiod in his *Theogony* lists a number of nonastronomical seasonal markers current among seventh-century B.C. Greeks: snails climbing plants meant that it was time to stop digging in the vineyards, migrating birds meant that it was time to get out the overshoes or summer sandals, depending, and so on. The American custom of Groundhog Day hints at such a flexible table: if the official ground hog of Punxsutawney, Pennsylvania, sees his shadow on the second of February, we get an intercalary month of winter, and then some.

The words *month*, *moon*, and *measure* all appear to come from an Indo-European root meaning "measure." (*Day* is of obscure origin, though cognate with *dawn*; *week* comes from a root meaning "turn" which shows up in Latin as the *vice* of *vice versā*; and *year* is quite possibly from the same root as *hour*, whose original sense was "season" or the like.) The Latin word for *moon* – *lūna* – is from an Indo-European root meaning "shine," whence Latin *lux* (light) and English *lucid* and *luciferin* (the pigment in fireflies' tails that emits light when oxydized) but not *luxury*. (Too bad. It also doesn't underlie Latin *lūcus* [grove], despite one ingenious grammarian's argument that a grove is so called because it admits no light – *lūcus ā non lūcendō*. Nice try.) Our most Latinate borrowing is *lunation* (lunar month), whose incommensurability to the solar year has given rise to much bother. Next in line, perhaps, is *lunacy*. While nobody much accuses the moon of *causing* madness anymore, there is some evidence that latent disorders are more likely to become florid at the full moon, as hospital emergency-room workers will readily tell you – regular as clockwork.

But just how regular is clockwork, anyway? The Roman *hōra* – whence our *hour* – originally meant a variety of things: season, period of time, part of the day. It only came to be used in the sense of a constant unit of time in 263 B.C., when the first sundial was imported to Rome from

Sicily. As it happened, the sundial was not all that accurate, having been calibrated for the latitude of Sicily, not Rome, a problem remedied a century later by the construction of a locally calibrated sundial which was then placed on its own pillar next to the Sicilian sundial in the Forum where both stood at least until the time of Julius Caesar. Unwary visitors to Rome from the provinces, asking locals why there were two sundials in the Forum and why, moreover, they didn't tell the same time, were told no doubt that if they both told the same time, there would only be need for one of them.

Shortly after the installation of the second sundial, Rome got its first public water clock – *clepsydra*, literally "water stealer" – a Greek invention as the telltale *y* suggests, the *c* being by now the standard Roman way of representing even borrowed [k]s. A clepsydra is basically a bowl of water with a hole in the bottom to let the water leak out at a constant rate (except on a very chilly day or a very hot one). Whether the Greeks experimented with other fluids whose viscosity varies wildly as a function of the temperature is not known. There is in any case no record of a *clepsomel* (honey stealer). Whatever its other limitations, the clepsydra had the advantage of working even when the sun wasn't shining, a vast improvement over the sundial. Furthermore, when calibrated against the public sundial, it could be used as a primitive stopwatch: Pliny the Younger alludes to its use in 100 A.D. or so in court – a lawyer was allowed so many water clocks in which to present his argument, the capacity of the judicial water clock being equivalent to approximately twenty minutes.

Minute comes to English from Late Latin – both as the measure of time and as the word meaning "tiny." The original Latin was *pars minūta prīma* (first[-order] little part) as distinct from *pars minūta secunda* (second[-order] little part), whence our second. The subdivision of the hour into sixty minutes and the minutes into sixty seconds each was an outgrowth of the astronomer Ptolemy's work (11 A.D.) in subdividing the circle into sixty degrees, the degree into sixty arc-seconds, and so on, a trick ultimately filched from the

Babylonians whose number system was hexigesimal. But if Ptolemy hadn't borrowed the notion of figuring in base sixty, someone else surely would have done so sooner or later, since this is a very useful bit of mathematics, sixty being divisible by two, three, four, five, ten, twelve, fifteen, twenty, and thirty, whereas ten of base-ten/decimal fame is only divisible by two and five, evenly. It is the exclusion of tidy divisibility by three that is one of the major drawbacks of the metric system: a third of a meter peters out in a string of repeating decimals while a third of a yard is a foot, period.

Ironically, the second has become a metric unit, and one talks of short-lived phenomena in terms of milliseconds (one-thousandths of a second) or nanoseconds (one-millionths of a second, literally "dwarf-seconds"). The quartz crystal in the modern wristwatch has a vibrating frequency of 2^{15} cycles per second (cps) – or, as cps are now called, Hertz, after Heinrich Rudolf Hertz, who in effect discovered electromagnetic waves – or one vibration every 30 nanoseconds. Since this is dead accurate to seven more digits than any ordinary person would even dream of caring about, a quartz clock can be used to regulate any number of mechanical contrivances to far greater tolerances than needed: it is a quartz crystal that controls the readout for the laser in an all-digital audio system, allowing a qualitative leap in what we know as high fidelity.

Not only did the Romans not have turntables (except as potter's wheels, whose fidelity has never been at issue), they weren't for the most part all that fussy when it came to reckoning the passage of time during an ordinary day. According to Censorinus's *De Die Natali*, the common division of the Roman day was as follows: *māne* (sun-up to about three hours later), *ad merīdiem* (forenoon; our A.M. comes from *ante merīdiem* [before midday] and is not to be confused with A.M. [master's degree, from *artium magister*, Master of Arts] or AM [amplitude modulation]), *dē merīdiē* (afternoon), and *suprēma* (from the ninth or tenth hour till sunset). (Our P.M. comes from *post merīdiem* [after midday], A.M. and P.M. being generally handy if you don't want to reckon hours by the twenty-four, but difficult when it comes to saying what twelve midnight and twelve noon are.) Civil business (if one had any that day) ended officially by the ninth hour, and thereafter prostitutes were allowed to appear on the streets, one Latin word for prostitute being *nōnāria*

(lady of the ninth hour). In the Christian liturgical day, *nones* – from Latin *nōna* (*hōra*) (ninth [hour]) – was around two or three in the afternoon, nine hours after the beginning of the day, the other liturgical hours being *matins, lauds, prime, terce,* and *sext* in the morning, and *vespers* in the evening, and *compline* at the end of the day. Eastern rite, as mentioned earlier, said to hell with the clock and, asserting the complete independence of sacred from secular time, didn't allow any mechanical timepieces inside the walls, perhaps discovering that people if left to their own devices tend to settle on an internally clocked "day" – circadian rhythm – of approximately twenty-five hours. *Nones* also gives us English *noon*, originally in the sense of midday meal, one's stomach being as good an internal clock as any. Compare the current British use of the *elevenses* and the sacredness of tea time, as immortalized in the music-hall lines "He would have said more/But the clock struck four/ And everything stops for tea."

L

IS FOR *LEGAL, LEGISLATE*, AND *LEGITI-mate* – all from Latin *lex, lēgis* (law). The *leg-* of *legible* and *delegate* may or may not represent a related root, the proximate derivations here being from the verbs *legere* (to read) and *lēgāre* (to choose, whence also *elect*) respectively. *Law* itself comes from the same Germanic root as "lie" and "lay" – thus, "to lay down the law" is not merely phonetically apt but etymologically solid as well – while *loyal* comes from Latin *legālis* (legal) via French, the idea being that a loyal person is one who goes by the book and can be trusted to do what's right by you.

Next to satire and the language itself, the civil law tradition of the Latin-speaking world is surely the most distinctly Roman contribution to Western culture. (Roman architecture and engineering, far-reaching as their effects on the empire were, owed a heavy debt to the Greeks.) Despite the legend that the Romans sent a council of ten to Athens to bone up on the statutes of Solon just prior to setting forth the Laws of the Twelve Tables, the Roman legal system was largely home-grown and certainly refined by Roman jurists speaking to particularly Roman legal problems, and addressing these in a peculiarly Roman way.

The origins of Roman law seem to have been in custom sanctioned by religious authority: all law, we are told, was at first *fās* (that is, divinely warranted) and, accordingly, its enforcement and adjudication were overseen by various priestly colleges. Offenses against the gods included murder, the slaying of a parent, incest, the selling of one's wife, the swearing of false oaths, and the moving of boundary stones, this last being a particular affront to the god Terminus. In all cases of this sort, a priest served as the presiding magistrate, and the penalties attached to such offense against the divine order could range from fines and forfeiture of property, if the crime was expiable, to excommunication, banishment, and even death if it was not.

Nonexpiable offenses against the gods – breaches of one or another of the *lēgēs sacrātae* – rendered the offender *sacer* in the eyes of the law and resulted in the sacrifice of his goods and person to the gods whom he had offended by his execrable behavior. (The word *sacer*, which underlies both *sacrifice* and *execrable*, as well as *sacrilege*, *sacrament*, and the first half of *sacrosanct*, originally meant something like "of or pertaining to the divine world" – in contrast to *profānus*, "of or pertaining to the regular, everyday, nondivine world," literally "before [i.e., just outside] the consecrated area [*fānum*, which is related to *fās* (divine law)]" – and got to be applied to bad guys not because they were holy but because they got top billing at the sacrifice, i.e., the ritual occasion on which the good guys made up to the gods by offing the culprit with all due ceremony. Compare the double use as "permission" and "penalty" of the word *sanction*, from Latin *sancīre* [to consecrate, make sacred], a form related etymologically to *sacer* and the basis of *sanctify*, *sanctuary*, *saint*, and the second half of *sacrosanct*.) Malfeasants fortunate enough to escape with their lives might be given a certain number of days to leave the country – originally, to leave the city of Rome and its suburbs, but extended in area as the Roman sphere of influence grew larger – and would be publicly interdicted "fire and water," which meant that everybody else was not to offer shelter or sustenance to the bad guy or his beasts. And, more to the point, no penalty would attach to anyone who killed such a convict, as he was effectively declared a nonperson, even in the sight of the gods – this being the real sense of *execration*. Or, as the man said after being tarred and feathered and ridden out of town on a rail, "If it hadn't have been for the honor, I'd just as soon have walked."

Historically, it appears that from *fās* (divine law) eventually split off *iūs*, *iūris* (human law) on the one hand, and *bonae mōrēs* (good rules of conduct) on the other. (*Iūs*, *iūris* underlies a raft of English juridical terms, including *judge* and *jury, justice, perjury,* and *prejudice.*) *Bonae mōrēs* had something less than the full force of law but the considerable weight of social custom still, the notion being that only a foreigner or a not-very-proper Roman would transgress them. *Mōrēs* – whence *moral* – is often glossed as "customs," as in Cicero's famous lament, *"O tempora! O mōrēs!"* ("O the times! O the customs!") or, as the more conservative among us might say, "What's the world coming to?" A gray area between *fās* and *bonae mōrēs* was supervised by the *Censor*, as an add-on to his original task of ascertaining, at periodic intervals, the number and age of the inhabitants, free and slave, of each household, together with the extent of family property – the *census*.

It is probably in the area of property that *iūs* arose as distinct from *fās*, for apart from the sanctity of boundary stones, the Romans early recognized the peculiarly human nature of disputes over who owned what. Or, to put it another way, the Romans found that things worked well enough if questions of ownership were adjudicated by purely human rules, as opposed to those thought to be divinely inspired. Perhaps the Romans recognized, too, that while in some instances a natural human impulse needed a higher law to check it – as in cases of murder, where the line of least resistance would be for a murder victim's family to exact revenge from the murderer's family in kind, thus setting in motion that most destructive of institutions to society as a whole, the blood feud – other sorts of disputes could be headed off by a submission to the good sense of qualified third parties, as in cases of inheritance, contracts, sales, rentals, and the like. That the notion of *iūs* evolved from that of *fās* is suggested by some of the formal procedures in effect well into the days of the empire: a law proposed by a presiding magistrate would be submitted to an assembly as a formulaic question beginning, "Is it the will of you citizens – and of the gods – that . . . ?" The assembly could veto such a proposal on the grounds that the sacrifice that had preceded the motion had either not been performed correctly or had resulted in unfavorable auspices.

Roman law, if thought of as a body of legislation, might

be seen as a formidable collection like the codification completed under Justinian, but this represents only the last stage in its classical evolution. At first, the laws were not written down, and they applied only for the benefit of those residents of Rome who were enfranchised citizens – a decided minority that excluded women, children, slaves, the poor, and foreigners. It was largely as a result of vocal dissatisfaction by the unenfranchised that the commission that went to Athens, supposedly to learn some law, set down on their return the code of Roman law on tablets of wood or bronze erected in the Forum where anybody and everybody – or anybody and everybody who knew how to read – could read them. (Literacy was, of course, still largely a privilege of the enfranchised, although a Greek slave was more likely to be literate than a Roman free proletarian.) Originally, there were ten such tablets, two more being added later to cover contingencies not adequately dealt with in the first ten, and it was these Twelve Tables that formed the basis of Roman law from about 450 B.C. on and also served as the schoolboy's bane well into the empire, as they had to be committed to memory, much as later generations of American children have been obliged to learn to rattle off the Gettysburg Address or the Declaration of Independence by rote – Cicero states that he and his fellows were required to "sing them out" until they had learned them by heart.

Unfortunately, the original tablets on which the Laws were inscribed were destroyed during the sack of Rome by the Gauls at the beginning of the fourth century B.C., so that what little we have left survives in the citations of more recent jurists of imperial times – though we may yet hope that some Roman kid's crib sheet will be discovered and we will have the lot. Still, we know that some of the Laws' stipulations included such penalties as clubbing to death of anyone who was caught singing or circulating scurrilous songs about someone – one of the few offenses, oddly enough, that *was* punishable by death. (Evidently this law eased somewhat by the time of the early satirists.) We also know that the Laws specified what the allowed procedures were for haling someone into court on an action for debt, and how far one could go if the defendant refused to come of his own accord: if the defendant was sick, the plaintiff could send a beast of burden for the defendant to be carried to court on, but if the defendant refused, the plaintiff was not obliged to send a carriage.

They further stated that an *inūria* (literally "unlawfulness," from *in-* in its sense of *un-* plus *iūs, iūris* [law], and the basis of English *injury*) could be requited in kind (*tāliō*, hence the expression *lex tāliōnis* to gloss the biblical "eye for an eye, tooth for a tooth," which should actually be more accurately rendered "the price of an eye for an eye, the price of a tooth for a tooth") but that money damages could be substituted, and went so far as to set a price for some instances: thus, "If anyone has bruised or broken a free person's bone with hand or with club, he shall undergo penalty of three hundred *assēs*; if a slave's, one hundred fifty." *Tāliō*, incidentally, made its first appearance in surviving print, apparently, in the Laws of the Twelve Tables, as did the word *prōlētārius* in the sense of proletarian, member of the lowest enfranchised class of society (*prōlētārius* being from *prōlēs* [progeny], the idea being that the proletariat's contribution to society was its children).

Again, if a thief (*fūr, fūris*, whence *furtive*) was surprised as he plied his trade by night, it was lawful to kill him, but unlawful to do so by day unless he resisted with weapons. (Similar distinctions in modern law may be found: if you stick up a bank while wearing a mask, that's more serious than if you didn't bother with the mask; and breaking and entering while somebody is home is much more frowned upon than waiting to do your b.-and-e. until everybody's left and the house is empty.) And there is at least one instance of a penalty being prescribed against anyone who caused someone else's crops to wither through the use of sorcery, although what that penalty was has unfortunately not come down to us owing to the fragmentary nature of the citation (in Pliny the Elder's *Natural History*).

The Twelve Tables were nuts-and-bolts affairs, dealing

very practically with practical problems and situations. Nevertheless, even at this early stage, a distinction was drawn between act and intent, a celebrated citation being the phrase "If a missile has 'fled' from one's hand rather than been 'thrown' . . . ," the accused being liable to make restitution to the injured person or surviving next of kin for accidental homicide and in much hotter water if the deed was done with deliberation, however brief: in the former case, the standard price was a ram, and suffice it to say that, in the latter, the hit was generally rather heavier. And a desire to restrain excessive spending on funeral arrangements (so that the money might go into the State's coffers in times of national need, rather than into the undertaker's strongbox, that profession's lobbying powers having apparently been somewhat less powerful in Roman times than today) was tempered with a respectful humanitarianism: the Twelve Tables forbade adding gold to a funeral pyre, but went on to say that if a person's teeth had been held in place by gold bridgework, it would not be necessary to remove this oral architectural device before cremation.

Further, provision was made for the guardianship of "a raving madman" (*furiōsus*) by his kinfolk – and, similarly, a spendthrift (*prōdigus*, whence *prodigal* [excessively openhanded], literally, "driving forth" as in the biblical "prodigal son," the openhanded person driving forth his money as though there were no tomorrow) could be forbidden to manage his own estate, this duty also being assigned to his relatives instead. These two provisions are noteworthy because they underscore the notion that laws existed to protect not only the individual but the individual's *gens* (clan) as well.

The *gens* was of great importance in Roman law because it was the clan that originally held a certain amount of property in common among all its members; and an individual family that might become extinct within the *gens* would normally have its residual property revert to the *gens* as a whole. Moreover, inasmuch as certain religious ceremonies were the collective duty of all heads of households within the *gens*, it was considered a sacred calamity if all of the members of the *gens* died out. This was one of the reasons behind the Roman penchant for adoption: to inherit was to acquire both the property of the deceased paterfamilias and the obligation to carry on the worship of the family gods.

Consequently, part of the magistrate's job before approving an adoption, which, by grafting the adoptee onto his new *gens*, permanently severed official connection with the one into which he had been born, was to make sure that there would be someone left to carry on the rites for the *gens* the adoptee was leaving behind. The act of being adopted was attended by what Roman law termed *capitis minūtiō* (literally "diminution of the head"), *caput, capitis* here being used in the specialized sense of "legal personhood," the sort of head counted in a head count: apart from the question of who would carry on the family rituals, the magistrate also had to make sure that by formally removing a citizen from one *gens* and placing him in another, he was not inadvertently placing a greater burden on the remaining members of the original clan if, for example, there existed a potential action for debt that the rest of the *gens* would be obliged to pay off, the adoptee having ceased to exist as a member of the *gens*, at least in a legal sense, in his own name and former persona.

Even before the Laws of the Twelve Tables, the proportion of property held by a *gens* as a whole to that held by individuals was on the decline, and one of the reforms of Servius Tullius, the penultimate king of Rome, had been to settle clear title to landholdings with their occupants. These titles were termed "quiritarian titles" because, after Servius's reforms, all landholding Romans were held to be *quirītēs* – i.e., citizens – and also, perhaps, because the ceremony by which one claimed title was performed with a Sabinian spear (*quiris, quirītis*) or at least a pole representing such a spear, which was stuck into the ground at the appropriate moment.

Indeed, quaint as it might seem to modern (and literate) eyes, much of the business surrounding property in general was accompanied by physical manipulation of the commodity in question according to a strict formula: the purchaser and seller would convene a party of five witnesses plus a *lībripens* (weigher, from *lībra* [pair of scales] and *pendere* [to cause to hang, weigh]) who held up a bronze set of balances that the buyer would then tap with a piece of copper money to represent the weighing out of the price of the thing being purchased and thereby signify that the deal was sealed (the word "deal" coming from Old Englilsh *dælan* [to divide, distribute], whose original sense is best preserved in the ritual vocabulary of card playing). Such a transaction was called a *mancipium* (from *manus* [hand] and *capere* [to take]) and was the only strictly legal form of purchase for certain types of property, including land, houses, rights-of-way, slaves, oxen, horses, mules, and donkeys. All other forms of property were considered *rēs nec mancipī*, that is, things not requiring *mancipium* for legal purchase or sale (including, for example, cattle and sheep): the distinction originally concerned those possessions that were reckoned as part of one's official wealth in the census, as opposed to those that were not part of the tally, a house being easy enough to count, but the number of the herd rather harder to estimate when the census-taker came around, since the cows might be just as likely as not to be off grazing on the public grazing grounds when it came time for counting head.

The problem with the *mancipium* was that it was often quite inconvenient to lay actual hands on a thing if you owned property in several mutually far-flung places, or if you were off on foreign service in Dacia or Ultima Thule. The Romans got around this with *ūsūcapiō* (literally "taking use of"), originally a form of squatter's right applying in cases of unclaimed land, salvage, and the like. (The Romans did not in the least subscribe to that fundamental principle of English common law, *nulle terre sans seigneur* [no land without a lord] – i.e., all land is owned by *somebody*; or to the notion that all land titles proceed ultimately from the head of state.) A person who had *ūsūcapiō* for two years on a plot of land, and a year on virtually everything else, in effect owned it, providing that there was no challenge to the title. This means, among other things, that you could sue someone for damage to land or objects to which you did not have a formal title through *mancipium*, and in later years this right was extended to include even those things that you did not yet fully own – because the period of *ūsūcapiō* had not yet run its course – on the not-unreasonable assumption that it would only be a matter of time. *Ūsūcapiō* should not be confused with usufruct (the use of the fruits of), a form of lend-lease whereby you bought the use of something (or someone, in the case of slave labor) while the legal owner retained ultimate title – which meant that if anybody damaged the goods, it was the owner, and not you, who had to file suit against the miscreant, invoking the rule of "you break it, you bought it."

So far, we have spoken of *iūs* as if that were all the official law, apart from *fās*, that the Romans had, and indeed this was the case, to all intents and purposes, down to the time of the first Punic War. From 450 B.C., the laws were right out in public in the Forum, and various magistracies had been established to adjudicate disputes in accord with those laws (for the pontifical colleges retained jurisdiction in matters of *fās* only), culminating in the establishment in about 370 B.C. of the office of *praetor* (chief magistrate), the term *praetor* being derived perhaps from **prae-itor* (the person who goes before everybody else, i.e., the leader), or perhaps from Etruscan *purθ*, *purθne*, itself a possible borrowing from Lydian via Greek. A new *praetor* was elected annually, and he would start out by issuing an edict declaring the principles according to which he would run his court. (Lest this degree of discretion seem altogether surprising, homely examples of comparable leeway are not unknown today: it is, for example, possible to enter a small-claims action by mail against a debtor in Freeport, Maine, but if you want to catch a deadbeat in Huntington, New York, you have to file in person.) These praetorian edicts were collected, and formed in later years a substantial body of legal precedent in the middle years of the empire – the total number of praetors would grow to eight a year under the dictator Sulla and twice that number under Augustus, making for a rather fat corpus of legal opinion for lawyers to slog their way through in search of a bolster for an argument.

Meanwhile, the increasingly cosmopolitan concerns of Rome in the third century B.C. had brought its citizens into contact – and legal dispute – with inhabitants of other Italic communities, many of whom became allies of Rome in the subsequent struggles with Carthage. Recognizing that Roman law was not altogether user-friendly to Rome's allies, Roman jurists pulled together a body of what came to be called *iūs gentium* (law of [other] nations) – *gentium* being the genitive plural form of *gens, gentis* (clan) – distinct from *iūs rōmānōrum* (laws applying to Roman citizens) – and created the office of the *Praetor Peregrinus* whose holder was chosen to handle legal difficulties as they arose between Romans and their foreigner friends, *peregrīnus* meaning "foreigner, stranger" and the basis of *peregrination* and *pilgrim*, the two involving wandering (into foreign territory). The *iūs gentium* was something of a least-common-denominator version of the laws of the people of Italy with any political clout, and came to be thought of as something like "natural law" in late Roman juridical philosophy.

The heyday of Roman civil law wound down with the accession of the first emperors, whose privilege it was to propose statutes and whose power was such that these were rarely voted down. Starting with the reign of Augustus – who established bodies of consultant jurists to give opinions in particular cases – and lasting until perhaps 250 A.D., Roman law was not so much formulated as elucidated, often through brilliant analogy and cold, inexorable logic. It is the glory of this phase of Roman jurisprudence that when a particular citation from the vast body of praetorian edicts of the Twelve Tables could not be found to act as legal precedent, an argument could be made by thoughtfully stretching the existing citations: thus, in expounding the point that concealment and the illegal laying-on-of-hands are both essential elements in an action for theft, the jurist Ulpian (who flourished in the early years of the third century A.D.) says, "Nobody is a thief through mere words or writing, for we follow the rule that theft as such has not occurred unless there has been some unlawful meddling with the actual goods," officialdom then, as now, holding firmly to the notion that there is more crime in the streets than crime in the suites.

Ulpian goes on to say that while a person who persuades a slave to run away is not guilty of theft, any more than the person who gives such bad advice as "Go ahead and jump off that window ledge if you want a really great experience" is chargeable with murder, the same egger-on may be liable as a co-defendant if he persuades the slave to run off merely so that a bounty-hunting friend can catch him for himself. Elsewhere, Ulpian writes that "*ruperit* [shall have broken] has been understood as well, by even the early jurists, to mean *corruperit* [shall have spoiled]" – whence English *corrupt* – and therefore an action under the same statute (the *Lex Aquilia*) could include such things as sowing wild oats among someone else's crops, or even adulterating wine or making it go sour: "There is nothing new in that a law, after giving some specific examples, should add a general term comprising particular instances." Such a view tended to make Roman law more useful than if novel – and eventually contradictory – laws were passed to amend old ones, as tends to be the case today.

Nevertheless, it was inevitable that after seven or eight centuries the total body of edicts and commentaries should have become cumbersome, and after a stopgap measure called "the Law of Citations" – the rule, promulgated under the eastern emperor Theodosius II in 426 A.D., that assigned primacy to five jurists (Ulpian among them) but said that other jurists could be accepted according to how many citations of their work existed in the literature, a sort of authority-by-nose-count – and several attempts at codification, the crowning work was completed under the Emperor Justinian, supervised in the main by his chief counsel, Tribonian.

The Code of Justinian assembled what were considered

to be the most reliable commentaries (in, we are told, a remarkably short period of time: the first draft was produced in a little over a year, and the *Digest*, commissioned at the end of 530 A.D., was completed by the middle of 533); and as an added safeguard to their authenticity, all the earlier manuscripts and authorities' rejected commentaries were destroyed – a tragedy from the standpoint of later classical scholarship but, from the viewpoint of a practicing attorney of the day, probably just as well, for rarely does the academic broom sweep so clean. It is ironic that this most Roman of institutions should have reached its most definitive form at a time when the western half of the empire had already ceased to exist, the last emperor of the western Roman empire, the cipher Romulus Augustulus, having fallen in 476 A.D., though Justinian's Code served the Eastern Empire well for another nine hundred years.

Thanks to the fortuitous discovery, in 1147 A.D., of a copy of the Code of Justinian squirreled away in a monastery in Amalfi, Italy, both French and Spanish lawmakers of the Renaissance and later had a solid body of Roman law to draw on for a model of the "new deal." The *Partidas*, an adapted condensation of Justinian compiled for the Spanish king Alfonso the Wise, eventually became the basis of the legal system of New Spain, and thence the underpinnings of the laws, particularly those concerning the ever-touchy question of water rights, in Texas and New Mexico. France after the Revolution, in part from the neoclassical fervor that helped to shape the new *République française* in so many other ways, used Justinian as the major source for the *Code Napoléon*, and when Louisiana was acquired by the United States, it kept much of the Napoleonic law intact – it is specifically as a result of these two historical accidents that married women in Louisiana and New Mexico, from the very start, have always shared equal property rights with their husbands, at least in the eyes of the law.

M

IS FOR *MAXIM, MOTTO,* AND *MUTABIL-ity.* A *maxim* was originally a *maxima prōpositiō,* an expression coined, apparently, by the Roman philosopher Boethius to refer to those "greatest of propositions" that are axiomatic in deductive reasoning, having a logical weight much like that of a syllogistic major premise, only more so. (Syllogistic reasoning works by taking a major premise – "All snarks are boojums" – and a minor premise – "Xanthippe is a snark" – and drawing a conclusion from the two – "Therefore, Xanthippe is a boojum.") *Maximus, maxima, maximum* is (are) the superlative flavor of Latin *magnus, magna, magnum* (great), to which the corresponding comparative is *māior* (from **magior* or the like), the underlying Indo-European root being something on the order of **meg-.* **Meg-* underlies Greek *méga* (as in *megalith, megahertz,* and *megabuck*), Sanskrit *mahā* (as in *mahārājā* and *mahātmā*), and English *much* (though not *more* and *most,* which don't seem to be related to much of anything other than each other, and the *-more* of the Scottish *Claymore* [great sword], in which the *-more* represents Gaelic *mōr* [big]). The *magis* of *magisterial* and *magistrate* (and, in mufti, *master* and *mistress* – whence *Mr., Mrs., Miss,* and *Ms.*) comes from Latin *magis* (more), a sort of afterthought formation, as if *māior* hadn't been more than enough already.

Of course, sometimes more is less: Latin *maximus, maxima, maximum* tend(s) to show up in English in somewhat truncated form, as in the name of the long skirt or coat – the *maxi* – that made a brief appearance in the 1960's, and the Game Theory dialect of Mathspeak's *minimax* (strategy for maximizing your gains while simultaneously minimizing those of your opponent[s], not necessarily in that order), the *mini* of which is short for Latin *minimum* (least, the superlative of *minor, minus* [less]) – though the productive suffix *mini-* (as in *minicourse* and *miniskirt*) is probably from a conflation of *minimum* and *miniature* (ultimately from Latin *miniāre* [to illuminate, literally, "to color with red lead (*minium*)"], an early Italian *miniature* being a [small] painting of the sort that might appear as the header in a fancy manuscript). And a *maxim* is a pithy statement of some presumptive universal truth, as "All men are created equal," Jefferson's formulation of the notion that all people – or at least all white freeborn males – should have equal access to the law, a *maxim* in both the traditional sense that much of the Declaration of Independence follows from it, and in the more commonplace sense that it has assumed the role of slogan or motto.

A *slogan* (from Gaelic *sluagh-ghairm* [shout of the troops]) was a Celtic chieftain's rallying cry and served the auditory function of a standard or heraldic crest: in order that, in the haze and confusion of battle, one's partisans might be able to rally around when, for example, one was on the verge of being overrun by the opposition, everybody in the MacWhosis clan could all holler out "MacWhosis Forever!" or some other such bright saying, and so get a fix on the rest of the platoon. Away from the battlefield, sloganeering has been refined to an art that has since served to rally people around the standards of a wide variety of causes, from the philosophical-political to the unashamedly commercial: "Hell No, We Won't Go," "Live Free or Die," "Make It in Massachusetts," "Nuke the Whales," "Nixon's the One," "Buy American," "Good to the Very Last Drop," "Honk If You're Jesus," and so on.

The Roman standard, or *uexillum*, a pole with the eagle, the letters SPQR (for *Senātus PopulusQue Rōmānus* [The Roman Senate and People]), and the particular emblems of the legion to which it belonged not only served as a visible rallying point but could be used (and abused) as an effective exhortation on to battle because of the almost totemic reverence with which the troops adored it: one Roman commander, to urge his troops ever onward, actually grabbed the *uexillum* and lobbed it into the enemy's ranks, correctly calculating that his soldiers would slash their way through anything and anybody that stood in the way of their getting it back; and on another occasion, a mutiny was quickly quelled because, when the legionaries tried to march (against the emperor Claudius), their standards stayed stuck in the ground and would not budge no matter how hard they were tugged at, and going without them would have been unthinkable. Again, when Varus lost the better part of three legions – and his own life – against the Germani of Augustus's time, the fact that three *uexilla* were lost as well was the crowning disgrace. At least two of the Caesars, Julius and Augustus, each bore the *uexillum* in battle (at least once) – the latter when the man carrying it was killed during one of the engagements with Marc Antony's troops; and the former when the regular standard-bearer, whom he had been threatening and generally verbally abusing during the heat of the moment, ran off, leaving the eagle in his commander's hand.

With all the importance that the Romans attached to the *uexillum* (which took on the extended meaning of "troops [who fight under a standard]" and, later, "[generic] flag, banner"), it is odd that Latin doesn't seem to have had a word for slogan *qua* war cry. A *clāmor* was simply a shout, cry, noise, not much to rally to, really; and the terms for slogan *qua* motto mostly seem to have shared the blander sense of "saying": *dictum* comes from the verb *dīcere* (to say), *adagium*, whence English *adage*, comes from a verb meaning "to affirm, say," (cf. *prōdigium* [omen, portent] whence English *prodigy*, from the same verb), and *prōuerbium* (set of words put forth) comes from the word for "word" – *uerbum*.

It is therefore more ironic than surprising that our words *motto* and *mot* (the former borrowed from Italian and the latter borrowed from French) both come from an unattested Late Latin word meaning something on the order of "grunt, mumble, mumph" – **muttum*, to which the onomatopoetic Latin verb *muttīre* (mutter, mumble) and the adjective *mūtus* (speechless, mute) may be compared. (French *motus* [not a word; mum's the word] is a latter-day Pseudo-Latin form based on *mot* [word].) In heraldry, a *motto* functions as a brief allusive gloss on the bearer's personality, principles, or acts of derring-do (or derring-did). Some heraldic mottoes undoubtedly started out as battle slogans, while others were cleverly crafted sayings specifically designed to go with the coat of arms – thus the motto of the Rural District Council of Chichester contains its own name: *Adhuc hic hesterna* (Here still are the things of yesterday); likewise, *non sinō sed dōnō* (I do not permit, but I give), the motto of the Sedon family, and – in translation – *Ostendō non Ostentō* (I show, I sham not), the motto of Sir Gyles Isham.

A catalogue of the state mottoes of the United States shows nearly half in Latin, of which perhaps the most infamous is Virginia's *Sic semper tyrannis* (Ever thus to tyrants), quoted by John Wilkes Booth as he fell and broke his leg at the Ford Theater after fatally shooting Abraham Lincoln. A Latin motto that was scuttled after only two years was that of Ohio from 1866 to 1868 – *Imperium in imperiō* (An empire within an empire) – which, having been passed by a Republican legislature, "gave offense to great numbers of our people," according to Rush R. Stone, and was "repealed none too soon" by the next Democratic majority.

Some state mottoes are originals – e.g., New York's *Excelsior* ("Higher," which, after being adopted as the trade name of a private company with its own lofty goals, gave us the word "excelsior" in the sense of shredded wood used as packing filler) – while others are culled from the classics with greater or lesser accuracy: New Mexico's *Crescit eundō* (It grows as it goes) is a direct steal from Lucretius's *De Rerum Natura*; North Carolina's *Esse quam vidērī* (To be rather than to seem) is a condensation of a line from Cicero's essay "On Friendship" which reads, in full, "*Virtūte enim ipsā non tam multī praeditī esse quam uidērī uolunt*" ("As to virtue itself, many wish not so much to possess it as to seem to possess it"); and the motto of Kansas, *Ad astra per aspera* (Through difficulties to the stars), appears to be either a fusion of two lines of Vergil – "*sic iter ad astra*" ("this way to the stars") and "*optā arduā pennīs astra sequī*" ("by hard work to follow the stars on wings") – or perhaps a misquotation of the second-century-A.D. poet, Silius Italicus.

Indeed, many mottoes are simply appropriated classical tags that have attained proverbial status, not the less for being in Latin, and much entertaining reading can be found in dictionaries devoted in part or in whole to listing them. The *Petit Larousse* obligingly prints its catalogue of "Latin and foreign expressions" on pink pages – the characters in Jules Romains's *Les Copains* who customarily decide what to do next by opening the *Petit Larousse* at random and sticking a pin in a random spot on one of the open pages (in a version of the *sortēs Vergiliānae*, the medieval method of divination by picking a quotation at random from the *Aeneid* and then acting according to its precept) express a particular fondness for the *pages roses*, where all the truly great stuff is. And a glance through a classic such as H. T. Riley's *Dictionary of Latin Quotations, Proverbs, Maxims, and Mottos* yields a mother lode of wisdom, some of whose nuggets are still famous, others having lost their luster, from Cicero's "*Detestandō illō crimine, scelera omnia complexa*" ("In that one detestable crime is all wickedness bound up"), Horace's "*Eheu! fugācēs, Postume, Postume, lābuntur annī*" ("Alas! Postumus, Postumus, how our years do fly away"), or Terence's "*Fortēs fortūna adiuuat*" ("Fortune favors the brave," said to have been quoted by Pliny the Elder shortly before he fell victim to sulfur dioxide and a stroke while investigating the eruption of Mount Vesuvius) to the proverbial "*Dūrum et dūrum non facit mūrum*" ("A hard thing and a hard thing [i.e., a brick and a brick without any mortar between them] don't make a wall"), "*Incidit in Scyllam cupiens uītāre Charybdim*" ("He falls to Scylla in desiring to avoid Charybdis" – although the allusion is Homeric, the source is actually the thirteenth-century French poet Philippe Gaultier de Lille), and "*Pā-ribus sententiīs reus absoluitur*" ("When the votes are equal, the accused goes free"), a legal maxim ascribed to the Tudor jurist Sir Edward Coke, but a *principle* that goes back at least as far as Euripides's *The Furies*.

Another favorite – if hackneyed – maxim is "*Omnia mū-tantur, nos et mūtāmur in illīs*" ("All things change [All things are changed], and we along with them"). (This catchy platitude we owe to one Borbonius, a second-century-A.D. poet otherwise reasonably forgotten.) *Mūtan-tur* and *mūtāmur* are passive forms of the verb *mūtāre* (to change) from which are derived the handy Latin phrase *mūtātīs mūtandīs* ("the necessary changes having been made") and the English words *mutual*, *mutant*, and *muta-bility*. That which is *mutual* is reciprocal or exchanged; a *mutant* is an organism differing from its parents as the re-sult of genetic or chromosomal change (*mutation*), whether through wholly natural processes or, for good or ill, through the agency of human tinkering; and *mutability* is "subject to change."

Metaphorically speaking, human languages are among the most highly mutable organisms going: given enough time, even without the outside assistance of invading for-eigners and the machinations of the purveyors of native Newspeak, the speech habits of any thriving linguistic com-munity are bound to change in all sorts of ways, from the level of sound to the level of meaning – indeed, even the very names that we use to designate our own and other people's theoretically unique ethnolinguistic identities are amazingly volatile. For example, consider – or, if you are a member of the linguistic community that survived the first week of second-year Latin, reconsider – the names of the various peoples mentioned in the opening line of that most famous of Roman works in the Latin language, Caesar's *Commentarii* (the *Gallic War*), "*Gallia est omnis diuīsa in partēs trēs, quārum ūnam incolunt Belgae, aliam Aquītānī, tertium quī ipsōrum linguā Celtae, nostrā Gallī appellan-tur*" ("Gaul is a totality divided into three parts, of which the Belgae inhabit one, the Aquitani another, and those who call themselves Celtae – and whom we call Galli – the third"), of which the majority, like the terms *Rōmānus* (Roman) and *Latīna* (Latin), have had a variety of applications.

While those Romans who thought about it generally figured that the name of their capital city had something to do with *Romulus* (and somewhat less with his brother *Remus*), the best guess among Latinists today for the origin of *Rōma* is that it was Etruscan. To be a citizen of the city was to be a *(cīvis) Rōmānus*, though later, as the city's military and political power expanded farther and farther beyond the city's borders, you could be a Roman citizen without ever having been to Rome. As part of this expansion, "Roman" came to be used, in some parts of the empire, to designate the kind of popular colloquial Latin spoken by the ordinary military grunt or working stiff in contrast to the more formal Latin of Roman officialdom. It is this particular use of "Roman" that gives us *Rumanian* and the various flavors of *Romance* – *Rhaeto-Romance*, the *Romance languages*, and the *Romance of the Rose*, the medieval French classic on the art of love, known in the original as *Le Roman de la rose*, the idea having been that Latin was for writing such serious stuff as philosophy or Literature with a capital L, while "Roman" was appropriate for the lighter, more popular fare. While to the modern French *homme de lettres*, a *roman* (novel) or a poem by one of the *Romantic* poets can be pretty serious business, few members of the contemporary American literary establishment would rate a Regency romance as much better than eye candy.

Not that "Latin" has been mummified while "Roman" has had all the fun: speakers of English talk of *Latin lovers* (with Roman hands) and of *Latin America*, i.e., the part of the continent in which one or another of the languages descended from Latin is spoken; and *(lingua) Latīna* has given its name to two colloquial tongues, the *Ladin* dialect of Italian, and *Ladino*, the language of the Sephardim. (Though, like the German-based Yiddish of the Ashkenazim, Ladino is customarily written in Hebrew script, the language resembles nothing more closely than Medieval Spanish, which is essentially what it was – cf. Hebrew *sapharad* [Spain] – when the Jews of Iberia and Northern Africa began to speak it.) It is at least thinkable that speakers of Ladin and Ladino were happy enough to call their language "Latin" because, unlike most other speakers of the Romance languages, they didn't have Latin foisted upon them.

The Belgae, Aquitani, and Celtae/Galli were, of course, another story. Caesar tells us that, while they all lived in a place called Gallia, they had different languages, customs, and laws. We know little more about the Belgae (who were kind enough to lend their name to modern-day *Belgium*) and the Aquitani (from whose stomping grounds Queen Eleanor of Aquitaine was to rise to power over France and England) than what Caesar tells us, though the *-tan-* of *Aquītānī* probably reflects a Celtic word for country, so the languages in question may not have been as different as all that, i.e., they may all have been Celtic. Why the Celts should have chosen to call themselves *Celtae*, as Caesar suggests, is no small mystery either, since the word is a borrowing of Greek *Kéltoi*, a term of obscure origin and rather vague meaning even in Greek. But then, stranger things have happened, as witness the bizarre tale of name-those-people that stars the *Gallī* and their cognates the *Volcae*, the *Wallachians*, the *Welsh*, and the *Walloons*.

The story begins with a Proto-Germanic form – **walh* – meaning "stranger, foreigner" that shows up in Old English as the word *wealh* (foreign[er]) and as the first major constituent of such compounds as *wealhstōd* (interpreter, translator) and *wealhgefēra*, which is variously glossed as "commander of the (Anglo-Saxon) troops on the Welsh border" and "reeve of the king's Welsh serfs." Since the Gaelic-speaking Welsh were there first, or at least before the Germanic-speaking Anglo-Saxons arrived on England's fair shores, one wonders at the apparent ease with which the invaders dubbed their new neighbors "foreigners" – the word *Welsh* is ultimately from Old English *wealh* – though it is only fair to say that the Welsh got some form of revenge by supplying the basis for the word *Gaelic*, the English name of the language that the Welsh, the Scots, and the Irish all speak, in one form or another: in Old Welsh, a *Gwyddel* is an "Irishman" – literally "wildman" – though the Irish who borrowed the Old Welsh term preferred to think of their version of the term as meaning "Celt," the sense in which the Scots borrowed the word.

Meanwhile (back on the Continent), the Romans made the acquaintance of the Volcae and the Galli, the former living in Gallia Narbonensis, i.e., the region surrounding modern-day Toulouse and Nîmes in southeastern France, and the latter in the region occupied by what the modern-day French proudly call *les Gaulois*, i.e., the French of France. Both *Volcae* and *Gallī* somehow worked their way into the Roman universe of discourse from Proto-Germanic **walh* – and, of course, both the Volcae and the Galli were "foreigners" to the Romans, at least in the same way that the Welsh were to the early Anglo-Saxons, though how the Volcae and the Galli came to be so named in the first place – since nobody involved was Germanic – is by no means clear.

Between them, the Romans and the Gauls seem to have pretty much gobbled up the Volcae without so much as a postprandial belch – sometimes conquerers come in and totally wipe out the so-called "substratum" language of the conquerees, though usually the losers manage to make some marks on the new official lingua franca, just as conquerors who don't ultimately manage to make their language stick get their taps in before being assimilated into the native Oldspeak (as happened with the Norse and Norman – both literally "Northerner" – invasions of the land of the Britons, the etymological confreres of the present-day Bretonese). Indeed, two of the reasons why the Romance languages plural aren't the Romance language singular are that (a) the locals whom the conquering Romans encountered in their various travels spoke differently from each other (and so left their individual imprints on the new official language – the descendants of the Galli and the Belgae are still at times not on speaking terms and they are all nominally speakers of French) and (b) the folks who came in and conquered the various parts of the Roman empire when it was on the skids let their own linguistic calling cards fall where they might – there's a lot more Arabic in Spanish than there is in French, and a lot more Slavic in Rumanian than there is in Ladino.

Other reasons for the nonuniformity of the Romance languages abound: for openers, the Romans took several centuries to win the hearts and minds of the peoples who now speak some version of their language, hitting different places in different times with different brands of spoken Latin, and who knows how seriously the new serfs took the imposition of Latin Newspeak anyway, especially if they'd already been on the pointy end of a whole bunch of different invaders' sticks (however softly the accompanying speaking was spoken) and so already knew full well that sooner or later another conqueror was bound to come along, fully equipped with a totally different way of saying "learn this language or else"?

N

IS FOR NŌMENCLĀTOR, LITERALLY "NAME-caller" (from *nōmen* [name] plus the root of the verb *calāre* [to call]). In Roman times, a *nōmenclātor* was a slave whose duty it was to accompany his master on public jaunts to act as a prompter when significant others approached on the street so that the master could correctly address them by name – "Ah, Marcus Flavius, *so* nice to see you!" – instead of having to fumble out something like "I never forget a face (but I have a terrible time with names)" or "Say, who was that masked man anyway?" The emperor Hadrian was said to have been so good at associating names with faces that he sometimes had occasion to correct his nomenclators on their lapses of memory, much, no doubt, to their professional chagrin – back to sweeping out the chicken coop for you, fella.

Roman males had a standard issue of three names – sometimes four. The first was the *praenōmen*, comparable to our first name – *Gaius, Marcus,* and *Lucius* being our *Tom, Dick,* and *Harry* – the literal meaning of the word *praenōmen* being the name that comes before (*prae*) the *nōmen*. The *nōmen* was the name of a male's *gens*, i.e., clan or tribe – family, in a broad sense. (The Romance derivatives of Latin *gens, gentis* generally mean "people," as in French *gens* and Spanish *gente*, the former being grammatically plural and the latter singular, though the French at one time conventionally assigned the surname *Gens* to foundlings on a first-come-first-served basis. *Name* and *nōmen* are cognates – nearly all of the Indo-European languages have a similar way of naming names and nouns: the word for *name* – and *noun* – is pretty much the same from language to language.) And the *nōmen* was followed up by the *cognōmen*, which corresponded more precisely to our modern-day "family name": *Publius Cornelius Scipio* would have been a fellow named Publius from the Scipionic branch of the Cornelian clan, who might have distinguished himself from all the other P. Cornelius Scipios in the neighborhood – a grandfather or grandson might have had the same moniker – by getting an *agnōmen*, a sort of honorific nickname tacked onto the end of the other three, as when one Publius Cornelius Scipio became P. Cornelius Scipio Africanus after conquering the Carthaginians.

Some *agnōmina* worked their way up to *cognōmen* status: Livy describes the capture by Etruscans of a soldier of the Mucius *gens* who, in order to show that he was not a sissy, held his right hand in his captors' fire until it was burned to uselessness, for which he got the honorific title of *Scaevola* (Lefty), borne with pride as a *cognōmen* by all of his descendants. But then the Romans seem to have had a fascination with leftiness, as witness the fact that Latin has three words for "left" but only one for "right": *scaeuus, laeuus,* and *sinister* all mean "left, on the left," while *dexter* is all she wrote for "right." Originally, *scaeuus* had the additional sense of favorable, since Etruscan augurs customarily faced south when doing their ritual stuff and the rising sun was on their left, which was a good thing. *Laeuus*, accordingly, had the secondary meaning of "favorable" but also the tertiary meaning of "unfavorable," since the Greeks tended to face north when it came to augury, thus placing the auspicious rising sun on their right. *Sinister* has a similar history: its basic meaning was "left," its secondary and tertiary meanings being "favorable" and "unfavorable," depending on your orientation or world view, the "unfavorable" sense being the survivor in English, French and Spanish having also found the whole business unsavory enough to have adopted other words for "left" – *gauche* and *izquierda* respectively, both borrowings from other languages.

The triple or quadruple scoop in Roman naming seems to have been an Etruscan innovation, the earlier Indo-European practice having been to jam two names together – *Hipparchus, Virasena, Mayfield* – and let it go at that. All

Nn

146

very well when there aren't all that many people in the universe of discourse, but a tax on the imagination when the
chosen few become too many and the community has to
resort to such jaw-breakers as "Rabbitears-Son-of-Hog-
farmer-of-Bog's-End" in naming their progeny in an unambiguous way unless they want to resort to the exotic,
which people seldom do when the question of naming their
kids comes up for real. The Etruscan system was clearly the
way to go: fifty *praenōmina* times a hundred *gens*-names
times two hundred *cognōmina* would yield a million possible first-name-middle-initial-last-name combinations –
and there was always the *agnōmen* for a backup.

Roman women were not given a *praenōmen*: if P. Cornelius Scipio had a sister (or daughter), she would be called
Cornelia Scipio, period – and so would her sisters, though
one would distinguish among them by calling the elder of
the two *Cornelia Maior* and the younger *Cornelia Minor*
or, if there were more than two, *Cornelia Prima*, *Cornelia
Secunda*, *Cornelia Tertia*, and so on down the line: if you
were born female, you got the feminine-gender version of
your father's *gens* name plus his family name with a numeral thrown in if you had sisters. When a woman married, she acquired the genitive-case form of her husband's
name: *Cornelia Scipio Fundani* was the daughter of *Somebody Cornelius Scipio* and the bride of some fellow named
Fundanus. Confusion could and, of course, did arise as a
result of this stinginess in naming: there were two famous
Agrippinas (Germanicus's wife and Nero's mother), two
Faustinas (Marcus Aurelius's wife and his mother-in-law),
a host of Julias – all relatives of Augustus and most of them
extremely feisty, if Suetonius is to be believed – and Clau-
dias – ranging from Claudia Quinta, who singlehandedly
unbeached the ship containing Cybele's meteorite as proof
of her questioned chastity, to that Claudia of little chastity
who was the Lesbia of Catullus's marvelous love poems.

The cynical reader might suppose that Roman fathers
gave their daughters only two names because women were
considered to be of little account in those days, and such a

supposition is not very wide of the mark: Roman men generally did have it a lot better than Roman women when all was said and done. On the other hand, the status of Roman women was a lot better than that of their Greek counterparts: Roman women were allowed to go out in public while Greek women of the day were largely confined to the dark inner recesses of the house. And, for what it was worth, a Roman woman could show off her social position with ornament: jewelry, fine trappings for her sedan chair, and a large number of slaves in attendance whenever she went outdoors. A second corollary is that by being able to leave their own households, Roman women had a great deal more contact with other women outside of their immediate families than had the women of Athens or Thebes. Moreover, the daughters of patricians were likely to have been taught how to read and write; and while very little written by Roman women survives, there is enough to show that Rome produced a number of female poets, several of whom flourished during the reign of Trajan and were friends of the younger Pliny.

One wishes that there had been contemporary female historians too: the women talked about in Livy and Suetonius are, one suspects, more than a little idealized, for good or ill. Livy's tableau of the Roman matrons bringing forth their jewelry to underwrite the second Punic War is painted in bold, broad strokes, but the Oppian Law, passed in 215 B.C. to curtail women's public display of wealth, was deeply resented for the twenty years that it was in effect, and even a "voluntary" surrendering of women's private wealth may well have had an element of coercion going beyond mere peer pressure: the Republic was in a jam and thousands of Roman men and their Italian allies had just fallen at Lake Trasimene and Cannae. Ironically, it was the mortality among patrician men that helped to concentrate a greater proportion of postwar Roman wealth in women's hands, since women could and did inherit property, and contributed to the repeal of the Oppian Law in 195 B.C. (for money talks, even when it can't vote): a widow with an estate of

250,000 in gold *aureī* or a bride with a dowry of 25,000 were forces with which to reckon.

Property ownership by women in the later Republic was hedged about with legal niceties. Technically speaking, only males had full citizenship and, therefore, a woman's property had to be nominally held by a man: in practice, this often amounted to no more than an absentee trusteeship exercised by an agent (*prōcūrātor*) only on formal occasions (such as the manumission of slaves) or in a clerical capacity. In law, such a trusteeship was analogous to the guardianship of a minor as, indeed, were other aspects of laws concerning women and their property. On the other side of the coin, legal cases frequently arose when minors and women sued to recover property embezzled by their guardians: such suits would, of course, have to be brought by sympathetic enfranchised adult males acting on their behalf.

The political uses of marriage did not escape the Romans, any more than did economic ones, and in a turbulent decade, a woman might be pressured to divorce and remarry several times as her kinsmen's political allegiances got reshuffled. (One woman who stood her ground was Octavia, sister of the future emperor Augustus: when her brother advised her to divorce Marc Antony, she not only refused but continued to care for their children after Antony's death, taking on his child by Cleopatra as well.) A man who married a patrician lady might see his son adopted by her childless, rich, and influential brother – the relationship between mother's brother and sister's son being a special one – and the Romans appear to have been far readier to divorce than to disinherit. Nevertheless, as time went on, wealthy Roman women seem to have been increasingly able to marry as they pleased, at least on the second or third go-round: witness Valeria's artful courtship of the dictator Sulla, which she initiated with a bit of grooming behavior (a common primate endearment), picking some lint off his cloak as she passed his seat in the amphitheater, excusing herself charmingly with "I wished only to share in your good luck." If, however, you had been betrothed at one and married at twelve, you hadn't much say in the matter: a bride could refuse a husband only if she could have it shown that he was an immoral character.

Morality itself was subject to a legal double standard: in Augustus's time, adultery by a woman was, at least in theory, a capital offense, and if the woman were still subject to her father's authority – some marriages transferred this power to her husband, but others did not – he could execute her himself if he so chose. A husband was in any case required to divorce his wife under these circumstances, and he could then bring an action against her in court: conviction deprived her of half(!) her dowry, fined her lover, and exiled them. (To separate places. Perhaps this explains why Ovid was sent off to Bithynia without his wife, though there is no public record of a trial.) A wronged woman, on the other hand, was not compelled by law to divorce her dallying husband, nor was he in any case liable to be prosecuted on his own account.

Again, *stuprum* (criminal fornication) was not held to include a man's relations with prostitutes; patrician women, on the other hand, were forbidden any sex outside marriage. One could get around that by registering with the *aedīlis* as a prostitute – *aedīlēs* were the magistrates who oversaw the market and trade, the word *prostitute* coming from the past participle of a verb meaning "to display for sale" – but women who did so lost the right to inherit property, and an edict of Tiberius would forbid the practice altogether. Women who were raped could not, moreover, sue on their own behalf; their guardian had to do this for them, and as a civil action (either under *uīs* [violence] or *iniūria* [injury]) rather than a public crime.

It has been suggested that the double standard perpetuated itself in part because of a very real fear that women might take such liberties with male slaves (eunuchs were a later import) as men already took with slave women – hence the compulsion under which Lucretia was said to yield to the son of the last Tarquin when he offered her the alternative of killing a male slave in her bed and then having them "discovered" together. Whatever the case, by the third century A.D., the jurist Ulpian was to remark wryly that it seemed most unfair to ask a woman to behave with greater decency than any husband ever could.

The condition of women of the not-so-well-to-do classes is not well documented, though one interesting fact that pops up in records of food funds set up for the maintenance of freeborn children in two Italian towns (Elea and Comum) in Trajan's time is that female children were allotted about three quarters of a boy's dole, a pattern not very different from Athenian public assistance during the Peloponnesian War. Some women, including freedwomen who continued to ply the same trades they had been taught as slaves, became successful and respected merchants: Eumachia of Pompeii, whose family owned a brickworks, got chosen as the patroness of the fullers, and during her lifetime gave the town several columned arcades, and at least one other woman at Pompeii ran a brisk business as a moneylender. Tombstone inscriptions of Roman women list such occupations as "nailmaker" and "physician" and just about everything in between. On the other hand, female membership in the crafts guilds, even by women pursuing the same callings as their opposite masculine numbers and masters of it, was unheard of.

Prostitution, as in Greece, probably offered a woman a clear shot at power and wealth, if not status. While Pompeii's brothels speak of women whose price was two *assēs* (i.e., about the same as the price of a loaf of bread), a topnotch prostitute in a brothel could demand eight times that. Brothels were regulated and taxed – part of the *aedile's* job, which perhaps accounts for the political graffito found on a wall in the ruins of Pompeii which reads: "*Sucula* ["Piglet"] says: vote Marcus Cerrinius for aedile." On the bottom of the heap was the prostitute unaffiliated with a brothel who sold herself on the street and consummated the sale in a *fornix* – originally, a "vaulted cellar" in which prostitutes and the Roman poor made their homes, later, a "brothel," *fornix* being the basis of *fornicate* in both its sense of "vaulted, arched" and "to indulge in sexual intercourse." On the top were free agents for whom sixteen *assēs* was chickenfeed: successful courtesans could retire wealthy if they managed their affairs well, a good example being Volumnia Cytheris, a freedwoman and former mime actress who had as lovers in the Republic's twilight such notables as Brutus, Cornelius Gallus, and Marc Antony, among others.

Freedwomen were in any case better off than slaves in the eyes of the law, for whereas a freedwoman was a *persona* (albeit a somewhat restricted one), a slave of either gender was a *rēs* (thing) and therefore of concern more as a valuable piece of property than as a human being. And it is no exaggeration to say that by the accession of Augustus, the Roman state survived largely on the fruits of slave labor, not free. This was due in part to a substantial influx of slaves captured in colonial wars (*captīuī*) – English *slave* comes from Medieval Latin *sclauus* (Slav), hence, "Slavic P.O.W. reduced to involuntary servitude" – and in part to the desertion of the free farmers to the city as larger landowners increased their estates and brought in slaves to work them.

The generic term for "slave" was *seruus*, which gives English *serf, serve,* and, by way of the verb *seruiāre* (to be a slave), the word *sergeant*. A *servomechanism* (sometimes called a Waldo, from Robert Heinlein's science-fiction story of the same title) is a tool that reproduces manipulation but scales it up or down or performs it somewhere else, such a device being quite handy when one has to tinker with something that is either very small or very radioactive, or both. A female slave was called an *ancilla* – whence English *ancillary* – the feminine-gender form of *seruus* – *serua* – being of late coinage and restricted in use to designating the purely judicial aspects of slavery. A *uerna* was a slave born into a household, as opposed to a *captīuus* or a *mancipium* (bought slave) – from *manus* (hand) and *capere* (to take) because, in the strictest form of witnessed legal purchase, the act involved the seller and owner physically laying hands on the thing (or person) sold, whence our *emancipation*. *Vernacular* talk (from *uernāculus* [little *uerna*]) is down-home talk. Any servant connected with the household was a *famulus*, the *familia* including both free family and re-tainers as well.

Individual titles went with the job. We began with *nō-menclātor*. Also accompanying the master into public might be an *anteambulō* (walk-ahead), whose job it was to clear a way through the crowd. Although a less-well-to-do patron might have to have one slave perform both offices, rather like a press photographer's trusty Speed Graphic, by the time of Augustus no self-respecting Roman *petit bourgeois* would appear in public with an entourage of fewer than eight. At home, the female slave in command would be the *uillica*, under whose instructions most of the actual domestic work got done. The *uillica* was subservient only to the male stew-ard, the *uillicus*. The doorman at the gate was called either an *ostiārius* (whence English *ostiary*) or a *iānitor* (whence English *janitor*), *ostium* and *iānua* being two of the words used by Romans to mean "door, gate, entrance": *ostium* comes from the word for "mouth" – *ōs, ōris* – and *iānua* is related to *iānus, iānūs* (passage) and *Iānus, Iānī*, the god of passages, entrances, and beginnings in general, for whom *January* was named. (Tripping over the threshold as you set out on a journey was considered a very bad omen indeed, and a very poignant reference to this occurs in Ovid's *Tris-tia*.) Two other Latin words for "door, gate, entrance" were *foris* (which is cognate with English *door* and which desig-nated, specifically, a door of a house that opens to the out-doors; cf. *forīs* [outdoors] to which *forum* and English *forest* are related) and *porta*, from which British English *porter* (doorman) is derived (but not American English *porter*, which comes from the related verb *portāre* [to transport, carry], the original sense of *porta* having been "passage").

Occupational names might apply whether a worker was slave or free: *notārius* (secretary, whence English *notary*), *tūtor* (from *tūtus* [safe], literally "watched over," a *tūtor* being responsible for the safety of his charges as well as for their education) or *paedagōgus* (a direct steal from the Greek that gives English *pedagogue*), *piscātor/piscātrix* (fisher or seller of fish), *aquārius* (water carrier), *argentārius* (silversmith, silver merchant). This last, in practice, would almost never have been a slave, for the job entailed certain features of banking and exchange as well. (The relationship between precious-metal workers and precious-metal currency has been alive and well ever since the first gold daric rolled out of Asia Minor in the fifth century B.C., if not before; New England's first real currency, the Pine Tree Shilling, was manufactured in the shop of Boston's then-foremost silversmith, John Hull.) By contrast, *aquāriī* were always slaves, and (according to Juvenal) the worst sort – the only way to get water to an upper-story apartment in one of Rome's tenements (*insulae*, literally "islands") was by somebody's back-breaking work. A *tūtor* was usually a slave too, a Greek *captīuus*, perhaps; but such a slave had a good chance of eventually being set free, partly, one supposes, because it is hard to dismiss as a nonperson someone fluent in more languages than the master, and literate to boot.

In law, a master's power over his slaves was as great as it was over his other property: he could flog or even execute a slave – in stark contrast to the punishment that the law might permit to be inflicted on a Roman citizen. (Paul, as related in Acts, though his was only the sort of second-class Roman citizenship that provincials of the day could attain, was immune from being tied up or beaten, and had the right to be shipped to Rome to plead his capital case directly before the emperor – who, as luck would have it, was Nero, never noted for his affection for Christians, or for Jews either.) In practice, however, the climate of opinion was shifting under the late Republic and early empire to call for more humane treatment of slaves: the emperor Claudius issued an edict ordering the manumission of sick and elderly slaves who had been abandoned by their masters on the island of Aesculapius in the middle of the Tiber, and providing for strict punishment for any master who arranged for the death of such slaves in order to be spared the expense of their care. Seneca, who was recalled from exile at Claudius's death and served as Nero's advisor (before being implicated in Piso's plot to assassinate him), publicly espoused the cause of human rights of slaves and may indirectly have been responsible for an edict that directed the Urban Prefect to investigate complaints by slaves against their masters' abuse. A senatorial edict under Domitian prohibited the castration of slaves, and the master who was caught at it was made to forfeit half of his property. This penalty was increased under Hadrian, and two other edicts (a) forbade owners to sell their slaves to gladiatorial schools and (b) required a magistrate's consent before a master could execute a slave. Antoninus Pius went so far as to state that a master who executed a slave on his own initiative was no more or less than a murderer.

One reason for this softening of attitudes was undoubtedly the practice of upper-class Romans who never considered a slave to be anything less than a human being. Pliny the Younger would go on afternoon walks with his better-educated slaves included in the literary conversations that accompanied them, and at least two members of the Scipionic circle were slaves who later rose to literary eminence: the playwright Terence and the historian Polybius. Another reason was the increasing number of citizens who had been slaves freed at the master's death or before: although in the early days of the Republic one-slave households were common enough that slaves got names like *Marcipor* and *Lucipor* (*Marcī/Luciī* [of Marcus/Lucius] plus -*por*, a suffixal form of *puer* [boy]), consolidation of estates (particularly during the civil wars) left many families with no slaves and a very few families with very many. Cornelius Sulla, whom Valeria courted, freed some ten thousand slaves in his will, all of whom adopted the *nōmen* Cornelius. A master still living might manumit his slaves (*manumission* coming from *manus* [hand] plus the verb *mittere* [send], another reference to the actual handling involved in property transactions): he could do so either in a formal ceremony, complete with sacrifice, in which the censor enrolled the former slave in the census as a free person, or the master could bring a fictitious action in the praetor's court, to the same end (*per uindictam*).

In either event, the freedman remained in the relationship of client to patron – the quasi-filial respect that the freedman owed his former master was called *obsequium* (whence English *obsequious*) – in addition to whatever actual financial obligations might have been involved. As mentioned previously, freedmen often kept on in the same occupation that they had pursued under their former master's roof. Under such conditions, a freedman might become very prosperous indeed, and the Trimalchio of Petronius's *Satyricon*, while clearly a burlesque, was a recognizable enough type, with his own houseful of slaves, estates in the country, and troops of hangers-on, all going to show that when the man you called a slave a couple of years ago invites you over for dinner tonight, name-calling has become a rather risky business.

O

IS FOR *ORIGINS* WHICH, LIKE *ORIENT*
and *orientation*, comes from Latin *orīrī* (to rise, hence, to
arise from). *Orīrī* is one of those verbs called "deponents"
(put-downs), not because they were derogatory but rather
because of their active sense but passive construction. They
were said to have put down, i.e., set aside, their active
forms. What actually happened was that such verbs were
originally conjugated in something called the "middle
voice" which the early Indo-Europeans used when the action of the verb had the speaker as its focus. The Indo-
Europeans also made use of an active voice and a passive
voice, all of which seems to have become sufficiently cumbersome that the middle voice eventually went out of business in Latin except in a handful of verbs – the deponents
and semi-deponents – which are conjugated in whole or in
part like passives but which signify like actives. Other de-
ponent verbs of note are *nascī* (to be born), whose past participle, *nātus*, gives us *natal* and *nativity*; *morīrī* (to die),
whose past participle, *mortuus*, gives us *mortal*, *mortify*,
and *mortgage* (which is a combination of the *mort-* of *mortuus* and a Germanic form meaning "pledge"); and *prōgredī*
(to set forth), whose past participle, *prōgressus*, gives us
progress.

The *Orient* is that direction from which the sun rises: to
orient a map was originally to draw it with the east at the
top, the convention that prevailed in Western mapmaking
until it occurred to someone that it might be nice to put the
north at the top instead. *Orientation*, then, is the process
of getting faced in the right direction, e.g., with the help of
your Freshman Week counselor or Senior Sister and accompanied by such rites of passage as the mixer dance, beer
blast, and compulsory funny hat, or perhaps in spite of

them: one scholar of our acquaintance states that his academic career began in earnest the afternoon he hurled his beanie into the river and watched it sink without a trace.

River comes not from Latin *rīuus* (stream, which is related to *orīrī*) but from *rīpa* (bank of a watercourse, which is not). *Rīpa* also gives us *arrive*, i.e., to reach the river bank, through French *rive* (as in *Rive gauche* [Left Bank], the side of the Seine that constituted the low-rent district where the artists lived. Because immigrants from Bohemia – the Czechoslovakia of today – lived there before the artists discovered it, *bohemian* came to refer to anybody who preferred low rent to relative respectability and high overhead for whatever reason.) *Rīuus*, on the other hand, gives us *rival*, which originally referred to a person who shared the same brook as you, the use of streams as boundaries being so ancient as to be shrouded in the mists of antiquity, especially on cold nights.

A fog of antiquity also coyly conceals the actual origins of Rome and the Roman people, though historians, archaeologists, and linguists have been able to piece together something like the following: The *Latini* were not the first inhabitants of the hills of Rome, excavations on the north side having uncovered artifacts of the so-called Appennine culture, Bronze Age Indo-Europeans who arrived in the Po valley sometime around 1600 B.C. and then began to wander south. Elsewhere within the city limits, archaeologists have discovered sites dating from the Stone Age and before. There is also evidence of a copper-working people who were already in Rome before the Indo-Europeans first came to town.

It is perhaps not too surprising that Rome was a popular place to live way back when: it straddles the Tiber, a handy source of water and, at its mouth, of salt, the lucrative salt route along the river being called the *Via Salaria*; and its famous Seven Hills (the Aventine, the Capitoline, the Caelian, the Esquiline, the Palatine, the Quirinal, and the Viminal) are relatively easy to retreat to and defend when you are fighting with little more than clubs and pointed sticks.

More than once the Capitoline Hill has proven a convenient refuge from hostile forces, as in 386 B.C. when the Gauls attacked the citadel on its top by night and were foiled only by the honking of the geese which, in spite of a dearth of rations, had not been slaughtered (because they were sacred to Juno) and so, according to Livy, awoke the sleeping defenders.

The Capitoline Hill seems to have been one of the last at Rome to have been continuously occupied down to the present day. The Appennine-culture Indo-Europeans were joined in about 1200 B.C. by iron-working people whose decorative bronze articles are reminiscent of the Mycenaean work of roughly the same period, i.e., the days of the Trojan War which Homer reported from the comfort of his armchair at a safe remove of several centuries. The original center of Latium was not Rome but Alba Longa, about thirteen miles southeast of Rome; and the Latini appear to have been a loose federation of communities with a common language – Latin's immediate precursor – and a common shrine – that of Iuppiter Latiaris, located at the summit of the Alban Mount, an extinct volcano, now called *Monte Cavo*, some three thousand feet high and surrounded with soil still fertile from the fresh potash and phosphates thrown up by successive eruptions, much like the rich earth surrounding the slopes of the intermittently active Mount Vesuvius eighty miles or so down the coast. The earliest tombs at Alba Longa date from about 1100 B.C.; the prospering Latini spread out all over present-day Campagna and had a foothold in Rome by about 750 B.C., dislodging or assimilating any older residents. The year traditionally accepted as the founding of the city – 753 B.C. – is probably reasonably accurate; and it is from this date that the Romans reckoned their official calendar, the year 1 A.D. being given as 754 A.U.C. – *ab urbe conditā* (from the founding of the city) – although most Romans actually dated historical events by who the consuls were that year. Though the tombs of the first Latini in the area can be dated with reasonable accuracy to a century before that, the middle of the eighth century B.C. marks the point from which the separate villages on the Palatine, Esquiline, and Caelian hills coalesced into a unified city-state (*cīuitās, cīuitātis*, the equivalent to the Greek *pólis, póleōs*, the first of which underlies *civil* and *city* and the last of which underlies *politics, policy,* and *police* – but not *polite*, which comes from the Latin verb *polīre* [to polish]).

One thinks of the Roman Forum as the civic center, and it is therefore somewhat surprising that this part of town, located between the Palatine and Esquiline hills, was first used as a cemetery before being built on and inhabited by the living. Much is made of the coexistence in time and space of two forms of burial practiced by the locals – cremation, which the Appennine-culture people seem to have brought to Italy with them, and inhumation, practiced by the Sabines, who were also of Indo-European stock, spoke a language closely related to Latin, and originally lived on the far side of the Appennines from Alba Longa. What do different burial practices prove? Not much, since how you dispose of your dead probably has as much to do with where you live as who you are, to the extent that these are distinguishable: a visitor to modern-day Vermont might draw a false distinction between those who buried their dead underground and those who made use of a general town vault above if not aware that the ground freezes so solid in winter that inhumation by hand-tool methods is impracticable five or six months out of the year. That there were Sabines in the vicinity of the early city of Rome is easily enough deduced from the linguistic evidence; that they were eventually completely assimilated is almost certain; and that they originally lived on the Esquiline and Quirinal hills – while the Latini lived on the Palatine – has now been largely discredited.

Far more easily distinguished are the influences of the non–Indo-European Etruscans, whose society collided with that of the Latini in the last days of the seventh century B.C. Livy says that an Etruscan named Lucumo – whose father, he claims, was actually a Corinthian in exile – seized power

Oo

at Rome and ruled, under the name of Lucius Tarquinus Priscus, from 625 B.C. It is more likely that various families simply moved south from Etruria, settled in Rome, and became important movers and shakers in the Roman aristocracy of the time through sheer prosperity, a success aided in part by their superior technology: the Etruscans were skilled iron workers, the largely pastoral Latini having a far more rudimentary command of the art. In any event, Etruscans were kings of Rome until around 500 B.C. – Livy gives 510 B.C. as the year of the expulsion of Tarquin the Proud, which is marginally credible, although the pretext (the rape of Lucretia by Tarquin's son Sextus) is suspiciously similar to the story of how the Athenians kicked out the sons of Pisistratus, down to the very date.

The Romans believed that by 508 B.C., their ancestors had established a form of republic. Their evidence for this date consisted of lists of consular pairs starting in that year (for which some of the names, at least in the earliest years, are questionable), and also a treaty between Rome and Carthage dated that year (probably erroneously), and cited by Polybius, in which there is no reference to a Roman king whatever, as there would surely have been were the Tarquins still heads of state. The new republic institutionalized certain differences in privilege between the commoners (*plēbēs*) and the aristocracy or patricians (*patriciī*), among whom the major families (*gentēs māiōrēs*) were generally accepted to be six: the Aemilii, the Claudii, the Cornelii, the Fabii, the Manlii, and the Valerii. If these names sound vaguely familiar, it is because people with these monikers performed great deeds in the subsequent history of republican and imperial Rome – or, put another way, every historian or poet of the day had to reckon with the influence of – or enmity of his patron toward – contemporary members of these same six families.

Thus far history, i.e., the part that's left over after the scientists have taken their cut. For the reasons just given, Livy, though entertaining, is unreliable in spots, for owing to the monumental nature of his project – to write the history of Rome from its foundations down to his own day, of which he managed to complete 142 books (through 9 B.C.) before his death in 17 A.D. – he was obliged to quote his sources somewhat uncritically. One of these, Fabius Pictor – the same Pictor who was sent to Delphi after the disaster at Cannae – had little good to say about the Claudii, toward whom the Fabii bore a perennial grudge. On the other hand, Livy was further hampered by the lack of Roman historians to draw on earlier than Fabius Pictor, who died about 200 B.C.; and until 130 B.C., the official city records kept by the *pontifex maximus* were supposed to be rubbed out and reinscribed every year, a practice which, if followed, made them terribly susceptible to tampering. Mucius Scaevola, who was chief priest from 130 to 115 B.C., supervised the writing down of the priestly chronicles in a permanent form; but he was not without his own biases and could, moreover, change sides: although originally a staunch supporter of the reform consulship of Tiberius Gracchus, Scaevola is said to have praised the latter's assassination in 133 B.C. This sort of partisanship had its effect not only the recording of things supposedly historical but also on the handing down of myth: as Livy believed that history ought to teach people to be good, so Scaevola believed that myth and religion were for keeping people quiet and obedient.

Roman myths of origin, then, reveal rather more about republican Roman morality than they do about ancient Roman religion. Still, it would do Ovid and Vergil an injustice to say that they were merely versifying the party line of late republican/early imperial Rome. After all, the gods and heroes that people their works were being talked about long before anyone wrote in Latin about them. Indeed, some of them were not even originally gods of the Latini but were of even older Italic provenance. *Juno*, for example, was apparently native to the peninsula, the patroness of women's generative power, and was only identified with the Greek *Hera* at a comparatively late date. Similarly, *Saturnus* (whose feast was the *Saturnalia*, falling in December) was a god of sowing, his name being akin to the Latin verb *serere* (to sow). As the husband of the goddess *Ops*, he got identified with Greek *Kronos* (because she was identified with Rhea). Ops was a harvest goddess, charged incidentally with the protection of the granaries from fire.

Mars, later identified with Greek *Ares*, was originally a god of vegetation who fostered crops and herds and defended them from attackers. It is presumably from wearing this last hat that Mars got to be a war god and gave us the word *martial*. Like Saturnus, Mars gave his name to one of the planets and to one of the days of the week as well. According to the Ptolemaic view of the universe, there were seven planets – the Sun, the Moon, Mars, Mercury, Jupiter, Venus, and Saturn – which revolved around the Earth. Each has lent its name to a day of the week in French and English, though neither language shares a single one: English has *Sunday* while French has *dimanche* (from Latin *diēs domenica* [the Lord's day]); *Monday* and *lundi*, while both meaning "the Moon's day," come from different words for moon; French has *mardi* (Mars's day) while we have *Tuesday* (Tiu's day, *Tiu* being the Germanic god of war and the sky comparable to Mars); French has *mercredi* (Mercury's day) while we have *Wednesday* (Wotan's day, the connection here being somewhat more tenuous but still in the same universe of discourse); *jeudi* is "Jove's day," i.e., Jupiter's day, while *Thursday* is "Thor's day," again not a perfect fit, but close enough; *vendredi* is "Venus's day" and "Freya's day" is *Friday*, *Freya* being the Old Norse version of *Venus* as near as no matter; *Saturday* is "Saturn's day" and *samedi* is basically the "Sabbath."

Another native Italic god whom the Romans adopted as their own in their characteristically eclectic way was *Faunus*, another protector, like Mars, of the crops and the herd. Faunus specialized in guarding against wolves and was given the epithet *Lupercus* (from *lupus* [wolf]), his annual festival being called the *Lupercālia*. It was during the Lupercalia that his priests, dressed in nothing but skins and somewhat drunk, ran around the city striking those in their way with goat thongs. Hitherto childless women would make sure that they either were or were not struck by the thongs, depending on whether they wished any part of the fertility that the whacks were believed to confer on the recipient. It was also during the Lupercalia that Marc Antony repeatedly offered the crown to Julius Caesar. Some say that Antony was sozzled at the time, as the ceremony allowed, but others said that he was cold stone sober. The feast fell on the Ides of February; and the month that followed was the last of Caesar's heroic career. On a somewhat more upbeat note, it may be added that Faunus was also known as *Syluanus* (from *sylua/silua* [forest, woods] and the basis of the names *Sylvia, Sylvester,* and *Pennsylvania*) and was considered to be a protector of the forest and of recently cleared land. Greek stories about *Pan* (whence *panic,* i.e., what you might do after dark in the forest) were transferred by the Romans to him.

Diana was originally worshiped at Aricia in Latium, whence her cult was transferred to the Avetine Hill in Rome. She was patroness of childbirth at first, a function later assigned to *Lucina* when Diana became identified with Greek *Artemis. Venus* was not originally a Roman *Aphrodite* so much as a goddess of the marketplace. She came to hold a special place in the Roman pantheon because of her divine parentage of the legendary Aeneas (whom some, at least, held to have been responsible for the founding of the city of Rome). *Fortuna,* on the other hand, seems always to have been worshiped as the abstraction of destiny, particularly when it came time to wonder how the harvest was going to turn out, and in this capacity had a shrine of respectable antiquity at Praeneste near Alba Longa. Curiously enough, Fortuna remained in the popular consciousness well into Christian times, and long past the dissolution of the Roman empire, for there is a picture of her commanding a wheel of destiny at the head of a medieval manuscript of songs by wandering scholar-poets that was found in the German Swiss monastery at Benediktbeuern, the celebrated *Carmina Burana.*

Sharing responsibility over storehouses was *Volcanus*, who was god of destructive fire (as was the Semitic god *Moloch*). He was patron of the docks at Rome's seaport at Ostia. *Neptunus*, later to be identified with the Greek *Poseidon*, was first and foremost a god of moisture, only secondarily a god of the sea, and his festival – the *Neptunālia* – was celebrated in rural areas of Italy until well into the fourth century A.D. *Vesta* was the goddess of the hearth and its benign fire; her worship was a central feature of Roman life, both private and official, and the six virgins who attended her altar in the Roman Forum were expected to be of unimpeachable morals – so much so that when one of the Vestals was debauched (as happened in 217 B.C. around the time of the battle of Cannae), she was buried alive and her lover publicly clubbed to death by the pontifex maximus. *Minerva* – later equated with *Athene* – was patroness of the rustic arts and crafts and seems to have been adopted by the Romans from the town of Falerii in Etruria.

The particular household gods of each Roman family were the *larēs* and *penātēs*. They were not considered to be of any particular sex. The *penātēs* were the gods of the larder (*penus*) and were numerous in proportion to the variety of eatables in store at any given time. Originally, there was only one *lar* to a household, he or she being the divinity that protected the plot of land on which the house was built. Later, the *lar's* function was broadened so as to include the protection of the building as well. *Ianus*, by contrast, was the god of doorways – anybody's doorway. The gates of his temple at Rome were closed only in time of peace, which is to say, rarely. He is said to have seduced the nymph *Carna* by promising to make her the goddess of hinges if she let him have his way, which she did. Renamed *Cardea* (Hinge), she had as her emblem a white thorn.

In addition to these native deities, the Romans took over a number of Greek ones lock, stock, and barrel, and not just gods but deified heroes as well: *Aesculapius* was imported as the result of the Romans' consultation of the Sibylline books – recorded oracles from the shrine of the Sibyl at Cumae in

Magna Graecia – during a plague in 292 B.C.: the snake that they were instructed to bring back from Aesculapius's temple at Epidaurus in Asia Minor leaped overboard and made for shore at an island in the middle of the Tiber that was subsequently dedicated to the healing "god" and set aside for his temple. Similarly, *Castor* and *Pollux* (*Kastor* and *Polydeuces*) had been worshiped at Tusculum, on the slopes of the Alban Mount, for such a long time that most Romans thought them to be native Italic gods, while in fact their rise to fame came when they were spotted coming to the aid of the Roman side at the battle of Lake Regillus in 496 B.C., when Roman troops fought against Praeneste (which had seceded from an alliance with Rome) and the exiled Tarquins. *Hercules* (the Greek *Herakles*), whom the Greeks saw as an intermediary with the Olympians to help mortals along in commerce and other highly practical activities, was gathered into the Roman fold very early on. His altar in the Forum was called the *āra maxima* (greatest altar); many a Roman swore *Herclē* (by Hercules) and his oath had long currency, being moreover revived in post-Revolutionary times by the ever classically minded French.

When Augustus Caesar came to power and the gates of the temple of Ianus were closed for the first time since the end of the second Punic War, literature flourished under (or, some say, despite) his encouragement and patronage, and it is significant that two of the greatest works to come out of this period should both have been (at least partly) about mythology: Ovid's *Metamorphoses* and Vergil's *Aeneid*. Under the general heading of "Things Changed," Ovid had a free hand to tell virtually any story that suited his fancy from the combined Latin and Greek mythic heritage, since almost every myth involved a metamorphosis of one sort or another. And tell he did, in gracious, easy hexameters, of Daedalus and Icarus, of the footrace that Atalanta ran, slowed just enough by three golden apples thrown at her feet for her suitor to win his life and her hand, of the greedy king Midas and how he grew donkey ears, and so on. These lively tales make nifty reading and, for the neophyte

Latin student, a rewarding introduction both to the Greco-Roman myths and to the nuts and bolts of Latin prosody, for Ovid has the charm of writing the hexameters borrowed from the Greeks with such facility that one forgets for the moment that the verse form did not originate in Latin at all but was yet another felicitous borrowing.

Vergil wrote sterner, grander stuff with all the dignity – and, some would say, starchiness – of a candidate's toga. (*Candida* was the bright white color obtained by pounding fuller's earth through cloth; a *candidātus* was a fellow who had got his toga as white as the fuller could bleach it before going out into the Forum to hustle votes.) Vergil relates how Aeneas, son of Venus and the Trojan Anchises, fled the burning, falling city and, aided by his mother and balked by Juno, eventually found his way to the Italic peninsula where, kindness of his son Ascanius, later renamed *Iulus*, the Roman people in general and the Julian house in particular would come into being. Its detractors have called the *Aeneid* a shameless piece of political propaganda, and perhaps it is; its champions, however, remind us that Aeneas is not just a polyunsaturated Odysseus, but a new type of hero, driven by a fate (*fatō profugus*) more powerful than, and often opposed to, his human sympathies. If Vergil between the lines was indeed saying that the *Pax Augustana* was bought at the melancholy expense of individual loves and alliances, it still may be asked whether this was obvious to his contemporaries, although conflicts between Vergil's and Homer's treatment of parallel situations would certainly not have gone unnoticed. At the very least, the *Aeneid* has its share of quotable quotes, such as "*Quicquid id est, timeō Danaōs, et dōna ferentēs*" ("Whatever it is, I fear the Greeks, especially those bearing gifts") – the book was an immediate hit in literate Roman society and has remained a staple for the past two thousand years.

Well, one might ask, why did the Romans care about their origins, real or imagined, or, for that matter, about the origins of their language (for etymology was a favorite sideline of virtually every Latin author)? Why, indeed, does anyone care about origins? What does it matter that *origin* comes from *orīrī* or that the Christians got their origin myth from the Jews or that the Claudii probably came from Sabine stock or that your great-grandfather came from Halifax? What human need does "knowledge" of where something comes from satisfy?

Maybe it's just that, when all is said and done, everybody likes a good story.

P

IS FOR *PETER, PAUL, PONTIFF, POPE, PAR-*
ish, parable, and a whole host of other church-related
words as well. Indeed, were it not for the church, Latin
might have disappeared many centuries ago, metamorphosed into the Romance languages of today. As it was, the
use of Latin for liturgical purposes gave it the status of a
lingua franca for medieval clerics and scholars, in which
the Scot could converse with the Spaniard and the German
with the Gaul. Moreover, notwithstanding Vatican II and
the celebration of the Mass in the vernacular, papal encyclicals are still written in Latin to this day.

Peter comes from Greek *pétros* (stone, to which may be
compared Greek *pétra* [rock]). Both *Petrus* and *petra* were
borrowed into Late Latin (in time to form the basis of
French *Pierre* and *pierre,* respectively, as well as English
petrify), replacing the old favorites *saxum* and *lapis, lapidis*
(rock, stone). (These are not without their English descendants, though some of them are pretty obscure: *saxicolous*
and *lapidose* are both botanical terms meaning "growing
among rocks," a *lapidary* is a gemstone cutter, and a *lapis*
lazuli is a gemstone, the best specimens of which come
from Afghanistan. Medieval painters ground up lapis lazuli
for pigment and charged for its use by the square inch.)
Saint Peter was really named Simon, his Aramaic nickname being *Kepha* (Rock). Before he became a follower of
Jesus, he had been a fisherman, like his brother St. Andrew,
and both were probably burly fellows. Jesus told him (Mat-
thew 16:18) that he was a rock on which to build the
Church ("*Et ego dīcō tibi, quia tū es Petrus, et super hanc*
petram aedificābō Ecclesiam meam"), and on this gentle jest
rests the entire notion of apostolic succession.

Saint *Paul* – the name is related to the *pau-* of *paucus* (few) and *pauper* (poor) – was originally Saul and had been a pupil of the celebrated Rabbi Gamaliel at Jerusalem before his astonishing conversion on the road to Damascus. A second-century source describes Saint Paul as short, bowlegged, and bald; his trade had been tent making before he gave it all up to preach Christianity to the Gentiles. There is a tradition that he and Saint Peter were executed at Rome on the same day for their rabble-rousing activities, but this seems to have arisen from the fact that they share the same feast day: June 29th.

Pontiff – the title of Saint Peter's designated successor – is from Latin *pontifex (maximus)* ([chief] priest). Latin speakers have repeatedly tried over the centuries to derive *pontifex* from *pons, pontis* (bridge) plus the suffix *-fex* (maker), the idea being that the priest was sort of a bridge between the sacred and the profane (*profānus* being, literally, "outside of the temple"), but this etymology is probably incorrect. Like many Latin words of obscure origin, *pontifex* has garnered its share of votes for having come from Etruscan. In any event, to *pontificate* is to speak with papal self-assuredness: papal pronouncements have always carried heavy clout, but it is only within recent times that the Roman Catholic Church has held that the Pope is infallible when speaking *ex cathedra* (literally "from the bench," a *cathedra* being originally a chair, hence a throne or throne of office, whence *cathedral*, "principal church of a bishop's see that contains his official throne"). *Priest*, incidentally, is from Greek *presbýteros* (elder), since that is what the first Christian priests were; the *presbyter-* in *Presbyterian* refers to the elders of the congregation. *Presbýteros* also underlies the *Prester* of *Prester John*, the mythical long-lived monarch who was supposed to have reigned over a Christian country at the far end of the known world (Asia or, as some said, Africa), of whom Sir John Mandeville (d. 1372) wrote,

"This emperor Prester John weddeth commonly the great Khan's daughter. . . . Prester John is Christian, and a great part of his land also, but they have not all the articles of our faith, but they believe well in the Father, the Son, and the Holy Ghost, and they are full devout and true to one another,"

a somewhat wistful fantasy of Christian utopia attractive to the medieval mind.

Pope comes from *Pap(p)a*, Latin for "Dad, Pop" – rather than, as one might think, from Latin *popa*, the assistant priest whose job it was at sacrifices to lead the intended victim to the altar and, on the command *"Hoc age!"* ("Do it!") to fetch the unfortunate creature a sharp whack on the head with a blunt instrument. (Sacrifices in which the victim's throat was cut instead were performed by a *cultārius*, from *culter* [knife], whence French *couteau* and English *cutlery*.) *Popa* may have been borrowed into Latin from Etruscan (which has contributed a number of masculine-gender nouns ending in what looks like feminine-gender -*a*) or it may have come from Oscan/Umbrian, in which case it may be related to the verb "to cook," whose Latin derivatives include *coquīna* (cookery, kitchen, whence French *cuisine*) and *popīna* (low-class eatery, greasy spoon), a term of Oscan origin that Romans used contemptuously in reference to a banquet (*cēna*) that fell short of expectations. *Papal*, *papacy*, and *papist* are all derivatives of *pap(p)a*.

Interestingly enough, another Latin children's word – *nonnus* – was occasionally applied to the Pope. *Nonnus* originally meant "uncle," and its feminine counterpart, *nonna*, meant "aunt." In the early days of the church, these terms, like the Latin words for the members of one's immediate family – father, mother, brother, sister – were used to designate members of the religious community. *Nonnus* and *nonna* were originally used in the sense of member of the religious community who has yet to receive the sacrament of ordination. *Nonna* eventually became Old French *nonne* (woman who has taken religious vows) and was borrowed as such into Middle English to become Modern English *nun*. *Nonnus*, by contrast, came to mean "senior member of a religious order" but eventually fell out of use in that sense, though it appears in Modern Italian as *nonno* (grandfather).

The sense of the Pope as Holy Father is perhaps more formal than the notion of "uncle" or "Dad," but the particular kinship relationship suggested is the same, not surprisingly, given the general patriarchal orientation of the Roman society in which the early church took root, an orientation embodied in the word *patricius* (patrician). *Patricius* is also the Latin name for Irish *Padraig* (Patrick). Saint Patrick was a Briton by birth; his father was named Calpurnius, and his grandfather was apparently a priest. His first visit to Ireland seems to have been fortuitous; he was carried away captive in a raid and spent his late adolescence there as a herdsman before escaping to the Continent. He studied for the priesthood in Gaul, probably under Saint Germanus (the French Saint Germain after whom the Parisian church of St.-Germain-des-Prés was named, the parish being technically a suburb at the time it was founded, much like St. Martin's-in-the-Fields), returning to Ireland as a missionary in 432 A.D. or so. It is doubtful whether there were any serpents in Ireland before his arrival, but there have certainly been none there since, save for those imported from off-island. The term *paddy wagon* for what criminologists now call a "mobile cell" derives either from the days when most of the people who got arrested in American East Coast cities were Irish, or were thought to be, or from the time when most of the police force was Irish (or was thought to be), in either case, at the end of the last century and the beginning of this one. In cities where the analogous ethnic group was Italian, the vehicle was called a *Black Maria* – no relation to the Black Madonna of Czestochowa, the patron saint of Poland.

It was presumably in part the Christian notion of God the Father, the one God, that got the early faithful in trouble with their pagan Roman neighbors, since insistent monotheism was clearly at variance with what one anthropologist has termed "pagan tolerance": You worship your gods and I'll worship mine, and every so often we'll get together and all worship the chief's. Pliny the Younger wrote a famous letter to Trajan asking, in fact, what to do about Christians who were informed on and who, on being questioned, refused to offer sacrifice to the emperor, to which Trajan replied that if they were caught and refused to sacrifice, there was nothing to do but execute them, but that informers ought not to be encouraged (to which his commentator would later add, "O would we Christians could use this moderation unto others"). *Pagan*, by the way, comes from Latin *pāgānus* which is, in turn, derived from *pāgus* (boundary fence or pale), which later came to mean countryside, district. A *pāgānus* was a country person (under Roman jurisdiction), i.e., someone within the pale. (*Pale*, while we are about it, comes from Latin *pālus* [stake] and came to mean, first, "stake used in making a fence," then, "fence [made of stakes]," then, "boundary." The original sense of *pālus* is suggested by the verb *impale*. No relation to *pale* [ashen], which comes through Old French from Latin *pallidus*.) *Pāgānus* eventually became Italian *paisano* and French *paysan*, the latter being borrowed into English in the fifteenth century to become our *peasant*. *Pāgānus* in the specific sense of "Roman provincial subject" was contrasted with *Christiānus* and as such survived to become the *pagan* of today, i.e., *heathen* – a heathen having been originally a "heath-dweller" (though some have suggested that the word is a garbling of Breton Celtic – or Armoric – *hethanos* [pagan]). A similar process gives *gentile/Gentile*, ultimately from Latin *gens* (clan), the idea being that *Gentiles*, whether in the sense of non-Jews, pagans, or non-Mormons, are members of the other clan. Compare *parish* and *parochial*, which come through Latin from the Greek *paroikós* (neighbor, alien, foreigner who lives in a place without enjoying any civil rights), a *paroikía* being an ecclesiastical district contained in the diocese (originally one of the lesser Roman provinces). Whether *parishioners* were so called because they were provincials or whether they considered themselves, as the *Larousse Etymologique* puts it, "strangers on the earth" is not clear.

What is clear, however, is that the word *cretin* is the result of the practice, once Christianity was firmly established, of referring to all souls (except the obviously non-Christian) as "Christians." Inhabitants of remote rural villages, given inbreeding and undernourishment, might be born with severe mental and physical handicaps, but they were considered Christians just the same. Swiss French *crestin* (later *creitin*) was a dialectal form of the word for Christian and got borrowed into Standard French in the specific sense of "deformed human being." As such, it migrated north into English as *cretin* and south to become Italian *cretino*. Modern English reserves the term in medical parlance for persons suffering from myxedema.

But back to *pons, pontis* (bridge) for a moment: the word probably has nothing to do with the surname *Pontius*, as in *Pontius Pilatus*, the hapless procurator of Judea who has come down to us as the epitome of the responsible official who tries to wash his hands of a disgraceful affair of state. (He was recalled to Rome under a cloud and ended his days by suicide or, as some say, in exile in Gaul, reminding one of W. C. Fields's epitaph: "On the whole, I'd rather be in Philadelphia.") *Pons* is, however, related to the Greek word *póntos* (sea) which was borrowed into Latin as the name for the Black Sea and the district surrounding it: *Pontus*. Ovid's *Tristia* (*Sad Tidings*) and *Epistolae ex Ponto* (*Letters from Pontus*) were written from Tomis, the border town near the mouth of the Danube to which Augustus had summarily exiled him in 8 A.D. *Hellespont* contains the same root but in probably its original sense of "means of getting from one place to the other" (in this case *Hellás*, i.e., Greece), the sea having been, to Greek lights, as handy a way as any of going to and fro. The same Indo-European root would appear to yield Greek *pátos* (trodden path) and probably English *path* itself (though not directly). Other derivatives include the *-pad* of *footpad*, i.e., pedestrian highwayman or thief, the *-put-* of Russian *Sputnik*, literally "fellow-traveler with the earth" (from s[o]- [earth] plus *-put-* plus the suffix *-nik*, the latter borrowed into English for use in such hybrids as *refusenik, nogoodnik, beatnik, shootnik* [gun freak] and the like), and English *find/foundling*. *Pons* is one of those handy words which serve as a nutshell example of sound change from Latin to Romance: compare Italian *ponte*, Spanish *puente*, Portuguese *ponte*, French *pont*, from the last of which (or, more properly, from the Old French ancestor of the last of which) come English *pontoon* and *punt* (the boat, not the football kick, which is apparently from *bunt*, a British dialectal term meaning "to butt with horns or in the like fashion," whence the baseball term, whose strategic similarity to the football punt should not be overlooked).

Although the *Peter/rock* joke stands as a rare example of early Christian boffo humor, there is much wit in the parables, those illustrative nuggets that Jesus used so skillfully in his teaching. The word *parabola* which underlies English *parable* is a Latin borrowing of Greek *parabolē*. (Indeed, much of the Latin liturgical vocabulary is borrowed from Greek, though the first Latin translation of the Bible actually came out of the North African colonies.) Greek *parabolē* – from the verb *parabállein* (to throw beside) which is also the source of English *ballistics* – means "a throwing side by side, an illustrative comparison" and was a tried and true pedagogic tool among the Jews long before Aristotle discussed its use in his *Rhetoric*, distinguishing between *parabolē* and *lógos* (fable) in a way that probably confused the Romans for whom a *fābula* was simply a "narration, story." (Some would say that the difference between a parable and a fable is a matter of the reality quotient: if the story could conceivably happen, it's a parable, and if it has talking animals in it or some other totally off-the-wall plot element, then it's probably a fable.)

That speakers of Latin were none too clear on the difference between *parabola* and *fābula* may be seen by what happened to these words as they wended their way into Romance. In French, *parabola* has become *parole* (word), and *parabolāre* (to tell parables) has become *parler* (to speak). English *parole* keeps the specialized sense of "word" as in "I

give you my word I won't run away (or do anything bad)."
Parabola also appears as Spanish *palabra* and Portuguese
palavra (word), whence English *palaver*, about which the
Oxford Dictionary of Etymology has this to say: "*Palavra*
appears to have been used by Pg. traders on the coast of
Africa for a parley with the natives, to have been picked up
by English sailors, and to have passed from nautical slang
into ordinary colloq. use." *Fabulāre* (to tell fables) is the
basis of Spanish *hablar* and Portuguese *falar*, both meaning
"to speak."

No mention of parables would be complete without a tip
of the hat to one of the most brilliant modern masters of the
form, Franz Kafka, who opens his *Paradoxes and Parables*
with a classic which may be paraphrased as follows: Somebody says that if you behaved the way people did in parables,
then you'd wind up becoming a parable yourself. Somebody
else says, "I bet that's a parable," to which the first somebody
replies, "You win." "Ah, but only in parable," says the second somebody. "No," says the first. "In reality. In parable,
you lose."

Q

IS FOR *QUERY, QUAESTOR, QUEST,* AND *question,* all of which come from the verb *quaerere* (to seek, seek to learn, ask). The past participle of *quaerere* is *quaestum,* the *r/s* alternation in the various parts of the verb being the result of the phenomenon called *rhotacism* (from *rho,* the Greek name for the letter of their alphabet corresponding to Roman *R*). The process of rhotacism involved the change of [s] between vowels to [r], perhaps via something like the [z] attested in Latin's close cousin, Oscan. Rhotacism was responsible for the *r*'s in such pairs as *honorable/honest, general/genus, temporal/tempo, oral/osculate,* and, of course, *query/quaestor, quest,* and *question.*

A *quaestor* was originally a magistrate in charge of criminal investigation, though the term later came to designate a magistrate in charge of various financial functions such as, presumably, the Roman precursor to the I.R.S. audit: to be a quaestor was to be empowered to ask the embarrassing questions and to hear the answers – *audit* comes from the verb *audīre* (to hear). Virtually all of the interrogative pronouns that a Latin-literate quaestor would have used begin with *qu-,* as most of their English counterparts begin with *wh-* (originally *hw-*): corresponding to our *who, which,* and *what,* Latin has *quī, quae, quod, quis,* and *quid; when* is either *cum* (originally *quom*) or *quandō; whither* is *quō;* and *why* is *cur* or *quārē.*

Other useful Latin interrogatives include *quālis* ("of what kind?") – which gives us *quality,* as *quid* gives us *quiddity;* and *quantus, quanta, quantum* ("how much, how many?") give us *quantity* (and the *quantum* of *quantum mechanics*). *Quot* ("how much?") appears thinly disguised as the adjective *quotus, quota, quotum* (from which English derives its *quota*) and also plays a cameo role in the word *quotidiānus* (daily, literally "of how many days"). English *quotidian* retains the sense of "daily" and derives from it a further sense of "everyday, commonplace." *Quotidian* has also been used in the specialized medical sense of "having a daily cycle," as in *quotidian ague*, a fever-and-shakes combination with a circadian rhythm. Compare *quartan fever*, with its four-day cycle of peak and break, and the traditional period of *quarantine* (from Italian *quarantina giorni* [period of roughly forty days]) while asking not for whom the bell tolls.

While questions have clearly been around since time immemorial in the Indo-European universe of discourse, the *question mark* has not. This handy graphic sign seems to have been formed from a *Q* with a little *o* under it as an abbreviation of the word *quaestiō* (query, question). Similarly, the *exclamation point* – a.k.a., "screamer" or "bang" – is derived either from an abbreviation of Latin *interiectiō* (interjection) or else from the interjection *Iō!* ("Hey!"). Both the question mark and the exclamation point – as well as all other early marks of punctuation – were developed as aids to reading aloud. (Writers of Spanish to this day obligingly warn the out-loud reader of what's coming up in the text by putting an upside-down question mark or exclamation point at the beginning of a sentence that is going to turn out to be a question or exclamation once you get to the end of it – which, in Spanish literary prose, can be a matter of days if you're not used to it.) Indeed, before punctuation was invented, it was virtually impossible to read much of anything more elaborate than the graffiti on the local bordello wall without moving your lips, since early writers didn't tend to waste much time putting spaces between words and could not even be relied upon to start each line of print at the same side of the page: a lot of early writing is *boustrophedon*, that is, with lines alternating left-to-right and right-to-left (or right-to-left and left-to-right) and back the other way whenever you hit the margin, the effect being that of staggering along a plowed field in which the farmer has driven an ox one length of the field and has then turned and come back the other way, a *boûs* being an ox and a *strophḗ* being a turn or twist in Greek.

Saint Augustine (354–430 A.D.) tells us that one of the unusual things about Saint Ambrose (d. 397 A.D.) was that he was able to read and understand a document of the day without moving his lips as he gave it a visual perusal. We do not know how many words a minute Saint Ambrose was able to read, presumably because literate people in Saint Augustine's day didn't fritter their time away trying to quantify such things when they could more profitably turn their energies to the question of how many angels could dance on the head of a pin. For those who do care about the relative amount of information grabbed by a "visual" reader (who eyeballs the page of text) versus the "phonic" reader (who sounds the text out, with or without concomitant movement of the lips or larynx), the sound-it-out person generally tops out at about 150 words per minute while the read-with-your-eyes person zips along at something like three times that speed – or substantially faster than that after the successful completion of one of the more reputable "speed reading" courses currently available. Not that speed has any intrinsic value in any endeavor worth doing well: speed readers tend to miss sound gags – puns and more elaborate plays on words – when they encounter them in print; and even the visually oriented tend to move their lips when reading stuff in a foreign language to which their introduction has been aural/oral.

Both sound-freaks and letter-crunchers – people who read with their ears and people who read with their eyes – are given a leg up with punctuation. The word *punctuation* comes from the Latin verb *pungere* (to puncture, prick), of which the past participle is *punctum*, a mark of punctuation having originally been a spot pricked with a writing implement. Other words derived more or less directly from *pungere* include *pungent* and *expunge*, the former meaning "prickly to the nose" and the latter "to zap out"; *punctual*, which refers to people who make a point of getting there on the dot; *pun* – probably – because of turning on a fine point; *punch*, in the sense of "tool for poking holes" and in the sense of "take a poke at, clout," the potable variety of *punch* coming not from *pungere* but from the Hindi/Urdu word for "five" – *pañc* – because the canonical version of the drink had five active ingredients; and, of course, *point*.

In French, *point* is used to mean not only point (of a pen or the like) but "period" (at the end of a sentence) and "dot" (over an *i* or as part of an ellipsis). In English, the word has a positively staggering number of uses: we speak of a *point of land*, a *point man* (who gets sent out ahead of the rest of the company as a sort of lone spearhead), the *point of an argument*, and being held up at *gunpoint*; of *decimal points* and the *points of a compass*; of *points of order, view*, and *no return*; of *brownie points* and *point spreads*; of *vowel points*, those dots that reader-friendly users of Hebrew and Arabic scripts put in under the appropriate consonantal letters to tell you which vowel comes next, the Semitic scripts being somewhat short on vowel signs – Indo-Europeans first grappling with the chore of having to learn to write might well have grumbled that when they were handing out vowels, the Near-Easterners were obviously out getting a second helping of consonantal letters (under and over which they are also known to put disambiguating dots, as in Persian ﹀ [*be*], ﹀ [*pe*], ﹀ [*te*], and ﹀ [*se*], or Hebrew שׂ [*sin*] and שׁ [*shin*]); and, not that this list is exhaustive, of the *point system*, which itself can refer to (a) a means of converting student letter grades to numbers, (b) a way of printing readable text for the blind, such as Braille, or (c) a convention for the measurement of characters and spaces in typesetting.

The earliest systematic exposition that we have of the art of punctuation comes from Isidore of Seville, a Spanish bishop of the early seventh century A.D. His *Etymologiarum*, which treats a variety of other subjects, classifies the then-current signs of punctuation as belonging to one or another of the following categories: *accentus, positūrae*, or *notae sententiārum*. The first category – *accentus*, whence English *accent* – contains signs to help the reader with the pronunciation of individual words in Latin and Greek: the acute accent (´), the grave (`), and the circumflex (ˆ) are dutifully cited even though writer-readers of Latin, unless they were reading Greek, didn't really need these, since they applied to the rising, falling, and rising-falling system of Greek accentuation and not the original Latin long/short vowel or later word-stress thumpty-dump with which Isidore was familiar. The French saved these three signs from the dustbin for their personal use, as may be seen in such words as *pré* (meadow), *près* (near), and *prêt* (ready).

Also included in the list of *accentus* are the so-called "smooth," and "rough" breathing marks – ' and ', respectively – which were originally ⊣ and ⊢ and derive, as Isidore correctly notes, from pieces of the letter *H*. Breathing marks are customarily written above initial vowels in Greek: compare *eugenḗs* (well-born), with its smooth breathing, to *heurískein* (to find, discover), with its rough breathing (for the want of which we get *eureka!*).

More useful for Latin readers-out-loud were the *breuis* (˘) and *longa* (‾) which told you whether a vowel was classically short or long, respectively, a good thing to know if you were trying to scan classical verse or attempting to tell the difference between, say, *pĭlus* (hair) and *pīlus* (company of veteran reservists) since, by Isidore's time, "long" and "short" didn't mean a whole lot when it came to talking about vowels – Classical Latin speakers took more time pronouncing the "long" vowels than their "short" counterparts, but speakers of Late Latin gave this practice up, going instead for the sort of "high" versus "low" distinction found in Modern English *beet* versus *bit*. The *breuis* and the *longa* are still used by writers of English to distinguish "short" vowels (as in *bit*) from "long" ones (as in *byte*) and "short" (unstressed) syllables from "long" (stressed) ones (as in *lōngĕr* and *shōrtĕr*).

Two other signs mentioned by Isidore under the heading of "Accents" are the *hyphen* – "*id est coniunctio*" – and the *apostrophe*, both of Greek invention. The hyphen was originally shaped like an upside-down eyebrow (‿) and was customarily written below letters that were to be run together (because they belonged to the same word) – *hypó* is Greek for "under" and *hen* is Greek for "one" – and the apostrophe was first and foremost a marker to show that a

Qq

181

vowel had been dropped before or after another vowel – elision. The under-the-letters form of the hyphen is a staple of the proofreading – pro_ofreading or pro͡ofreading – trade, while most non-proofreaders make do with the modern (flattened out and raised) version of the sign (-) both to show that the two parts of a word that breaks at the end of a line go together (as *to-gether*) and to show that the two (or more) word-length parts of a compound go together (as *mother-in-law* or *user-friendly*). The apostrophe has made itself equally at home if not more so – good proofreaders strike it out in such locutions as *"The Smith's are at home"* and *"Thank's"* – but it has a number of legitimate uses as well: to mark possessives (as *John's* and *the Smiths'*), contractions (as *I've* or *it's*), and the omission of a letter or letters (as *rock 'n' roll*), and to make the plurals of individual letters, numerals, and other typographic signs not look so peculiar (as *p's* and *q's, 6's* and *7's*, or *$'s* and *¢'s*).

Isidore's *positūrae* – "things that get put in place," a rough rendering of Greek *thésis* (a setting, placing, putting down; the latter part of a metrical foot in which the voice drops) and referring essentially to marks of intonation – include the *comma,* the *period,* and the *colon.* These terms come from Greek too: a *kómma* is a "cut, section," hence, a clause of a verse or sentence, and a *períodos* is a "circuit, cycle," hence, a "well-rounded sentence," hence, mark of punctuation found at the end of a sentence, a *sentence* being originally a Latin *sententia* (thought, opinion, thought expressed in words) from *sentīre* (to sense, be sensible, feel, perceive). *Colon* comes through Latin *cōlon* (a subdivision of a line of verse containing at least one principal accent), from Greek *kôlon* (limb).

Periods, colons, and commas have been used in a number of ways since their first appearance on paper. In mathematical notation alone, these three signs have had a long, illustrious, and confused history: both the colon and the period have been used to express proportions, and it wasn't until the 1850's that the period finally won out over the comma as the standard decimal point, both having been used as such up until that time. The raised dot as a sign of multiplication enters the picture at about this time too, creating some initial confusion (since the dot as decimal point was often written raised before settling down to its modernday position). The dot was also pressed into service in the early 1700's to show repeating decimals: ⅓ = .33 . . . , 1/27 = .0037037 . . . , and so on.

Period was used to mean "sentence" in English starting with the Tudors, Sir John Harington's *Metamorphosis of Ajax* providing the earliest known citation. During this same era, the period and the comma were also known as the *jot* (ultimately from Greek *iŏta*) and the *tittle* (from Latin *titulus* [superscription, label, title]). As for *dot*, the word seems originally to have meant head of a boil or pimple.

Isidore doesn't really have very much to say about periods, commas, and colons, but he more than makes up for this in the third section of his treatise, *"De Notis Sententiarum."* *Notae sententiārum* are essentially orthographic figures used for marking passages of text in one way or another. Isidore lists twenty-six such figures, some of which are still in use today (whether in their original form and function or not). One of the handier of these is the *asterisk* which, we are told, is put in to show that something has been left out, a function which this sign has continued to serve to this day (see below). The asterisk takes its name from the Greek word for "star" – *astĕr*.

Other *notae sententiārum* that are named after things whose shapes they resemble are the *obelus* (−) and the *lemniscus* (÷). Isidore describes the *obelus* as a *uirgula iacens* (recumbent *uirgula*), the original literal meaning of *uirgula* having been "little rod, switch" (from *uirga* [slender branch, rod, wand, scourge]). Later meanings attached to *uirgula* were, to quote the *Oxford Latin Dictionary,* "a small longitudinal mark; a line of colour, streak; a mark put against spurious verses (i.e., obelus)." *Virgula* has subsequently come down to us as *virgule*, which is used in French to mean both "comma" and "decimal point" and, in English, to designate the slash mark (/) – also known as a diagonal, separatrix, shilling (mark), slant, slash, or solidus – that we use to separate the divisor from the dividend in fractions, the month from the day from the year in numerical dates, one run-in line of verse from another, and the elements of such choices as *and/or*.

The *obelus*, then, was a dashlike mark placed before a passage considered to be spurious. The word comes from Greek *obelós*, which originally meant "skewer, spit" and later took on the meaning with which it was borrowed into Latin. An *obelós* could also be a pointed pillar, i.e., an *obelisk* (from *obelískos*, the diminutive form of *obelós*). *Obelus*, *obelisk*, and the verb *obelize* (to mark with an obelus) are all used in English: *obelus* may refer either to the Latin mark of punctuation or, more commonly, to the *obelisk* (†), also known as the "dagger" and from which the "double dagger" (‡) is derived. The *obelisk* originally served much the same function as the *obelós/obelus* but is now used chiefly as a footnoting device, as a lexicographical sign to show that a word is obsolete (or, in a text, nonsensical), or, when placed next to a biographical date, to signify the year of death.

Besides the canonical version of the obelus, Isidore mentions two others: one written with a dot over it (÷) and used to mark dubious (as opposed to definitely spurious) passages, and the other written with a dot below and a dot above (÷). The latter was used in Greek to mark passages considered superfluous, while writers of Isidore's day placed this mark beside portions of Holy Scripture which had been translated differently by different translators. The Greeks referred to this mark of punctuation as the *obelós periestígmenos* (*obelós* with two dots), while the Latin grammarians called it the *lemniscus*, a borrowing of Greek *lēmnískos* (ribbon attached to a victor's wreath).

Considering its form and functions in Greek and Latin, one might have expected the *obelus* to show up as the *dash* in English and the Romance languages, all of which borrowed heavily from the Late Latin grammarians for their marks of punctuation. But no. English *dash* comes from the Middle English verb *daschen* (to rush, strike with violence), the idea being less that the written mark is mightier than the sword (or dagger) than that it is something done in a hurry, something "dashed off," so to speak. The English dash, for all its hasty origin, has gained a certain respectability, several varieties being now standard in a regular font of type: the *en dash* (–) takes up half a square the size of a (large-sized) letter and looks for all the world like a hyphen, while the *em dash* (—) takes up a whole square, the *two-em* and *three-em* being twice and three times as long, respectively. The *en dash* is chiefly used to indicate that the items between the beginning and the end of a series have been left out but are to be understood, as 5–10 (five through ten, i.e., five, six, seven, eight, nine, ten). The *em dash* is used to indicate abrupt transitions — *What?* — and quasi-parenthetical expressions — such as this one. The *em*, *two-em*, and *three-em* are all used (often in combination) to indicate ellipsis as well, as when the speaker is cut off in the middle of a sentence, or in a bibliographical entry in which the author is the same as the preceding one.

In French, the word for "dash" is *tiret*, not to be confused with the word for "hyphen" – *trait* – however inextricably bound the two terms are from an etymological point of view. *Trait*, originally the generic term for any kind of throwable weapon, comes from the verb *traire* (from Latin *trahere* [to pull, draw, drag away with violence]), while *tiret* comes from the verb *tirer* (to pull, shoot, which is probably derived from the Old French verb *martirier* [to martyr], the *mar-* of *martirier* being read as the adverb *mar* – a contraction of Latin *malā hōrā* [in bad time] – and the rest being connected with *tiranz* [executioner] – from *tyrannus* [tyrant] – who was as likely as not to draw and quarter you if you were so unfortunate as to have run afoul of the local judicial system). *Tirer* replaced *traire* in its more general senses, violent and not so violent, with *traire* remaining in use in the sense of "to milk," while *trait* and *tiret* gradually settled into middle-aged linguistic domesticity.

The *trait* and the *tiret* are used in French much as the hyphen and the dash are used in English, though the French go us one better in inventive purposes, to which

the latter may be put by using their dash to indicate the
beginning of some spoken dialogue by a new speaker, reserving the *guillemets* (« ») for quoting individual words
(foreign or otherwise noteworthy), dialogue embedded in a
sentence, cited text, and so forth. The French *guillemets*,
like our quotation marks (both double and single), are derived from another of Isidore of Seville's *notae sententiārum*, the *diple* (>). The word comes from Greek *diplê*, the
feminine-gender form of the word *diploós* (double, literally
"two-fold"). The *diple* had been used among the Greeks as
a marginal mark to indicate rejected passages and, in dramatic works, a new speaker. Isidore reports that Medieval
Latin writers used the *diple* in ecclesiastical works to set off
text taken from the Holy Scriptures. Several other rather
arcane versions of the *diple* are also mentioned in passing.

Other noteworthy *notae* treated in the *Etymologiarum*
include the *chi-rho* or *Chrismon* (☧) – a sort of shorthand
for the name of *Christ* formed from the first two letters of
Greek *Christós*, *chi* (χ) and *rho* (ρ) – and the similarly
formed hybrid from the Greek letters *phi* (φ) and *rho* (ρ),
(Ⳏ), short for the Greek word *phrontís* (care). This latter
sign was customarily placed at the beginning of an obscure
passage to be read with caution, much as a musician of
today might write a skull-and-crossbones above the beginning of a particularly tricky passage of music. The Greek
letter *theta* (θ) placed next to a soldier's name on a Latin pay
list signified that he was deceased, *theta* being short for
thánatos (death), the ultimate mark of punctuation.

But fortunately life goes on and the literate continue
cheerfully to suggest new marks of punctuation without
which the spoken language cannot be accurately reproduced
in print. The most serious candidate in recent years has
been the *interrobang* (‽), for use in such sentences as
"What the hell ‽ " One reason that this sign has a leg up
in the fierce competition for the adoption of new marks of
punctuation is that it can easily be produced in typescript by
overstriking a question mark with an exclamation point,
though it is only fair to say that when it first got a name and
made it into standard typefaces, *Esquire* magazine included

in it its annual "Dubious Achievements" section as the silliest punctuation mark of the year.

Other suggestions have included the *crescendo mark* ($\rlap{/}{\circ}$) – as in "And awaaay we GOOO $\rlap{/}{\circ}$" – the *sigh-mark* ($\curlyvee$) – as in "Gosh, you're wonderful, Mr. Murgatroyd $\curlyvee$" – the *delta-sarc* ($\triangle$) – as in "Yeah, and he cried all the way to the bank $\triangle$" – all suggested by Lewis Burke Frumke in his *How to Raise Your IQ By Eating Gifted Children* – to which may be added the *deflation point* (i) – as in "Ah, a jar of your calf's-foot jelly, Aunt Mable. How nice i" – and the *sapostrophe* (-'-'-') – for people who aren't sure how to punctuate the possessive form of a name ending in the letter *s*. The sapostrophe and the deflation point are, perhaps understandably, the inventions of one Carl Huss, the punctuation of the possessive forms of whose last name poses many a trap for the unwary. The present authors, for their part, would like to urge the adoption of the *facetio* ($\rlap{/}{\wp}$) as an orthographic sign to mark the end of a passage of tongue-in-cheek $\rlap{/}{\wp}$.

New orthographic signs, like new anythings, tend to have a hard time breaking into the business: it's always a temptation to push the tried-and-true a little bit harder instead of trying to lobby for the untried-and-potentially-untrue. So the faithful exclamation point is used by biologists to indicate that a certain plant claimed to be a new discovery has in fact been attested; mathematicians use the same sign for "factorial" (as in 5!, which means "5 times 4 times 3 times 2 times 1"); and in some dialects of Computerese, the same character signals the beginning of a comment written into a file – you can look at the nuts and bolts of the file, but if you print the whole thing out, the comment is demurely invisible.

The asterisk has also been made to do more than an ordinary day's work. Indeed, the asterisk may hold the all-time record for orthographic versatility. Genealogists sometimes use the asterisk for "born" along with the obelisk for "died" (see above). Linguists use the "star" in a couple of ways: specialists in the history of language use it to show that a form is hypothetical – **pHter-* is the hypothetical root underlying Sanskrit *pita*, Latin *pater*, English *father*, and so on – and specialists in modern grammatical theory use the same sign to mark a saying that is hypothetically impossible – or at least extremely unlikely – our favorite being "*For what job is Sam no man?*," the question to which Dr. Forthcoming Larynx-Horn (in *Studies out in Left Field*) suggests that the answer is not "*Sam is no man for the job.*"

In Computerese, the asterisk – or *splat* – has several uses. It can be an ornate form of the raised dot as a multiplication sign; it can be a prompt sign, that is, a sign that tells the computer user that it's time to issue a command; and it can be the sign for a *wildcard*. The *wildcard* is an ingenious invention that serves a number of time-saving functions. For example, if you have a bunch of files – FOO.DMS, FOO.DMI, FOO.DMC, FOO.ERR, and the like – and you wish to delete them all in one fell swoop, wildcarding allows you to type DELETE FOO.*, hit the carriage return, and – *shazaam* – all of the FOO files are no more, a much quicker procedure than having to type DELETE FOO.DMS, hit the carriage return, type DELETE FOO.DMI, hit the carriage return, and so on. Again, if you wanted to delete all of your files with the extension .MEM, say, you could simply type DELETE *.MEM and they would be as gone as gone can be. (Reader queries concerning wildcarding should be addressed to *.HUMEZ.)

In addition to its use as a typographical ******framing device****** and as an itemizer, as in "Check out these uses of the asterisk:

> * *prompting*
> * *multiplying*
> * *wildcarding*
> * *itemizing*
> * *and much, much more,*"

the asterisk has also been known to moonlight as an indicator of missing letters in a sort of job-sharing arrangement with the dash family. The latter are nicely represented in Hugh Rawson's A *Dictionary of Euphemisms and Other*

Doubletalk in the entry "f – , f---, f--k, ----," to which may be compared the "f**k" entry in Eric Partridge's classic *Origins: A Short Etymological Dictionary of Modern English.* The advantage of the asterisk over the dash in such cases is that one knows exactly how many letters have been deleted: "f—k" could, as the schoolboy joke attests, be short for "firetruck," while "f**k" could not.

It is this euphemistic use of the asterisk that is doubtless responsible for the sign's regular inclusion in the cartoonist's *maledicta balloon*, the conventional device for the representation of a character's swearing that will not blemish the Sunday funnies. Indeed, it is in cartooning that some of the richest use is made of orthographic signs to represent the many nuances of human language in its various manifestations – speech, thought, body language, or what have you. All comic-book devotees are familiar with *plewds*, those teardrops flying off the head of a character who is suffering an attack of extreme anxiety or exertion. *Crottles* are the plus-signs in place of eyes on the face of a character who has fainted from concussion or excessive drink – these are sometimes also called *oculamae*. Often accompanying cartooned drunkenness are the signs of the *boozex*, those *x*'s suggesting potency on the labels of bottles, and, over the drinker's head, *squeans* – the little centerless asterisks that look like bursting bubbles or "seeing stars" (*phosphenes*) – and perhaps a *spurl* or two, spurls being helixes going up from the character's head as he or she faints dead away. A tiny window reflected in a shiny object is called a *lucaflect*, and the dust cloud made by characters in rapid motion is a *briffit*, the multiple image of moving feet being *blurgits*.

Two other symbols from maledicta balloons worthy of note are the *quimp* – a shorthand image of the planet Saturn – and the *jarn*, a name applied both to the tiny spiral and to the crosshatch. The *crosshatch* (#) is also known as the *double hashmark, pound sign, number sign, octothorn,* or, in Computerese, the *crunch*. The pound sign/number sign/octothorn/crunch has a variety of uses. Like the asterisk, the crunch is sometimes a prompt sign. It can stand for *pound(s)* when it comes after a number (5# is "5 pounds"), and can mean "number" when it comes before a number (#5 is "number 5"). It also serves as a proofreader's mark meaning "insert a space," presumably because the shape of the sign is more than a little suggestive of the musical sharp sign (♯), a signal to put in a musical space of a halftone up between the note as written and as it is to be sounded: sharps, flats, and naturals in musical notation all go back to variations on *b*.

The *hatch* of *crosshatch* and the *hash* of *hashmark* and *corned-beef hash* both derive from French *hacher* (to chop up) – compare *hache* (axe) and its diminutive, *hachette*, whence English *hatchet* – this mark being the sort one might make with an axe (the culinary masterpiece quite logically following from doing a Lizzie Borden on a cow). The French inherited the word from Late Latin, which had previously borrowed it from Germanic. The underlying Indo-European root seems to have meant something on the order of "cut, scrape" and shows up in such English words as *shave, scab, shaft*, and – surprise! – *comma*.

It is ironic that the publishing industry – than whom no fellowship of the educated should be more committed to the preservation of literacy – should have one of the most comprehensive inventories of signs to substitute for words; but this is less astonishing when one considers that proofreaders' marks must of necessity be confined to interpolations and marginalia. One of the commonest signs in use is the "delete" symbol – ℒ – which is most surely derived from Latin *delendum*, the future participle of the verb *delere* (to obliterate, blot out). The use of the left bracket and right bracket for "move left/right to this line" is clear enough on the face of it, though less obvious is the convention of underlining roman text to make it italic (and circling italic text to make it roman). The *caret*, for insertion, is from Latin *caret* (is lacking). And, for those who have marked up some text and then thought better of it, the marked section can be underscored with a row of dots, accompanied with the marginal note *stet*, the third person singular present subjunctive of the Latin verb *stāre* (let it stand).

R

IS FOR *ROSY, RUFOUS, RUBIGINOUS,* AND
rubricated – all having to do with the color red. *Rosy* is
"rose-colored, i.e., the color of a rose," the word for this
perennially popular flower having been borrowed into Old
English from Latin *rosa*. Though convention has it that
roses are red (and violets blue), *rosy* is generally understood
to be *pink* (cf. French *rose* [pink]): rose-colored glasses do
not cause you to see red but rather a mellow pink haze. The
Latin word *rosa* is of obscure origin, though the root that
underlies it shows up in the *rhodo-* of the Greek *rhodóden-
dron* (literally "rose-tree") and the *jul-* of *julep*, a Franco-
Arabic distillation of the refreshing Persian rosewater-based
concoction, the *gulāb* (of which the *gul* is the "rose" – no
relation to the heraldic *gules* [red] which comes from Latin
gula [throat] by way of Old French *goule* [red, red necker-
chief] – and the *āb* is the "water" – the *Punjāb* being the
place of the "five waters," i.e., five major rivers in what was
the Persians' first and foremost administrative base of operations in precolonial India), so call its origin Mediterranean
and see if any hands go up.

Not that the origin of the word *pink* is much clearer than
that or *rosa/rose*, though the mug shots of the primary suspects have long been on file with the authorities. It is generally agreed that the name of the color comes from the
name of the flower, a *pink* being a plant of the genus *Dian-
thus*, the most famous representative of which is the *carnation*. (The original meaning of *carnation* was "flesh-
colored," from Latin *carō, carnis* [flesh, meat].) The
question is whether the word is to be traced back through
French to Late Latin **pinctiāre* (to prick, pinch, a variant
of *punctiāre*, from *punctus* [prick, point]) because the
plant's leaves look "pinched," or whether the underlying

form is to be found in Dutch *pinck oogen* (little eyes, the literal meaning of *pinck* having been "little finger," whence English *pinkie*) because the flowers reminded people of conjunctivitis.

About *rufous* there is a different kind of doubt. The word comes clearly enough from Latin *rūfus*, a popular word meaning "red, red-headed" and the basis of the name *Rufus*, as in *King William Rufus* of England, son of the Conqueror, who was felled by an errant arrow from the bow of one Wat Tyrell during a hunting expedition, to nobody's great sorrow. (Compare *Eric the Red*, who was presumably so called not because of his radical politics – that *Eric* was *Eric the Pinko* – but because of the color of his hair.) The confusion appears when we have a look at what *rufous* is supposed to mean: "reddish-brown, as a *rufous* (chestnut) horse," "yellowish-pink to moderate orange," or "dull-red deficient in chroma," all depending on which dictionary you happen to consult.

This sort of disagreement is commonplace when it comes to color terminology: is turquoise (or teal, for that matter) a bluish green or a greenish blue? What's the difference between purple and violet? It is all very well that the visible spectrum is objectively confined to those colors produced at wavelengths of 4000 to 7500 angstroms (one angstrom – named after the Swedish physicist Anders J. Ångström, who died in 1874 – is equal to one ten-billionth of a meter), violet being at the shorter and red at the longer extreme; but how one chooses to divide up the spectrum and name its parts varies considerably from person to person, not to mention from culture to culture. Among the Hanunóo of the Philippine Islands, for example, there are four broad color categories: "blackness," "whiteness," "redness," and "greenness," with subdivisions within these. This apparent oversimplification belies the fact that the Hanunóo have an impressive pharmacological sophistication that rests on their ability to make accurate distinctions among poisonous, innocuous, and medicinal plants, and that correct color categorizing is an integral part of the process. While English-speaking color theoreticians talk of the dimensions of hue, value, and intensity or chroma, when asked about how we differentiate among colors, most of us simply try to make do with a handful of color terms that we like to think are unambiguous, whose basic meanings are agreed upon: black is black and white is white. What could be more straightforward?

In fact, so much as a glance at the etymological underpinnings of the most common Indo-European color terms reveals a decidedly unstraightforward picture. The English word *black*, for example, comes from an Indo-European root *bhel-* that seems to have meant something on the order of "burn, flash, shine," something black being something "burnt" (rather, one suspects, than something that absorbs all light). Cognate with *black* are *blue, blaze, blush, blende* (shiny metal), *blond*, and *bleach*, all, with the possible exception of *blue*, retaining something fairly obvious of the original Indo-European sense of the root from which they are derived. To these may be added *blanch* (to turn white), *blank* (as in a *blank* sheet of white paper), and *blanket* (originally a piece of white woolen cloth), all borrowed through French from the Late Latin borrowing from Germanic, *blancus* (white), the source of the vanilla-flavored term for "white" in nearly all of the modern Romance languages – Rumanian has *alb* from Latin *albus*, the "white" word that underlies *alb* (long white robe), *album* (originally, "white tablet on which to write," hence, register), *albino*, and *albumen* to which Old High German *albiz* (swan) and medical Greek *alphosis* (lack of skin pigmentation) may be compared.

Other "shine, burn" roots provide additional words for black and white. The Greeks, for example, commonly described things clear or white as being *leukós* – compare *leukocyte* (white blood cell), *leukoderma* (lack of skin pigmentation), and *leukoma* (white corneal opacity) in modern Medicalese – *leukós* being from the root that has also given us *luster, translucent*, and *lunar* (the Latin moon being, etymologically, "that which shines"). The Romans used the term *candidus* in similar fashion: *candēre* is "to shine, be brilliant," a *candēla* is a "candle," *candor* is "clearness," and *candidus* is "clear, shining white." (A *candidātus* [candidate for office] was originally someone in a white toga.) *Candidus* was considered to be the antonym of *niger, nigra, nigrum* ([shiny] black), a term of obscure origin. The opposite of *albus* was *āter, ātra, ātrum* (black, dark, gloomy) which seems to have originally meant "burnt" or the like, or so its Avestan cognate, *atarš* (fire), would suggest. *Niger, nigra, nigrum* eventually displaced *āter, ātra, ātrum*, though the latter may be discerned in *atrium* (perhaps originally the room through which the household smoke was vented), *atrocious* (savage, cruel, violent: the epithet of a black-hearted person in a black mood), and *atrabilious* (suffering from melancholy, i.e., an excess of black humor, *melancholy* being from Greek *mélas, mélanos* [black] and *cholē* [bile], *cholē*, for its part, being from the same root that gives English *gold, yellow,* and *yolk,* as well as Greek *chlōrós* [pale green, as in *chlorophyl*]).

Our own native *green* is cognate with *grow* and *grass,* and our borrowed *vert* (in post-Conquest English forest law, "green vegetation serving as cover for deer, or the right to cut such vegetation" and, in heraldry, "green"), *verdant* (green with vegetation), *virid* (bright green), and *viridian* (bluish-green pigment) all come, ultimately, from the Latin verb *uirēre* (to be green [of plants]). *Verdigris* (green or blue copper acetate) gets its first syllable from the same source, the original literal meaning of *verdigris* being "green of Greece," the -*gris* here being no relation to the -*gris* of *ambergris,* literally "gray amber": the -*gris* of *verdigris* is a reflex of Latin *Graecus* (Greek), while the -*gris* of *ambergris* is the upshot of the French borrowing of one of the Germanic forms cognate with our *gray* (or *grey*), *griseous,* and *grizzly.*

This is not to imply that the Indo-Europeans have restricted themselves to borrowing color terminology from each other: speakers of English may have borrowed *azure* from the French, and the French may have borrowed their *bleu(e)* (blue) from Germanic and their *azur(e)* from the

Spanish, but the Spanish got their *azul* (blue) by extrapolation from the Arabic *allazaward* (lapis lazuli), apparently a borrowing from Persian. The Arabs also played a role in the derivation of *crimson* and *scarlet*. *Crimson* comes via Old Spanish from Arabic *qirmizī*, *qirmiz* being the Arabic rendering of Sanskrit *kṛmija* – literally "worm-born" – a term applied to a kind of red dye made by crushing the dried bodies of females of the insect species *Kermes*. *Scarlet* has come to us by a more circuitous route: English borrowed the term from Old French, which got it from Late Latin (in which *scarlāta* was "scarlet cloth"), which got it from Persian (in which *saqirlāt* was "silk material dyed red"), which got it from Arabic, which had originally borrowed the underlying term, *sigillātus*, from Latin, *sigillātus* meaning "decorated with little figures," *sigillum* (little figure, image) being a diminutive form of *signum* (mark, sign) and the basis of our word *sigil* (seal, signet; magical figure or sign) and *seal*.

Scarlet and *crimson* bring us to the one color term on which the Indo-Europeans seem to have managed some semblance of an accord, that which underlies Sanskrit *rudhira* and *rohita*, Greek *erythrós*, Latin *rūfus* and *ruber*, Lithuanian *raudonas*, Irish *rūad*, German *rot*, and English *ruddy* and *red*, all of which refer to the blood-colored hue at the long-wave end of the spectrum – indeed, the *red* of *red-eye* (a beverage notorious for producing bloodshot eyes) and *red-handed* (*in flagrante delicto*, i.e., before you've had a chance to wash the blood off your hands) is a stand-in for blood itself. And what is "to be red in the face" but a case of having the blood run to your cheeks as your cardiovascular system deals with your embarrassment or rage, a condition to be unfavorably compared to being in the pink, which is the result of engaging in healthy physical activity as opposed to spiritual tussling with the emotions.

Latin *rubēre* was the standard verb used for blushing as well as simply being ruddy or red, and to it may be compared *ruber* (ruddy, red). *Ruber* had a rustic variant, *rōbus*, that was chiefly used in Standard Latin in the specialized sense of "red-roan color of the pelt of a bull or ox." The rare but still current English word *rubiginous* (rust-colored) comes from a *rōbus* spin-off, *rūbīgō*, a variant of *rōbīgō* (rust – both the kind that forms on iron and the disease that blights wheat). (English *rust* is a native development of the Indo-European "red" root.) The Romans had a god named *Robigo* who was the personification of wheat rust and in whose honor an annual feast, the *Robigalia*, was held on the seventh of May, the god having the power to go easy on the rust if properly placated, much as Apollo had the job of sending or averting plague. And wheat rust was quite properly a matter of concern, for not only does it attack the crop but, when ingested with the harvested grain, it can cause bellyaches and hallucinations: indeed, it is from derivations of rye rust – ergot – that Albert Hoffman of the Sandoz laboratories succeeded in synthesizing the powerful hallucinogen LSD-25, and it has been convincingly argued that a physical cause for the delusions of the "afflicted girls" of Salem Village's witch hunt lay in their having ingested black bread contaminated with the rust attendant on the previous year's rather dank growing season.

The *rōbus* of *Robigo* is related to – but distinct from – another *rōbus:* Old Latin *rōbus* (red oak), later, *rōbur*, the source of English *corroborate* (to strengthen, i.e., to make the other guy's testimony as strong as an oak, though a more fanciful etymology derives the testimony–oak connection from the practice – rather more druidic than Roman – of swearing by the oak tree) and *roborant* (restorative). *Rōbus* the oak underlies our word *robust*, something that a victim of *rubeola* (measles) or *rubella* (German measles) by definition is not, rubeola and rubella being but two of the several English offspring of Latin *rubeus*, the "red" that eventually supplanted *ruber* as Latin evolved into the Romance languages: *rubefacient* (causing redness, especially of the skin), *rubescent* (reddening), *rubicund* (ruddy-skinned), *ruby*, and *rouge* are the most noteworthy of the other *rubeus* progeny in our language.

Actually, *rubeus* wasn't the only replacement for *ruber* that fought its way to the head of the class in Late Latin/ Early Romance times: *russ(e)us*, *rubeus*'s close relative, underlies the generic word for red in Italian (*rosso/rossa*) and Spanish (*rojo/roja*), and makes an appearance in French as *roux/rousse* (red-headed), the basis of English *russet*. (*Rubeus* shows up in Spanish as *rubio* [blond], and all of the Romance languages have their share of learned Latinate "red" words beginning with *rub-*.) All of which goes to show that if languages were animals, they'd be pack rats, never really throwing anything away: witness the exemplary tenaciousness of Latin *ruber* which, in the face of overwhelming competition from *rubeus* and *russ(e)us*, managed to hang on long enough to enshrine itself in the words *rubric*, *rubricate*, and *rubrician*, all from *rubrica*, originally the Latin word for "red ocher" and later the word for "red ink," then "decorative title or initial letter (in red)" – it is the practice of highlighting festival and holy days in red in liturgical calendars that gives us our *red-letter* days – and, still later in Ecclesiastical Latin, "direction (in red) in a liturgical book."

Henry Ford is famous for saying, among other things, "Let them have any color they want as long as it's black." While Ford was speaking of the Model T – the vehicle that reoriented the public vision of the automobile from Rube Goldberg device (*Rube* being not "Red" but short for *Reuben*) to household word – the same dictum (in Latin, of course) could just as well have been uttered by the Director of Publications in any medieval monastery, there being at that time an increasing interest in the use of red ink in liturgical manuscripts to highlight the rules that direct the celebrant's performance of various of the ceremonies of the Church – as opposed to the text of the rituals themselves, which appeared in ordinary black ink. (The history of *ink* is messy: the word comes from Greek and involves melted wax, the verb "to burn," and various dyes, some of them palpably poisonous.)

Among the reforms of the austere Cistercians, who seceded from the Benedictine order in the twelfth century to follow a stricter observance, as they saw it, of the Rule of Saint Benedict, one stipulation was that manuscripts were to be written in one color of ink only – black – and without elaborate initial capitals: this was in keeping with their philosophy, as one scholar has put it, of "disengagement from the world of the senses as the primary way of reaching spiritual enlightenment." (William of Saint Thierry, co-author of the first biography of the Cistercian Saint Bernard of Clairvaux, reasoned that "a spirit that is intent on interior things is better served by an absence of decoration and trimming in the stuff around them.") Elsewhere, however, the use of *rubrics* – (red) flags – in liturgical handbooks was so widespread that it was commonly said that "you have to read the red in order to understand the black" (*"lege rubrum sī uīs intellegere nigrum"*).

It is probably no great exaggeration to say that, as far as medieval Europe went, the Church had a near monopoly on literacy; indeed, the Premonstratensian canons – founded at around the same time as the Cistercians and deeply indebted to them for architectural ideals that successfully reconciled the quest for simplicity with the reality of being in what would today be called a "growth industry" – served faithfully in secular posts, as did their fellow canons, the Gilbertines and the Augustinians. In fact, such was the extent of participation of these members of the Church in everyday life that one contemporary critic was led to complain that the canons "deny that they are monks because they wish to be called preachers and rulers of churches." But far more than that, the canons were capable administrators in the opening-up of northern England to government by its Norman conquerors. Yorkshire had been a hotbed of literacy long before the Normans arrived. One of its archbishops was no less than the scholar-monk Alcuin (735–804 A.D.), who later went to France where he served as abbot of Saint Martin of Tours and oversaw the refinement of the so-called Carolingian minuscule style of writing, a synthesis of the best features of the Lombard script, then in its ascendancy in Italy, and the Mercian hand that Alcuin had learned back home in England, itself an offshoot of the manuscript tradition best exemplified in the seventh-century Irish *Book of Kells*, which displays not only a fine, legible hand but great beauty of illustration and intricacy of ornament and exuberant use of color. Ironically, one feature of the Carolingian manuscript was the use of classical architectural motifs for border decoration: where the *Book of Kells* has sinuous borders (almost serpentine – surely the only snakes in Ireland), Alcuin's followers introduced pillars, arches, leaf moldings, and so forth, drawn largely from Roman buildings at second or third hand.

By the time of Alcuin, the Roman practice of writing first titles and initial letters and then textual annotations as well in red ink had given the word *rubrica* two distinct meanings, one referring to the embellishment of individual letters in such illuminated manuscripts as the *Book of Kells*, and the other referring to the practice of highlighting ritual instructions in the missal and other liturgical books. Pope Gregory the Great – after whom Gregorian chant is named – made a collection of rubrics in this latter sense, according to tradition, during his papacy (590–604 A.D.), though, curiously, the earliest attestation we have of *rubrica* qua instruction is quite late – the 1300's – by which time a distinction was already being drawn between *mandatory rubrics* and *directive rubrics*, the latter being, strictly speaking, not so much canon law as matter of conscience. In the end, the Vatican established a Sacred Congregation of Rites to correct, establish, and – in some cases – suppress these proliferated rubrics. The Congregation was founded by Pope Sextus V, whose other noteworthy accomplishments included a futile attempt to quash English Protestantism by routinely excommunicating the Tudors and backing their Spanish foe King Philip's ill-fated Armada.

Modern Spanish, incidentally, has a couple of additional, secular meanings for its *rúbrica*, a "learned" borrowing of Latin *rubrica* rather than what would have been the native development of the word, had it not disappeared with *ruber* in the great *rubeus/russeus* wars. One use of the term is in the world of the theater, where a *rúbrica* is any stage direction, annotation, or description of the *mise-en-scène* that accompanies the text of a play, the sort of thing that would appear in italics in an English-language script. A *rúbrica* can also be the flourish at the end of a signature on an official document by, for example, an examining magistrate or notary public. In certain cases, a person's personal *rúbrica* (without the signature that it is supposed to embellish) is considered sufficient unto the legal day and is accepted as though a full John Hancock. A notary's particular rubric is registered when he or she is sworn in and it is understood that there will henceforth be no further doodling around with it.

S

IS FOR *SPECIES* AND A BUSHEL-BASKET-
ful of related words: *specie, spice, special, specimen, specific,
specious, specter, spectator, spectacle(s), spectrum, speculate, speculum, aspect, inspect, respect, suspect, conspicuous,* and *despicable,* to mention a few. All are ultimately
derived from the Latin verb *specere* (to look [at]), from
which the Romans themselves effortlessly produced the fre-
quentative stand-alone verb *spectāre* (to gaze [at], examine)
and the combining forms -*spic*- and -*spex,* as in *haruspex,
haruspicis,* although here they may have had some help
from the Etruscans: a *haruspex* was a "reader of entrails,"
hence, a soothsayer, the -*spex* component of the term being
the visionary part and the *haru*- part being either from the
Etruscan word for liver or else from an Indo-European root
that shows up in the sense of "intestine" in a smattering of
Old Norse (*gorn*), Lithuanian (*žárna*), and Greek (*chordē̆*,
whence English *chord, cord,* and *cordon*) and in the extended sense of "string" in English *yarn*. For those of more
delicate constitutions, there was always the *auspex, auspicis*
(from *auis* [bird] plus -*spex,* -*spicis*) who based his prophes-
ies on the observation of birds in flight, or so he made it
appear. We get *auspicious* out of all of that and should probably
ably be grateful.

The Indo-European root which Indo-Europeanists re-
construct as **spek̑* and from which Latin *specere* sprang
seems to have had all of the ambiguity of English *look* as it
appears in "Samantha looked high and low" (which can
mean either that Samantha made a thorough visual search
or that she seemed to be strung out on a combination of
chemically enhanced personality disorders) and in John
Lennon's *jeu de mots* "Got to be good-looking/'Cause he's
so hard to see." The depth of this ambiguity has been most

ingeniously probed in recent years by Carol Chomsky, who found that if older English-speaking kids were told to "make this doll hard to see" they would hide it under the table or behind their backs while younger kids would, as often as not, cover the doll's eyes. The explanation for this difference in behavior is that, grammatically, "the doll is hard to see" looks like "the doll is nice" on the face of it but, actually, the logical subject of each of those statements is different, and less sophisticated speakers tend to parse anything that looks like subject-verb-whatever as logical subject-verb-whatever until somebody takes them aside and explains about how the grammatical subject of a sentence isn't always the logical subject – if the doll is hard to see, somebody else is doing the looking – by which time the kid has probably already discovered de Morgan's rules or the opposite sex and couldn't care less.

The problem is, of course, that seeing involves something of an existential conspiracy between the looker and the subject of the looking – person, place, or thing, animal, vegetable, mineral, or what have you: you can't see it if it isn't there in some sense, though, of course, you can look for all you're worth and (a) not see anything or (b) not be seen or (c) both or (d) none of the above. Erving Goffman's *Strategic Interaction* may well be the last word on the dynamics of looking at and being looked at (and adjusting one's looks): singing in the shower or screaming in your car is what Goffman terms "naïve behavior" when you're the only person in the shower or car and you assume that nobody's watching – a crucial point – and if I watch you singing in the shower or screaming in your car, then what you're doing is "observed behavior"; and if you see me watching you, you may pretend to be doing something else, such as giving various parts of your anatomy a healthy if somewhat unconventional workout – "deceptive behavior" – and if I'm not fooled I can either pretend to be fooled so that you'll continue wasting your time or I can let you know that I'm not fooled and why don't we cash in our chips and go out to lunch? This is "acknowledged behavior."

This is the end of the show, according to Goffman: once you let the other guy know that you have in fact been staring, it's time for something new to happen. If it's a case of boy-meets-girl, it may be all for the best – or at least all for the better or worse – and if it's spy-meets-spy, that may be all for the best too, since even spies need time out (as when they have been trying to outwait each other at a local pub and somebody has to heed the call of nature). The words *spy* and *espionage*, however conspiratorily, also come from Proto-Indo-European *spek̂: *spy* comes to us from Old French, the Old French having swiped it from the Germanic Franks – good neighbors make good fences for such hot linguistic items – and *espionage* comes from somewhat later French from Old Italian (from some loose-lipped or heavy-bladdered eyeballer of Germanic persuasion).

Indo-European *spek̂ appears in Greek as the root of the verb *skopeîn* (to see), the *k* and *p* having changed lobsters through the not-uncommon linguistic quadrille of metathesis (a Greek term whose literal Latinate gloss is "transposition" and whose common English handle is *Spoonerism*, after the Rev. Mr. W. A. Spooner, the slippery-tongued warden of New College, Oxford, to whom such classics as "The Lord is a shoving leopard" and "Kinkering kongs their titles take" are credited). *Skopeîn* and its mediopassive look-alike *sképtesthai* underlie such English words as *skeptic, periscope, telescope, microscope*, and the like, as well as the psychiatric term *scopophilia* (peeping Thomism, the original Tom having been, according to tradition, the naughty fellow who eyeballed Lady Godiva through the crack in his shutters during her celebrated equestrian streak through downtown Coventry). *Episcopalian* and *bishop* are also derived from *skopeîn*, "overseer" being the connection in both cases.

The Romans, who undoubtedly did miss a trick from time to time, were apparently right on the money when it came to the two-way-streetedness of *spek̂: a *specula* was a "watchtower, lookout" (not to be confused with a *spēcula* [glimmer of hope], from *spēs, speī* [hope]), while a *specu-*

lum was a mirror. *Speculum* is still with us as Medicalese for an instrument whose vernacular name is "duck-bills," while *specula* flashes itelf in our pan as the shaker and mover in the verb *speculate* – to look at the odds and, we hope, make a killing in the market by wheeling and dealing in tulip or soybean futures, real or fake estate, or whatever else looks like a good bet at the time, the *specter* of Christmas Yet to Come being down the street visiting someone else with any luck, presumably a *despicable* person addicted to *conspicuous* consumption, *despicable* being "that which is worth looking down upon" and *conspicuous* consumption being "ostentatious tuberculosis as the result of putting the money you made on the commodities market into a tried and true species of gas-guzzling automobile (whose name may be discreetly coughed into one's monogrammed linen handkerchief)."

A *species* was originally an "aspect," i.e., an "appearance-on-its-face." This sense is fairly well preserved in English *specie* (money whose face value is self-evident, from the ablative singular form of Latin *speciēs*, *specieī* [look, sight, appearance, likeness]): this money is worth a shilling because it is a shilling. (And is to be contrasted with paper money, especially *scrip* – from Latin *scrībere* [to write]. An American political cartoon from the 1840's deplores the employer practice of issuing scrip, redeemable only at the company store, by showing two merchants, one with a sign saying "All goods to be paid for in specie" and the other with a sign saying "No goods to be paid for in specie" – the good guy being easily distinguishable from the bad guy even without black and white hats – though recent labor-law cases involving migrant-worker camps have shown that the issue is by no means dead and buried.) *Species* is also used by some musicologists to distinguish among various types of counterpoint; but by far the most familiar use of the term is in the vocabulary of the taxonomic classification of living creatures developed by Carl von Linné, better known by his Latin name: Linnaeus.

Linnaeus was born in Sweden in 1707 and seemed destined for a life as a churchman like his father and maternal grandfather before him, but he showed so little inclination toward the profession that his father almost heeded the advice of friends and neighbors to bind the boy apprentice to a shoemaker or tailor instead. Fortunately, his bent for botany impressed a physician in his native Råshult – one Dr. Rothman – and Linnaeus went off to study at the University of Lund, transferring to Uppsala a year later. While a student at Uppsala he was sufficiently strapped for funds that he applied for the vacant post of university gardener – for which he was turned down as being overqualified – but, after a couple of years of starving studenthood, his fortunes improved dramatically when he was taken under the wing of Olaf Celsius – not the [Anders] Celsius after whom the centigrade measurement of temperature was named – who was a theology professor with a keen side interest in botany and who graciously housed and fed his budding protégé. During this time, Linnaeus boned up on all the available botanical works, including two Latin treatises that directed his attention to the stamens and pistils of flowers. Convinced that here lay the meat of plant classification, Linnaeus wrote a short work on the subject that so impressed Olaf Rudbeck, who held the chair in botany at the university, that the latter took him on as adjunct professor, putting under his direction the same university garden that had turned Linnaeus down as maintenance man just two years before.

In 1732 the Academy of Sciences at Uppsala financed Linnaeus's expedition to explore Lapland, then a virtually unknown frontier as far as the together-huddling folks of the south were concerned. During the grant-funded adventure, Linnaeus roughed it, on one occasion being shot at by a hunter – an honest mistake, apparently, and not the work of a burned-out graduate student – and, on another, sleeping in a hut with sixteen naked deer herders. *Flora Lapponica* was the result, to be published in Amsterdam in 1737.

For a short time thereafter, Linnaeus thawed out while lecturing on metallurgy at Uppsala, but on the advice of friends at Uppsala – some say that these included his future father-in-law – he left Sweden to pursue a medical career on the Continent. This was to prove a happy accident, for while in Holland Linnaeus met Jan Fredrik Gronovius and showed him a draft of his *Systema Naturae:* Gronovius was so impressed with Linnaeus's painstaking taxonomy that he sent the work to the printers at his own expense.

Gronovius, like Linnaeus, was quite literate in Latin, the university lingua franca of Europe even in his eighteenth-century day, as it had been in medieval times. Indeed, so pervasive was Latin as a second language in academic circles that anyone embarking on a scholarly career without it was at a severe disadvantage. Thus John Bartram, an American naturalist of the early 1700's, began by going to Philadelphia and buying some botany books and a Latin grammar, and enlisting the aid of a schoolmaster to coach him in the rudiments of the language. When Bartram later shipped some rocks – including some fossils – to Gronovius and received a delighted thank-you note back saying, in the midst of some English, *"Transeundum nunc est ad tales lapides, qui simul[a]crum animalis . . . ,"* the American wrote back somewhat plaintively saying, "Please to write all thy further observation in English. Latin is troublesome to me." Gronovius was quick to suggest that Bartram consult another New-Worlder – Dr. Cadwallader Colden – to act as translator (English being, apparently, somewhat troublesome to Gronovius) – the troublesome Latin meaning, in this case, "Let us now pass on to such stones as bear a resemblance to animals."

Linnaeus's *Systema Naturae* was itself (as the title warns) entirely in Latin, though in highly streamlined prose – his succinct descriptions of particular organisms are without verbs, an unusual stylistic zip for an academic work at the time – which may well have boosted its immediate appeal to his colleagues (since they probably weren't much more fluent in Latin than he was). By far the most appealing feature of the system was its orderliness: in dividing classes of plants, for example, according to whether their flowers had simple pistils (the *Monandria*, from Greek *mónos* [one] plus *anér*, *andrós* [male], all tricked out in Latin garb), two pistils (*Diandria*), and so on, and similarly giving names to the orders of plants according to whether they had single stamens (*Monogynia*, the *gynia* part being from Greek *gynē* [female]), double stamens (*Digynia*), and so forth, Linnaeus put his finger on easily verifiable features that could be counted upon to run true to type. Subclassifications again relied on distinctive features – shape of fruit, shape of leaves, habitat, and so forth.

All of this was a tremendous improvement on previous taxonomies that had either been so unwieldy as to be un-learnable in the classroom or so simplistic as to prove useless in the field – an example of the former being the description of the common ground cherry, which an earlier classifier had dubbed *"physalis amno ramosissime ramis angulosis glabris foliis dentoserratis"* ("bladder-fruited, many-branched, with the branches angular and with smooth, toothily serrated leaves"), which Linnaeus, seizing on its most distinctive features, called *Physalis angulata*. No mat-ter that in shorthanding it by juxtaposing salient character-istics Linnaeus made errors that, by today's standards, might be considered ludicrous – among members of the genus *Homo* he classified *Homo troglodytus*, which included not only the fabulous semihumans (supposed to live in Ethio-pia) cited in Pliny the Elder's *Natural History* but also the orangutan (*Pongo pygmaeus*, its original Malay gloss being "man [*orang*] of the forest [*hutan*]") – the important thing for Linnaeus being to be able to distinguish among orga-nisms that were truly different and to classify together things that were apparently the same. The implications of such a system of taxonomy – that similar organisms might have descended from a common ancestor – were not, so it seems, a matter of great concern at the time. And, given the reli-gious climate of Protestant Sweden in the 1700's, Linnaeus himself would probably have been horrified at the suggestion that his work might be a prerequisite for Darwin's *Origin of Species by Natural Selection* a century and a half later.

We are so used to thinking in terms of the Linnaean view of the world that it may come as a surprise to learn that Linnaeus actually divided the world into three parts: animals, vegetables, and minerals. The *Systema* begins with a short section entitled *"Imperium Naturae"* ("Nature's Empire"), in which he says that "Natural things are bodies made by the hand of the Creator, the constituents of the surface of the earth, and divided into three Kingdoms of Nature . . . : minerals – assembled bodies (*corpora congesta*), neither alive nor feeling; vegetables – organisms (*corpora organisata*), alive but not feeling; animals – organisms both alive and feeling, and able to move of their own accord." (He adds parenthetically that "the lithophytes [i.e., corals] are a borderline case.") In fact, nowadays nobody thinks in terms of Linnaean taxonomy for rocks, for advances were shortly to be made on the front of geology by others, not the least on account of the puzzle posed by the sorts of fossils Bartram had sent to Gronovius; but Linnaeus's system proved eminently workable for the other two kingdoms and, more to the point, made for the addition of many other sorts of creatures in an orderly way, whether found under the microscope (e.g., the giant amoeba, *Chaos chaos*) or brought in from hitherto unexplored places by Linnaeus's students.

One of these, Peter Kalm – whom Linnaeus mentions in a list of sources at the beginning of the 1757 edition of the *Systema* – was to write to Cadwallader Colden via Benjamin Franklin's post office in Philadelphia; and it should be mentioned here that one of the most useful services that Franklin could and did perform in his capacity as postmaster was to allow scientific correspondence and shipments between America and Europe at reduced rates or even duty free. Kalm mentioned to Colden that he came with letters of recommendation from Linnaeus (with whom Kalm had studied for two years), adding in Latin, *"Ignoscas, quaeso, Vir Nobilissime, si minus bene lingua uestra uernacula utar"* ("Overlook it, I pray, Most Noble Man, if I am some-

what less facile in your vernacular tongue [i.e., English]").
Kalm, who arrived in Philadelphia in late 1748, would go
on to collect botanical samples in Canada as well. Other
students whom Linnaeus cited in the 1757 edition of the
Systema Naturae were equally diligent in scouring Egypt,
Palestine, Italy, Spain and her American colonies, China,
Java, Surinam – and the list goes on and on. Meanwhile,
the indefatigable Linnaeus – knighted in 1755, one of the
first Swedish scientists to be made a member of the Order
of the Polar Star – continued revising and reprinting his
work, and calling for new information from travelers, mu-
seums, and other scientists – in short, from any and every
source available to him – to refine his taxonomy, until dis-
abled by a stroke in 1774 at the age of sixty-seven.

As it happened, the work of Darwin was to introduce a
special problem into the taxonomic process Linnaeus established; for in building a convincing case for evolution, Darwin made it possible to assign fossil remains to their place
in the scheme of things, but created a third dimension for
classification: time. Easy enough to assign a contemporary
animal to its proper place in the Linnaean plan – human
beings are of the kingdom *Animalia*, the phylum *Chordata*
(having backbones), the class *Mammalia* (having milk-
producing breasts), the order *Primates* (principal), the family *Hominidae*, the genus *Homo* (from Latin *homō, hominis*
[human being]) – and give them the species name *Homo
sapiens* (literally "knowing human being"). But what happens when a paleontologist finds fragmentary remains of an
early hominid? In one instance, such a creature was tenta-
tively named *Pithecanthropus erectus* (Apeman [the] up-
right). Later finds of the same creature, far less fragmentary,
suggested to anthropologists that this creature was in fact
more humanoid than apelike, and accordingly they renamed it *Homo erectus*. But by this time, the earlier term
had gained more than a little currency – the eminent jazz-
man Charles Mingus was to name one of his recordings
Pithecanthropus erectus — and the same sort of thing happened later on when Mary and Louis S. B. Leakey uncov-

ered fossils of a three-million-year-old hominid whom they named *Zinjanthropus*. Later finds would result in the distinction between *Australopithecus africanus* (Southern-ape of Africa) and a contemporary dubbed *Homo habilis*, *Zinjanthropus* being now reassigned to the former species. (The morphological differences between *A. africanus* and *H. habilis* are recognizable but not great, the principal distinction being that the latter used tools of a sort while the former apparently did not.) Clearly, this was more than Linnaeus could have bargained for.

Another unexpected result of the Linnaean system is that it has given Latin a contemporary utility that has outlasted by a century the use of the language as the common academic tongue. (While to a great extent its place has been taken over by English, this is due perhaps more to the particular role played by America in world politics and warfare than to any innate superiority of the language as a scientific tool.) "Cat" may be *chat* in French, *billī* in Hindi, *aílouros* in Greek, and *mao* in Chinese, but say "*Felis domesticus*" to any biologist the world over and your meaning will be unerringly understood.

T

IS FOR *TRIANGLE, TRIUNE, TRICYCLE,*
trillion, trivia, testimony, testament, tertium quid, tercel,
sesterce, triumvirate, trine, and *trinity.* All are derived from
Latin *trēs, tria* (three), one way or another, and are related
to virtually every other down-home Indo-European "three"
word in the current universe of discourse – English *three,*
the *Drey-* of the German name *Dreyfus* (Three-Foot), the
troi- of Russian *troika* (three-horse sleigh), the *si-* of Hin-
dustani *sitār* (from Persian *si-* [three] plus *tār* [string]), and
so on. *Triangles* are the stuff of which *trigonometry* is made,
the *tri-* part being the combining form of Greek *treîs, tría*
(three), the *-gono-* part being from Greek *gonía* (angle, cognate with Latin *genū* [knee], as in *genuflect*), and the *-metry*
part being from *métr(on)* (measure) plus the noun-forming
suffix *-ía*: trigonometry works because a triangle is unique
given the length of its three sides, or the length of two sides
and the angle that joins them, or two angles and the side
between them – a corollary of which is the structural stabil-
ity in real-world carpentry of the triangle (such as that
formed by nailing up the small brace that props the cross-
piece of a gallows). *Triune* means "three in one" (from Latin
tri – the combining form of *trēs, tria* – plus *ūnus* [one]) and
is usually given as an attribute of God as Father, Son, and
Holy Ghost, i.e., the *Trinity* (Latin *trīnitās* meaning,
simply, "threeness"). *Trine* is an astronomical/astrological
term meaning "offset by 120 degrees," this being one third
of the 360 degrees that make up a circle.

Tricycle and *trillion* are a little trickier. *Tricycle* is a fusion
of the Latin combining form *tri-* and the Greek word for
wheel (*kýklos*). That the *tri-* is the Latin rather than the
Greek one may be inferred from the fact that the one- and
two-wheeled relatives of the tricycle are the *unicycle* and

bicycle and not the **monocycle* and **dicycle*, a tip-off that the coiner of the terms was not a native speaker of either of the two constituent languages. (Compare *automobile*, which the astrophysicist William Sarill has suggested ought to be called either an *ipsomobile* or an *autokinetikon*.) *Trillion* is a conflation of Latin *tri-* and the word *million*, which came into English in the fourteenth century from Old Italian via Old French, *million* – originally *milione* – having been made by taking *mille* (plural *milia*) (thousand) and adding to it the augmentative suffix *-one* (which shows up in Spanish as the *-ón* of *hombrón* [husky man, man of parts] – cf. *hombre* [man] – and *cabezón* [big-headed, headstrong] – cf. *cabeza* [head] – and, in English, as the *-oon* of *buffoon* – cf. *buffo* and *boff-yock* – and *garboon* [large trash receptacle, ashcan]). Thus, a *million* is literally "a great thousand," namely, a thousand thousand. Note that British and American usages differ: an American *billion* is "a thousand million," whereas British *billions* are "million millions." The Romans apparently had few enough occasions on which the notion of a million had to be expressed that they did it by nuts and bolts: *deciens centēna milia* (ten hundred thousand) was the ponderous name for this figure, which would have been even more cumbersome to write in Roman numerals had it not been for the convention of drawing a line over a numeral to multiply its value by a thousand (and by drawing lines on either side to multiply that by another hundred). Despite the size of the empire in its prime, and the devaluation of its currency in its decline, even the tax accountants of the Roman state had apparently little need for discrete terms for "billion" and "trillion," which are both of fifteenth/sixteenth-century French origin and made their way across the English Channel by the middle of the 1600's.

Trivia is worth a comment – trivia *are* worth a comment? Like *data* (things given, the neuter nominative/accusative plural form of the past participle of the verb *dare* [to give]), *trivia* is/are plural but, when the subject of a verb, apt to be treated as a singular: "Trivia is my hobby" and not *"Trivia are my hobby." Several things are at work here: (a) nobody ever uses the Latinate singular *trivium* in the sense of "one piece of trivia," just as *datum* is almost never used (except at the bottom of USGS topographic maps); (b) *trivia* and *data* function as collective nouns, a category that has always made Indo-Europeans nervous – is it "The committee always *meets* at Posby's Pub" or "The committee always *speak* with one voice"? (American English tends toward the singular verb, while speakers of British English seem to prefer the plural: "The band always play 'God Save the Queen' at the end of the first act.") And (c) any veteran of first-year Latin knows that there are some nouns that end in -*a* in the nominative singular, so the clever student might well conclude that *trivia* is singular because it comes from *tri*- plus *uia* (road), which, in a sense, it does. Or, realizing that *trivia* is really a neuter plural, the student might conclude that it takes a singular verb because in the older layers of Indo-European speech, neuter plurals customarily took singular verbs (as in Greek *tà paidía paízei* [children play, i.e., "boys will be boys" or "louts will be louts"], *paidía* being the nominative plural form of the neuter noun *paîs*, *paidós* [child] and *paízei* being the third person singular present active indicative of the verb *paízein* [to play]).

As it happens, both of these latter notions, while ingenious, are – like those perpetual-motion machines invented by night-school students sophisticated enough to attempt a violation of the second law of thermodynamics – flawed. (Oh, all right: the first law of thermodynamics says that there is conservation of energy – "you can't get something for nothing" – while the second says that the tendency of the universe is in the direction of uniformity, i.e., increased entropy – "you needn't even bother trying.") The real story is this: *triuia* is the nominative/accusative plural of the neuter noun *triuium* (place where three roads converge), or, in the urban-planning vernacular, a "Y-square," with which may be contrasted the *quadriuium* (place where four roads converge), or, "X-square," the -*uium* in both cases being from *uia* (road, way). In medieval times, *triuium* designated the core curriculum of grammar, logic, and rhetoric. Those who survived the first course got to have the *quadriuium* – geometry, astronomy, arithmetic, and music – for dessert. It is likely that *trivial* in the sense of "elementary" comes from this division of learning, though an appealing alternative is that *trivia* is the conversational fluff blown about at a Y-square (as while waiting for the bus, presumably for longer than one has to wait at the central node of an X-square). "Tedious but trivial" is gaining currency as a cliché for problems that are simple in concept but involve huge amounts of computation.

Testimony and *testament* both derive from Latin *testis* (witness), itself most probably from *tristis, i.e., *tri-* plus a reduced form of the verb "to stand" – *stāre* (whence *stance, stanchion, staunch, instant, constant, status, stationary,* and *stationery,* to mention only a few). The notion of threeness in witnessing is either that of the "third party" so dear to modern jurisprudence or, more likely, that of the requirement in some Roman courts that three people had to swear that they saw you do it before you could be convicted and given your comeuppance. Indeed, the number of people necessary as witnesses has always been a lively issue: in William Bradford's chronicle of Plymouth Plantation, we find a case in which Bradford felt obliged to write away to his colleagues in Connecticut to ask whether, with a capital crime to which the culprit confessed "voluntarily," the corroboration of a second witness was really necessary, this being the customary minimum ordinarily required by the common law in effect at the time. The defendant was a young man who, having been accused of having intercourse with a mare, confessed to also having had relations with a cow, several sheep, and a turkey – "I forbeare particulars," wrote Bradford.

A last will and *testament* was and is so called because you need witnesses – still two others, at least in Massachusetts – to make it legal. Popular etymology has it that *testēs* (testicles) are so called because they are "witnesses" to a man's virility. A somewhat less popular etymology suggests that speakers of Latin gave the meaning "testicle" to *testis* (witness) as the result of some confusion as to the relationship of Greek *parastátai* (testicles) to the legal term *parastátēs* (defender, supporter): *parastátai* means "twin supports for a mast, butresses," and the like, and by extension also means "testicles." The singular of *parastátai* is *parastátēs* which means, among other things, "support(er)." Indeed, *parastátēs* is better glossed as "one who stands nearby," hence, comrade-in-arms on the flank and part of a set with *epistátēs* (rear-rank man) and *prostátēs* (front-rank man) – whence the medical term *prostate* – the -*stat*- of all these terms coming from the Greek verb *sistemi* (to stand). A third possibility, which has nothing to do with the number three, is that any resemblance between *testēs* (testicles) and *testēs* (witnesses) is purely coincidental and that the word for testicles is to be derived from *testa/testum/testū*, which originally meant "shell, carapace" and later took on the extended sense of "earthenware vessel," forming the basis for the popular word for "(person's) head" in various of the Romance languages. (See the chapter on "C" above.) The idea would presumably be that the globular shape of a pot was suggestive of both parts of the human anatomy. Who knows?

Tertius/tertia/tertium (third) appears in the expression *tertium quid* (that which belongs to neither of two categories supposed to be mutually exhaustive, e.g., "neither mortal nor immortal"). Literally, *tertium quid* means "third whatsis" and is a gloss for the Greek expression *tríton ti*, a natural enough invention for speakers of a language with a grammatical number that was neither singular nor plural – the *dual* – and a grammatical gender that was neither masculine nor feminine – the neuter (literally "neither"), *tríton*, like *tertium*, being – appropriately – the neuter form of the adjective here. The Latin feminine form – *tertia* – appears, filtered through Old French, as *tierce* or *terce* (third of the canonical hours; liquid measure equal to a third of a pipe [a pipe being 126 gallons]; three-card straight of the same suit; musical third); and the masculine form –

tertius – appears in similar disguise as *tercel* (male hawk used in falconry), so named because of the popular belief that the third egg of a laying was bound to produce a male.

Tertius also shows up embedded in *sesterce*, the English rendering of Latin *sestertius*, a coin equal to two and a half *assēs*. The term literally means "half" (*sē[mi]s*) "a third" (*tertius*) – compare German (and British) usage in telling time, where *halb Drei* (half three) means "2:30." *Sestertius* was commonly abbreviated HS, that is, the Roman numeral II with a line through it, plus S (for *sēmis*); and from the genitive plural form of the word in the expression (*milia*) *sestertium* ([a thousand of] sesterces) came the word *sestertium* (1,000 sesterces, i.e., 2,500 *assēs*). The *ās* was originally a pound of copper, the old-time basic unit of Roman currency. Indeed, it is in this sense of basic unit that *ās* has worked its way into English as *ace*. The *ās* was later divided into twelve *unciae*, whence both English *ounce* and *inch*. Ten *assēs* made a *dēnārius* – the word is related to Latin *decem* (ten) – which got borrowed through Greek into the Arabic-speaking world where it still survives as the *dinar*. *Dēnārius* also underlies Spanish *dinero*, the generic term for money, and was the basis for the British abbreviation for "penny" prior to the decimal currency reform of the 1960's: 6d = sixpence.

Let us here lament the passing of the old system of pounds subdivided into shillings, in turn subdivided into pence: unlike a decimal currency, divisible only by multiples of two and five, the old British pound was divisible by multiples of three as well (and pennies were further divisible by four – breathes there a Britisher who does not miss the tiny copper farthing with its sparrow on the back?). The pound sign (£) stood for *lībra*, Latin for pound (originally "pair of scales," still the name of the zodiacal sign), possibly cognate with Greek *lítra* (silver Sicilian coin; twelve-ounce pound) which survives as today's *liter*. *Lībra*, meanwhile, gave rise to the Italian *lira*. Folk etymologists have also suggested a connection with the 1960's term *lid* in its sense of "ounce of marijuana," but this is more convincingly explained as deriving from the use of a visual gauge – the lid of a peanut butter jar – in lieu of a set of scales, there being nothing incriminating, on the face of it, about possession of a peanut butter jar just so long as it doesn't happen at the time of search and seizure to contain any controlled substances. It should be noted that while convention held that a lid was equivalent to an ounce, there was frequently some disparity between the two, the lid generally being smaller, there being, during a bullish market, as many as twenty lids to the pound.

Pound comes from Latin *pondus, ponderis* (weight) – whence also *ponderous* and *preponderance* – to which may be compared the verb *pendere* (to cause to hang, hence to weigh [out], hence to pay), whose present stem is found in the words *pendant, pendulum,* and *depend,* and whose past participle – *pensum* – forms the basis of *pensile* (hanging loosely), *pensive* (from French *penser* [to think, i.e., to weigh in one's mind]), and *pension* (regular payment as a retirement benefit). *Pensum* also gives the *-pois* of *avoirdupois* (literally "to have some weight"), the system whose sixteen-ounce pound prevails in English-speaking countries today. (The other kind of standard pound – *Troy* weight – comes from the medieval French trading center of *Troyes,* the Troy pound being divided into twelve ounces, albeit heavier ones than their avoirdupois cousins. For the record: the Troy ounce is divided into twenty pennyweights – approximately eighteen of which make up an avoirdupois ounce – which are further divided into twenty-four grains each. Thus, the Troy pound is 5,760 grains, while the avoirdupois pound is approximately 7,000.) *Pensum* also underlies the Spanish *peso* and *peseta.*

The observant reader will already have noticed that the names for units of currency tend to be woefully hyperbolic: it would take a considerable stretch to make the *peso* or the *lira* anything like a *pound,* even with a nonmetallic standard such as Styrofoam. The reason for the disparity is, of course, devaluation, which is the way in which any monetary standard usually changes if it changes at all, the exception being during times of severe economic hardship when it is a buyer's market because everybody is out of work and nobody has any money to spend. The first instance of planned currency devaluation is fabled to have been under Solon of Athens, who ordered coins minted that were worth five percent less than their face value as metal.

Naturally when the metal in a coin comes to be worth more than the coin itself, the danger arises that clever but unscrupulous folks will create a currency shortage by melting down as much coinage as they can get their hands on for resale at something more like its real worth as scrap metal. Indeed, this practice was considered so problematic in England in the late Middle Ages and early Renaissance that coin melters (and their relatives, the coin shavers and clippers) were subject to mutilation on conviction, on the theory of "you clip my coin, I clip your ear." No such Draconian penalties attend inflation, which in many beleaguered countries today can run to three digits annually, and Germans can still recall the terrible inflation of the last days of the Weimar Republic, when one took a wheelbarrow to market not so much to bring home one's groceries as to get one's paper money to the store in the first place, and when many pianos were bought by people who couldn't play a note, just as a means of converting their rapidly depreciating fortunes into something of real resale value.

Rome was by no means immune to this sort of thing. The first Roman mint was established, according to tradition, in 289 B.C. under the direction of a three-man board (*tresuirī*), though the Roman marked bar of bronze (*aes signātum*) had been in circulation in central Italy for some time before that. The mint's tutelary deity was Juno Moneta (Juno of the Mint), *monēta* being a probable Carthaginian borrowing and the origin of our words *money* and *mint* (no relation to the herb, Greek *mínthē*). The first Roman silver coin, equal to the Greek two-drachma piece, was issued in 269 B.C., and first devalued silver coin, a lighter-weight *didrachm*, was issued during the first Punic War a couple of decades later. By 235 B.C., the *ās* was down to half a pound, a devaluation of fifty percent in not as many years. A hundred years later, the *ās* had shrunk to one *uncia*, or a twelfth of the original, by which time it was clear that the relation between the coin and the amount of the same metal that it could purchase was merely nominal. Furthermore, the currency "reform" at the time of the Gracchi brothers revalued the *dēnārius* at sixteen instead of ten *assēs* in recognition of the smaller size of the *ās*; and, during this same period, plated *dēnāriī* started turning up on the market alongside of solid silver ones, a situation recalled in the switch from silver to copper-sandwich coins in the United States as the cost of the Vietnam War began to skyrocket in the 1960's. The *ās* went to half an *uncia* in 80 B.C. after the bloody Social War staggered to a close.

The mint was closed from 40 B.C. to 20 B.C.. When Augustus reopened it, he undertook a reform of the currency which included issuing both *dēnāriī* (eighty-four to the Roman pound) and the gold *aureī* (twice as heavy) in the ratio of 1:25 – in other words, the *aureus* was worth 100 *sestertiī* or one tenth of a *sestertium*. Nero reduced the weight of both the *dēnārius* and *aureus* by about fifteen percent. In addition, he increased the percentage of alloy in the silver *dēnārius*, a practice which, once begun, led to the abandonment of a bimetallic standard in favor of one resting entirely on gold. In 215 A.D., Caracalla issued the so-called *antōnīniānus*, whose face value was supposed to be two *dēnāriī*, and this coin came to supplant the *dēnārius* almost entirely. By 259 A.D., the *antōnīniānus*, like the Gracchi's *dēnārius*, had become a copper sandwich.

Into this deteriorating situation eventually stepped Diocletian, who issued new coins and, defining their relation in his Price Edict, set the *aureus* at sixty to the pound in 294 A.D. Fifteen years later, Constantine minted a new, somewhat lighter *aureus* (seventy-two to the pound), the *solidus* (literally "whole, complete, firm, enduring," and the basis of English *solid* and *solder*), which became the standard currency in which taxes had to be paid. Its minting remained the special prerogative of the emperor, the provincial mints which had sprung up along the way being restricted to coining the lesser denominations – which after this period became increasingly confusing and worth less and less.

Ironically, it is the *solidus* that gives us our word *soldier*, originally a "mercenary": "pay" in Old French was *soulde*, and one who fought for pay was a *souldier*. And lest it be thought that the *solidus* held firm while all other currencies were dwindling away to nothing, it should be pointed out that it is the *solidus* that gave its name to the smallest-possible coin in French: the *sou*, as in "not worth a *sou*," to which may be compared the British "not worth a brass farthing" and the American "not worth a red cent," not to mention the adjectival "penny-ante," "nickel-and-dime," and "two-bit," all signifying "insignificant." Erasmus is credited with coining the phrase "not worth a brass farthing," the ordinary *farthing* having been one *fourth* of a silver penny, though the early 1600's saw the introduction of the *Harrington* (more properly *Harington*), a farthing made of brass and so named for John, First Baron Harington to whom James I granted a patent to mint this form of money. It was James II who was responsible for the brief appearance of the so-called "gun money" minted in Ireland from old brass cannon, pots and pans, and just about anything else metallic and close at hand.

The *cent* – red or other – comes through Old French from Latin *centum* (one hundred), there being a hundred cents to the dollar, just as there are a hundred *centimes* to the French franc, the Algerian dinar, and the Haitian gourde, and a hundred *centavos* to the Mexican peso, the Guatemalan quetzal, and the sol of Peru. Similarly, the *dime* is ultimately from Latin *(pars) decima* (tenth [part], tithe), there being ten such to the dollar. (*Dollar*, while we're on the subject, comes from a shortening of *Joachimsthaler, Joachimsthal* – Joachim's Valley – being the name of the Germanic town in which this popular unit of currency originated.) The *nickel* is named for the substance that makes up one quarter of the coin's weight (the other three quarters being copper). *Nickel*, the metal, was so named by Axel F. von Cronstedt, the Swedish minerologist who separated it out in 1751 from the nickel-copper ore called in German *Kupfernikel*, literally "copper demon" (because it looked as though you could extract copper from the ore but, in fact, early eighteenth-century refiners couldn't, presumably because of the machinations of some resident malevolent sprite).

A *quarter* is, of course, a *quarter* of a dollar. A *quarter* is also *two bits*, a *bit* being, literally, "a piece bitten off, a morsel." As an extension of this sense, *bit* came to be used to designate any relatively small coin and was used in America to refer specifically to the Mexican *real* (also known as the *Mexican shilling*), a silver coin valued at twelve and a half cents. The *British* shilling, which went the way of the farthing with the introduction of decimal currency, was a twentieth of a pound, or twelve pence. And the *penny?* The origin of this staple of British and American currency is by no means clear. Some would derive the word from the adjectival form of *Penda*, the eighth-century Mercian king who is said to have minted the first pennies. Others suggest a connection with the word *pan*, either because the metal from which pennies are made is melted in a pan or because pennies are pan-shaped. Still others derive *penny*, ultimately, from Latin *pannus* (cloth, rag) – whence also *pane*, *panel*, and *pawn*, the earliest *windowpanes* being made of cloth rather than glass, the first *panel* being a piece of cloth placed under a saddle, then, by extension, a piece of parchment (attached to a writ) on which the names of a "panel" of jurors were written, and a *pawn* being something (such as an article of clothing) given as security for a loan. A *penny*, like a *pawn*, would have been a piece of cloth or clothing used as currency.

If this seems a bit farfetched, consider the colloquial American use of *buck* or *skin* for dollar, *buckskins* having been a common unit of trade in frontier days. The *sawbuck* – ten-dollar bill – is obliquely related to the one-dollar *buck*: a *sawbuck* is really a *sawhorse* with X-shaped legs, and X is the Roman numeral for ten. Even more remote is the connection to the *buck* of "to pass the buck," which is short for *buckhorn knife*, i.e., a knife whose handle was made of *buckhorn*, it having been the practice among frontier poker players to use such a knife as a pointer to the next dealer – if you didn't want to deal, you could pass the buck, i.e., point the knife at the next guy. It is this last *buck* that appears in Harry S Truman's famous dictum: "The buck stops here."

U·V·W

IS FOR *UNCIAL* AND *UNICORN*. *UNCIAL* comes from Latin *uncia*, which was a twelfth of the Roman pound (and, thus, a twelfth of the original copper/bronze *ās*, which originally weighed a pound) and, by extension, a twelfth of a foot, that is, an *inch*. Indeed, both *inch* and *ounce* as units of measurement come from *uncia*, the former via Old English and the latter via Old French. (*Inch* in the sense of "small island" comes from the unrelated Scots Gaelic *innis*, and *ounce* in the sense of "snow leopard" comes from Old French *lonce*, which in turn comes from the Latin borrowing of Greek *lýnks* [lynx].) The Modern French inch, by the way, is a *pouce*, i.e., a thumb (from Latin *pollex, pollicis* [thumb]), to which may be compared such body English as the *foot*, the *hand* (used in measuring horses), the *span* (the distance from the tip of your pinkie to the tip of your thumb when your hand is splayed – nine inches, by convention), and the *fathom* (the distance from the tips of your fingers on one hand to the tips of the fingers on the other hand when your arms are stretched out perpendicular to your sides – six feet, by convention, Old English *fæþm* being from an Indo-European root meaning "stretch").

Uncia, for its part, is related to the Latin word for "one" – *ūnus* – which, like the words for "two" and "three," has cognates in nearly all of the other Indo-European languages. *Uni-* is the standard combining form of *ūnus* and appears in a large selection of (mostly) Latinate words, such as *unique, university, unit, unisex, Uniat* (from Russian *uniyat*, from Polish *uniat*, from *unja* [union (of the Roman Catholic and Eastern Orthodox Churches)], from Late Latin *ūniō, ūniōnis* [union]), *Unitarian* (Unitarians being said, by some of their more orthodox brethren, to believe in, at most, one God), *uniform*, and *únionized* (when it refers to workers, as opposed to *uníonized* when it refers to gases, e.g., helium). *Uni-* is in fact a pretty productive prefix in English and may be used to make one of just about anything, as long as the anything in question, according to the rule of thumb, begins with a consonant (compare *unanimous* [of one mind]) and has a Latin look to it: the Latinate adjective meaning "of or pertaining to a pogo stick," for example, would be *unipedal*, while its Hellenistic synonym would be *monopodic*, either being far classier than the plain English *one-footed*.

The use of *uncial* in English to refer to the style of writing characterized by somewhat rounded capital letters comes from Saint Jerome's prologue to his translation into Latin of the Book of Job. While Jerome's translation was not the first Latin rendering of the Bible, it soon supplanted its predecessors: it is called the "Vulgate" not because it was written in what we now think of as "Vulgar Latin" – spoken Latin with its own nonclassical peculiarities of inflection and innuendo – but rather because it was written in plain style for the *uulgus*, i.e., the common folk, who were not generally familiar with Greek, Aramaic, or Hebrew, the languages of the New and Old Testaments. One of Jerome's sources was, in fact, a translation of the Old Testament into Greek that had been completed in the third century B.C. by a committee of seventy-two Jewish scholars at Alexandria; it was called the Septuagint from the Latin word for seventy, *septuaginta*.

Jerome's prefatory notes to Job read, in part, *"Habeant qui uolunt ueteres libros, uel in membranis purpureis auro argentoque descriptos, uel uncialibus, ut uulgo aiunt, litteris"* ("Let those who so desire have their old books, whether on purple parchment with gold and silver lettering, or, as the common folk say, 'uncial' letters"). There is some dispute as to whether *unciālibus litterīs* should be read as *initiālibus litterīs* ([illuminated] initial letters) or, as some have suggested, *uncinālibus litterīs* (hooked letters), or as *unciālibus litterīs* (inch-high letters), but the subtext is clear enough: an affected style of penmanship more concerned with ornament than with intelligibility is to be shunned. Jerome goes on to say that, in doing his translation, he had to work from "*pauperes . . . schedulas, et non tam pulchros codices*" ("poor . . . little *schedas*, and not from such pretty *codices*") – a *scheda* being a sheet of papyrus (such as would be glued side to side to make a roll, or *uolūmen – uolūmen, uolūminis* being from the same Indo-European root, meaning "turn," that gives both *volume* and *voluminous* as well as *revolver* and *convolution*), and a *cōdex* being, originally, a slab of wood (little ones being used for dispatches being known as *cōdicillī*, whence our legal term *codicil*), then a quire of ten sheets or so stitched together and bound between two slabs, the sheets being originally of parchment and usually written upon on the smooth (nonhairy) side only. (The *cōdex*, thanks to its ease of use for reference, eased out the *uolūmen* in state record-keeping by the fourth century A.D.) We should mention in passing the *tabula* – a piece of wood with a raised edge into which black-colored wax was poured to form a temporary surface on which to write with a stylus. A *tabula rāsa* was a "scraped tablet" (*rāsa* being the feminine nominative singular form of the past participle of *rādere* [to scrape, shave], whence *eradicate* and *razor*) and was used during the Enlightenment as a metaphor for the impressionable and as yet unwritten-upon mind of the small child. The Greeks also contributed the term *tómos* (cut, whence our *tome*) for a roll of papyrus cut to length but as yet uninscribed, called by the Romans *charta* (as in the *Magna C[h]arta*), whence our *chart, charter, cartography,* and *card*.

Whatever they were written on, the letters that came to be called *uncials* developed around the fourth century A.D., probably following earlier Greek trends in penmanship (*pen* being from Latin *penna* [feather] to which may be compared German *Feder* [pen]); but it was not until two centuries later that uncials would gradually supplant both the earlier square capitals that modern typographers refer to as "Trajan capitals" (because probably the finest surviving ex-

UVW

225

ample of this script can be found in the inscription at the base of Trajan's column, erected at Rome ca. 113 A.D., that served as a paradigm for the Renaissance type-cutters) and the so-called "rustic capitals," which were their most popular handwritten offspring. The transition from square to rustic capitals had been marked by a shift in angle of the broad-nib quill pen (low slant – perhaps thirty degrees – for square; high slant – some sixty degrees – for rustic) and, more important, an increasing roundness of form. This last tendency was accentuated even further with the uncials, and certain letters began to assume the shapes of the lowercase letters that we know today – particularly *a*, *d*, *e*, *f*, *h*, *l*, *m*, *q*, and *u* (which had hitherto been written V in both its vowel and consonant forms). Thus, AVDAX (bold, whence *audacity*) came to be written *audax* in the new script.

U, then, started life as the uncial version of V, which, like *F* and *Y*, comes ultimately from the Phoenician letter *waw* (Ⲩ). In pre-uncial days, V was used to represent both the vowel [u] (in its long and short flavors) and the corresponding consonant (really a semivowel) [w], V-as-[w] appearing before vowels and V-as-[u] appearing pretty much anywhere else in Latin. Eventually, "Standard" Latin [w] became [v] – what was pronounced [we:na] and spelled *uena* by the Romans became *veine* with a [v] in Old French before it was borrowed into English where we know it as *vein*. (Again, *uenīte* [y'all come] was pronounced [weni:te] by the Romans, became [veníte] in Medieval Latin, and is pronounced *"v'nightie"* by modern Anglicans.) Accordingly, many printers today use *v* for prevocalic Latin V, but *u* for V-as-vowel. To this practice may be compared the former convention of using V for all capital V's and U's and *u* for all lowercase *u*'s and *v*'s: "VIRTVES we haue; uices we shun." An alternative usage had *v* for lowercase *u* and *v* at the beginning of a word, and *u* word-internally – "For vnto vs . . . a son is giuen." Stonecutters undoubtedly still have a preference for *v*.

Although the letter that we call "double U" and the French call *"double vé"* appears as early as the first century

A.D. in Roman inscriptions bearing Germanic names (e.g., VVITILDES), W as [w] first came into use among the Anglo-Saxons after the Norman Conquest, just as U came to stand for [u] and V for [v]. (In the earliest printed books, W customarily appeared as *uu* in louuercase uuords and as VV IN VPPERCASE VVORDS.) The Anglo-Saxons had previously used runic letters – prevalent among the Germanic folk of northern Europe and undoubtedly derived from the Roman alphabet – to represent their [u], [w], [v], and [f] sounds, these last two having been essentially in complementary distribution until foreign borrowings started to muddy the waters. The Anglo-Saxon runes for [u] and [w] were *ur* (ᚢ) and *wen* (ᚹ) respectively. A runic-alphabet poem in Old West Saxon (translated by Linda Hecker) contains the following entries for these two letters, whose names, like those of the other runes, were also words in their own right:

ᚢ   *ur*   Wild ox is rash, high-horned, moody;
(the aurochs)   Fiercely he rushes, fearless in battle,
                Goring and gouging, that great moor-
                    stepper.

ᚹ   *wen*   He who knows joy knows little of woe,
(joy)   Sorrow or soreness; But his spirit
                Is blithe, and his storerooms rich.

So why did the Anglo-Saxon literate trade in their runic writing for the continental spread? A number of factors suggest themselves, though it should be said that the change-over was neither immediate nor complete, the runic letters *edh* (ᛞ), *thorn* (ᚦ), and *yogh* (ᣇ) for the initial fricative consonants in *thy*, *thorn*, and Old English ᣇ*eolu* (yellow, cf. German *gelb*) – having been retained rather longer than the rest. One reason for the demise of runic script may perhaps be seen in the word *rune* itself: in Old English, the verb *rūnian* meant "to whisper" (whence the archaic Modern English *round* [to whisper]), and the noun *rūn* meant "secret council." (*Rūn* in this sense is preserved in the place name *Runnymede* – literally Meadow on the [Secret] Council Island, Old English *mæd* [Middle English *mede*] being "meadow" and *ī3* being "island" [and cognate with Latin *aqua* (water), an *island* with its spurious *s* being, literally, "water-land"] – famous as the site of King John's signing of the Magna Carta in 1215.) If runes were a big secret, they were presumably of rather limited use to all but the initiated in their mysteries, unlike the Roman alphabet that the early Christian missionaries were happy enough to make accessible so that converts could read the Scriptures. It is further possible that the transition to the Roman alphabet was hastened by the bad press that Christians tended to give the pagan philosophy implicit in the runes themselves: to the early denizens of the cloisters, a letter was just a letter, by God – nominalism, the philosophy that asserted that the mind can frame no concept corresponding to any universal or general term – or, in its extreme statement, that only individual examples and no abstract entities exist – being as yet unformulated, waiting to be proposed in its best and most classical form by William of Occam in the fourteenth century.

The medieval cloisters, in which much of the writing of the day took place, often had menageries attached to them, and, though these may have originated as mere livestock pens, the acquisition of more exotic and inedible fauna led at least one Bishop of Paris to order that all the animals were to be cleared out from the cloister of Notre-Dame-de-Paris except for the residents of the fishpond whose official function it was to supply the monks with nonmeat protein on Fridays and during Lent. In the meantime, however, clerics had evolved a genre of book to record all that was known about animals, both the ones in the abbey and those much further afield, some so fanciful as to boggle less credulous minds of today. Such a book was called a *bestiary* and ranged from recountings of the lore of chickens, oxen, and other equally familiar creatures of the farm all the way to chronicles of the more exotic gryphons, manticores, phoenixes, and unicorns.

The *unicorn* – "one-horn" – was given considerable credence, being duly catalogued in such respectable works as Pliny the Elder's *Natural History*: while skeptical about many other beasts, such as the pegasus, the gryphon, the tragopan, and the sirens that he had encountered in the writings of the Greeks, Pliny was nevertheless prepared to accept the unicorn as a genuine creature hunted – but never taken alive – in India. Moreover, Christian writers had the authority of Scripture, thanks to a creature called the *re'em* mentioned in Job 39:9–12 in the passage that begins, "Will the *re'em* be willing to serve thee, or abide by thy crib?" and rendered by the Septuagint as *monokérōs* (Greek "one-horn"), though the Biblical animal was probably in fact the aurochs. (It is only fair to add that elsewhere in *Job* the question is posed, "Canst thou draw out leviathan with an hook?" and the Septuagint scholars had undoubtedly never seen a leviathan either, though the notion of this huge sea-creature was appealing enough for the seventeenth-century English political scientist Thomas Hobbes to adopt it as a metaphor for the State.) In consequence, Saint Bernard of Clairvaux, while castigating his contemporaries for building elaborate churches with fanciful decorative carvings, seems to have taken deliberate care not to mention the unicorn by name when fulminating against "a snake's tail spliced onto a quadruped, the head of a mammal on the body of a fish, a beast that is half horse and half goat, another with horns and a horse's arse. . . . If they aren't ashamed of producing such nonsense, oughtn't they at least to be appalled at the cost?"

But you can't keep a good fanciful beast down. One of the attractions of this mythical creature was that its horn, when made into a drinking vessel, was supposed to be proof against poison, and for uneasy monarchs unwilling to submit to Mithridates's legendary prophylaxis – this eastern potentate having accustomed himself to a number of the commoner poisons by swallowing them himself in increasingly large doses – or to waste perfectly good retainers by making them taste everything first, the unicorn's horn was a prudent investment. Indeed, in the days before refrigerators when king and commoner alike ran a high risk of accidental food poisoning from badly preserved meat, the unicorn's horn, whole or powdered, remained a much-sought-after commodity and a stock item of English pharmacists at least until the beginning of the eighteenth century, narwhal teeth and the spiral horns of various nonmythical beasts being passed off as the genuine nonpowdered article – whether the French for "narwhal" – *licorne de mer* (unicorn of the sea) – originated as a gloss on this particular practice of phonus balonus or merely as an innocent likening of the narwhal to the unicorn is not clear. But then, for everything that's lost in translation, there's usually something gained: the French got their *licorne* (unicorn) from the Italian *alicorno*, an argle-bargling of Latin *ūnicornū*, and the English borrowed French *licorn(e)* for use in designating an eighteenth-century variety of howitzer on wheels (much as *unicorn* was used a century later, sans gunpowder, to refer to a three-horse carriage with one horse leading the other two).

Apparently the original Western source for much unicorn lore was the Greek physician Ktesias, who was personal medic to Artaxerxes Mnemon, treating the spear wound that the Persian king received at the hand of his upstart brother Cyrus at Kunaxa, where Xenophon's Ten Thousand helped win the battle and lose the war. Ktesias passed on a number of stories about India, including the bit of lore that the unicorn's horn, whether hollowed out as a cup from which to partake of healthy food or ground into a powder to provide a literal spice of life, made a nifty antitoxin. Some have suggested that Ktesias's Indian unicorn was really no more than the *rhinoceros* (literally "nose-horn"), albeit several times removed and embellished in the retelling, while others have suggested that by ascribing an Indian reality to this otherwise totally fanciful concoction, the author was simply using the tried-and-true strategy of legitimizing something totally off the wall by saying that it exists among people of whom one has heard and whose existence is granted but with whom one has no actual firsthand experience, the assumption being that if you accept the existence of these unknown people, you might as well accept any equally unknown aspects of their world into the bargain at no extra cost.

And occasionally it all pays off, as with the story of the Chinese unicorn, or *kilin* (*ch'i-lin*). This mythical beast, with its deer's body, ox's tail, and single horn, is said to have made its first appearance during the reign of Fu Hsi nearly five thousand years ago. (Fu Hsi, for his part, is said to have developed the Chinese system of writing from copying the magical signs that he observed on the back of the beast.) Henceforth, the *kilin* was associated in its rare appearances with great things for the current ruler, one such appearance, by tradition, having presaged the birth of Confucius. Ho hum, you say: show me one.

Well, in the early fifteenth century, the enterprising Cheng Ho managed to do it, after a fashion, by spearheading a series of expeditions to such foreign parts as Java, Sumatra, the coast of India, the Gulf of Hormuz, and the coast of modern-day Somalia and Kenya (whose port cities of Brava, Mogadishu, and Malindi were even then major trading centers), the idea having been to get some mercantile action going in a way that would be acceptable to the officially trade-disdaining Confucian emperor. Cheng Ho's credentials were excellent: he was a Chinese Muslim from Yunnan who rose to the rank of court eunuch – eunuchs were privileged to the extent of being trusted in many matters, such as shopping, by the court – and he apparently had a flair for adventure. The relevant upshot of his various trips to the west was the discovery of the giraffe – hitherto totally unknown in China – and the fortuitous fact that this animal was called, in Somali, *girin* – close enough to *ch'i-lin/kilin* for folk music, as they say: this strange animal was presented to the emperor with all due pomp and circumstance as the latest appearance of the traditional unicorn with all its auspicious-omen baggage, and everybody thought it was a great thing.

The fact that the giraffe, on close inspection, didn't in

fact match the specs on the packing slip for a unicorn seems to have gone by the boards: the giraffe was apparently so novel a reality to the Chinese of Cheng Ho's day that the fact that it had a long neck instead of a horn growing out of its forehead was a matter of not much concern. And when the Japanese borrowed the word *kirin* – for "giraffe" – it still had the flavor of things exotic: in Japan, the *kirin* has been a rich and wildly varied motif in decorative art, perhaps best known to modern Westerners as the logo on the outside of Kirin beer, beer itself being originally as nonnative to Japan as the unicorn.

Pliny described the unicorn as "an extraordinarily wild beast . . . which has a stag's head, elephant's feet, and the tail of a wild pig; the rest of the body is horselike. . . . It is said that this animal cannot be taken alive." These words were echoed by Julius Solinus in whose *Polyhistoria* the unicorn is called "a most savage [*atrocissimum*] animal with a horrible bellow. . . . Its horn sticks out from the middle of its forehead, wonderfully bright and about four feet long, so that whatever it rushes against is run through easily with the blow. . . . While it may be killed, it cannot be taken alive." It is not impossible that what the authors were describing was, again, a transmogrification of the rhinoceros, and it is certainly this creature that Marco Polo saw, with ". . . elephant feet and buffalo hair . . . the head, like a wild boar's, carried close to the ground. They take pleasure in living in the mud – a hideous beast to see, nothing at all like what we call and think of as a unicorn in our land, i.e., a beast that allows itself to be captured in the lap of a virgin."

The virgin's-lap trap, pregnant with sexual imagery, seems to have become a part of the unicorn's mythic lore thanks to Christian bestiarists, who saw images of the heavenly order of things in the very animals – the lion, for example, was thought to be born dead and to have life breathed into it as a three-day-old cub by its sire, a metaphor for Christ's death and resurrection; tigers were supposed to be the embodiment of evil because they were striped with vices; and so on. Such a ruse as baiting the unicorn with a maiden is in line with other peculiarities of medieval justice – the notion that witches would float if thrown into the duck pond, or the good guys would be able to carry a hot iron without getting burned (well, nobody's *perfect*) – and, under the circumstances, it may be fortunate that unicorns were as rare as the medieval mind thought they were, else sister might have had some very fast talking to do once they dragged her home to the manor after the hunt.

Oddly enough, if there are no natural unicorns, it has at least been demonstrated that veterinary surgeons can manufacture one, if they care to go to the trouble to do so: despite Baron Georges Cuvier's contention, in 1827, that a single-horned animal could not have a cloven hoof because such creatures would have to grow that horn right at the joint of their divided frontal bone, W. Franklin Dove of the University of Maine demonstrated that a day-old calf could have the bud of its future horns transplanted and fused to grow right in the middle of its forehead, Cuvier's assumption that the horns were an integral part of the skull structure having been only partly correct – they do fuse with the skull, but not until the bones of the skull have hardened into place. Which being demonstrated, scientists have since pondered whether primitive societies might not have produced the occasional one-horned sheep, cow, etc., as a showpiece (perhaps to beguile visiting explorer-traders from far-off lands). The Dinka of the Upper Nile tinker with the horns of their young cattle in order to get them to grow in distinctive ways for easy identification later in life, and the Kafirs of Nepal were known to produce one-horned sheep, though by what process or to what purpose remains a mystery. Again, Pericles of Athens was reputed to have been sent a one-horned ram as a token of his power as head of state.

Ironically, Pliny the Elder may simply have failed to put one and one together to make one, for his *Natural History* contains a passage about the horns of oxen which reads:

"incīsa nascentium in dīuersās partēs torqueantur, ut singulīs capitibus quaterna fiunt" ("being cut when [the oxen are] young, the horns are twisted in several directions so that out of a single head there come to grow four horns"), something like the reverse procedure giving us the motto *ē plūribus ūnum* (out of many, one).

UVW

X·Y·Z

AREN'T FOR MUCH OF ANYTHING, IN
Classical Latin at least – the X, Y, and Z entries in the
exhaustive Oxford Latin Dictionary span pages 2124 to
2126 all told – basically because the Romans didn't have
much use for these letters except when it came to representing Latin's [ks] sound cluster, which only occurred in
the middles and at the ends of words, and transliterating
borrowed Greek words featuring the [ks], [ü], or [z] sounds
of that furrin tongue. Unlike the other letters of the Roman
alphabet, X seems to have come not from Etruscan but directly from West Greek, as though, once having been offered the opportunity to acquire the alphabet from the
Etruscans, the Romans decided to do a little comparison
shopping before rashly buying the system lock, stock, and
barrel.

It is reasonable to assume that the Etruscans went
through a similar process when they were first introduced
to alphabetic writing by the Greeks, only this time it was
presumably to the Phoenicians to whom the comparison
shoppers turned. Whether the Greeks looked over other Semitic scripts when considering the adoption of the Phoenician syllabary is not clear, nor is it known exactly how the
early Semitic scripts evolved from the Egyptian pictographic
system of writing, but a certain amount of trial and error
and looking over your neighbor's shoulder to see if you got
the same answer is probable.

The upshot is that while the Romans got most of their
alphabet from the Etruscans (who got it from the Greeks
who got it from the Phoenicians), they neither felt obliged
to take all that the Etruscans offered nor refrained from
picking and choosing what they wanted elsewhere: they
passed up the Etruscan letter 8 for the Greek digamma

(F) when they came to represent their [f], even though 8 seems to have represented Etruscan [f] while F pretty clearly represented Greek [w] – earliest Roman use involved writing [f] as FH – and they again went to the Greeks for the letter X.

Just why the Romans thought they needed a special letter for [ks] is by no means obvious, since they could just as easily have represented these sounds by K plus S. Actually, the Greeks didn't really need a special letter to represent their [ks] either, though here the story is a little more complicated and is worth a brief digression, since it illustrates two phenomena that almost invariably occur when a writing system is passed from one set of speakers to another. These are the tendency on the part of the borrowers to borrow more than they really need and to adapt what they've borrowed to suit their sound system (which is, as like as not, different from that of the people from whom they got the writing system). The early Greeks borrowed the Phoenician syllabary letter for letter even though this meant acquiring a number of signs that represented sounds found in Phoenician but not in Greek. Phoenician seems to have distinguished between [š] (as in English *ship*) and [s] (as in English *sip*), representing the first sound by *shin* (W) and the second by *samekh* (∓). The Greeks wound up using *shin* in modified form – it eventually became *sigma* (Σ, σ) – to represent their single sibilant [s], leaving *samekh* up for grabs. In Ionic Greek, *samekh* was retained for use to represent [ks] – waste not, want not – while in West Greek, *samekh* simply disappeared.

This is not the whole story, however, for Greek had a set of sounds – the so-called aspirate stops, [ph], [th], and [kh] – which were not found in Phoenician and which, consequently, the Phoenicians did not bother to represent in their script. What seems to have happened is that the early Greeks took the Phoenician letter *ṭeth* (⊗) and fiddled with it until it became the prototype for *phi* (φ), *theta* (θ), and *chi* (χ) in Ionic; and *phi* (⦶) and *theta* (⊕) in West Greek. West Greek seems to have adapted the Phoenician letter *kaph* (⤵ , ⤷), which underlies Pan-Hellenic *kappa* (κ) and our own *K*, to make their *chi* (Υ), while using X for [ks], having perhaps thought better of jettisoning *samekh* in such haste. The West Greek *chi* (Υ) shows up in Ionic Greek as *psi* (ψ) at the end of the alphabet with the other "new" (i.e., non-Phoenician) letters, *phi* and *chi*.

The Romans, then, may be presumed to have borrowed West Greek's X partly because it was there and partly because that was the letter that West Greeks used in spelling such names as *Xanthippe* (the most famous Xanthippe having been Socrates's sharp-tongued wife) and *Xerxes* (the great king of Persia whom the Greeks trounced at Salamis) as well as the words for such useful cultural items as the *xylon* – which in Latin meant "cotton plant" and in Greek "wood," hence, "tree," hence, "cotton tree" – and the *xenium* (gift given by a host to his guest, cf. Greek *ksénos* [foreigner, stranger]). Once having this handy letter, the Romans put it to further use in native words in which [ks] occurred in other than word-initial position – *ex* (out of, from), *rex* (ruler, king), *dīxī* (I said), and so on.

Y and Z were tacked onto the end of the (Roman) alphabet later on for use in transliterating such borrowings from Greek as *zingiberi* (ginger) and *zēlotypia* (jealousy). Actually, Z went out and came back in again: this letter, originally written *I*, appeared in the early Greek, Etruscan, and Roman alphabets between the letter *digamma/F* (Phoenician *waw*) and what was to become *eta/H* (Phoenician *chet*), but since the Romans had no voiced sibilant, *I* = Z was tapped on the shoulder and ushered into an early retirement (a process for which the term in Japanese labor relations is *katatatake*) to the Oscan countryside, where it retained a part-time job standing for the Oscan [z]. Even after Z had straggled back into the alphabets of Europe in relatively late Latin times, taking its place at the rear, it was often seen as something of an anomaly: thus the Earl of Kent in *King Lear* says (II:2), "Thou whoreson zed! thou unnecessary letter!" – *zed* being from *zêta*, the Greek name for the letter, and the name by which most speakers of non-American English know it.

Zingiberi (from which the word *ginger* is derived) originated in Sanskrit, in which *śṛṅgavera* literally meant "horn-body," *śṛṅga* being in fact cognate with English *horn*. *Zēlotypia* was a native Greek invention based on the word *zêlos* (eager rivalry, zealous imitation, emulation, jealousy), the basis of English *zeal, zealous,* and *jealous*. The doublets *zealous* and *jealous* are derived from Late Latin *zēlōsus* (full of zeal, full of envy), the earlier standard Latin words for "jealousy, envy" having been *inuidia* and *aemulātiō*. *Inuidia* (ill will, spite, envy) comes from the verb *inuidēre* (to look askance at, look at with ill will) and is the basis of English *invidious*. The original meaning of *aemulātiō* was probably something on the order of "imitation," a sense that survives in English *emulation,* but the word seems to have acquired a flavor of "rivalry" and, on the part of the unsuccessful rival, "envy."

Y's career as a member of the Roman alphabet has been more checkered than that of any other letter. Like *F, U,* and, later, *V* and *W, Y* is a manifestation of Phoenician *waw* (Ψ). The early Greeks used this letter both in its original consonantal value – [w] – and in what was for them its corresponding vocalic value – [ü], a sound made by simultaneously rounding the lips and saying, "*ee.*" In its [w] value, *waw* retained its original place in the alphabet and was renamed *dígamma* (double gamma) because it looked like one gamma (Γ) on top of another: Ϝ . In its [ü] value, *waw* went to the end of the alphabet and was renamed *upsilon* (bare, plain *u*): Υ, υ. The Greeks eventually lost their [w] sound and sometime thereafter dispensed with *dígamma*. The Romans, however, had already acquired *waw* for use in both consonantal and vocalic functions. As already mentioned, consonantal *waw* became *F* and was used to represent the consonant [f]. The end-of-the-alphabet vowel letter *V* (*Y* without its tail) was used to represent both the vowel [u] – "*oo*" – and its consonantal counterpart, [w], no problem since [u] and [w] were essentially in complementary distribution in Latin: [w] only occurred before vowels, and [u] only occurred elsewhere. Later on, then, *Y* made its reappearance in the form in which we know it today when the Romans decided that it would be a good idea to have a letter suited to representing the Greek [ü] sound (with which speakers of Latin seemed to have as much trouble as speakers of English do today with the same sound in French and German).

Not that Y was the only candidate to represent this sound: the emperor Claudius, maintaining that they were "absolutely necessary," attempted to introduce by imperial edict three new letters (to go at the end of the alphabet, naturally): one to represent the unstressed upsilonlike vowel sound in the first syllable of *lubīdō* (today's *libido*) and the second syllable of *optimus* (sometimes spelled *optumus*), another to replace V in its consonantal value [w], and another to represent the consonant cluster [ps]. The first of these letters was to be Ⱶ , the second an upside-down *F* (called, appropriately, *digamma inuersum*), and the last a backward *C* (called *antisigma*). However, despite their inclusion in a few inscriptions by dutiful stonecarvers, none of these letters ever caught on, so it was back to the Greek alphabet for Y, which the Romans called by the same name as their letter *I* (pronounced "*ee*"), sometimes dubbing it more precisely "*I Graeca*" (pronounced "*ee gryca*" or, in Late Latin times, "*ee grecka*") or "Greek *I*," since *I* was the letter that the Romans used to represent their "*ee*" vowel, and "*ee*" was the way in which most Latin speakers tended to pronounce Greek *upsilon* by the simple expedient of not bothering to round their lips when uttering the vowel for which that letter stood. Even after Y came to be used consonantally in non-Greek words such as Late Latin *yomanus* (yeoman) and *yeresiua* (gift made to an official at the beginning of a year in office), the name still stuck: speakers of English may somewhat atavistically call it "*wy*" – which railroaders spell "*wye*" (from *wī*, originally *uī*, i.e., V plus *I*) and the Germans call it "*üpsilon*," but in Spanish it's "*i griega*," in French "*i grec*," and in Russian, a contemporary poet (Elena Sergeevna Ventzel) took *I*. *Gregova* as her pseudonym "Ms. Y," or as we might say, "Ms. X."

The use of X, Y, and Z to stand for unknown quantities

in algebraic notation may be traced back to René Descartes, who so used them in his *La Géometrie* (1637), reserving A, B, and C for known quantities in the same work. It was also in *La Géometrie* that Descartes advanced X and Y to stand for spatial coordinates on a grid, a practice continuing to this day, whence they are known as *Cartesian coordinates*. (In three-dimensional analysis, the third coordinate is, naturally enough, Z.) J. Tropfke, in the 1902 edition of his *Geschichte der Elementar-Mathematik*, suggested that Descartes got the idea for X as the sign for an unknown from having seen the symbol $\mathfrak{X}$ so used in the works of Clavius, $\mathfrak{X}$ being a thinly disguised German blackletter A ($\mathfrak{A}$), but the presence of $\mathfrak{X}$ side by side with X in a letter from Descartes to a colleague in 1619 casts considerable doubt on this hypothesis, and Tropfke himself retreated from it in a subsequent edition. In any event, the dissemination of X, Y, and Z as geometric coordinates was facilitated by Gerard Kinckhuysen's *Algebra* (1661), De la Hire's *Nouveaux élémens des sections coniques* (1679), and other works by Euler, Bernoulli, and Pitot in the forty years following.

The French were so sold on the use of X in mathematics that they came to use the expression "to be strong in X" to mean "to be good at math," and "to have a head for X" to mean "to have a mathematical mind." This gave rise to the following logical wheeze: A person with a mathematical mind (*tête à X*) was never drafted into the army, because this would make the draftee an *ex*-conscript. Symbolically expressed, this would be:

$$\textit{ex}\text{-conscript} = \theta X \; (\textit{theta-X, i.e., tête à X})$$

If both sides are divided by X, we get

$$e\text{-conscript} = \theta$$

Dividing both sides by *e* gives us

$$\text{conscript} = \frac{\theta}{e}$$

The result has conscript equal to the pun *theta sur e* (theta over e)/*tête assurée* (literally, "guaranteed head," i.e., person whose life is definitely not in danger), the latter sense suggesting a reductio ad absurdum if ever there was one, though one cannot help but be reminded of Pierre de Fermat's Last Theorem, an annotation of a postulate in a mathematical treatise in which Fermat scribbled the marginal note: "I have discovered a truly wonderful proof of this, which, however, I have not the space to reproduce here." As it turned out, Fermat may have been fudging: his Last Theorem was recently proved wrong by a combination of sound reasoning and not a few hours of computer run-time number-crunching.

The Romans were at a distinct disadvantage when it came to anything remotely resembling number-crunching, largely because of the clunkiness of the way in which they chose to represent their numbers: Roman numerals may be easy to carve in stone, but they are the pits when it comes to doing multiplication, division, or square roots. No matter: Roman numerals have imprinted themselves so firmly on the collective consciousness of the school-going Western-world kid that still lurks within us all that it would be mean not to say something about their origins here, so we will:

I is the basic unit – one. It probably originated as a simple slash – score – or tally stick. II = 2, III = 3, IIII = 4, IV (one before five, V) being the replacement for IIII in along about Renaissance times. Indeed, none of the subtractive forms (CD = 400, MCM = 1900) seem to have been used until well past classical times, the Romans having apparently been just as happy writing LIII or IIIL for 53, perhaps more so in instances in which it was desirable to prevent forgery or at least cut the losses – compare the modern advice to novice check-writers always to start the written part as close to the left as possible.

V is five. Mattheus Hostis, a Dutch writer on ancient mathematical notation, suggested in 1582 that V represents an open hand with the thumb off to the side and that X (for ten) was for two of them – send me a mongoose and, while you're about it, send me another one. This derivation of V as the Roman numeral for five has a certain appeal, though it has also been suggested – *ignotum per ignotius* – that·V, which also appears upside-down for five in some inscriptions, was half an X (ten). For what it's worth, the English words *fist, finger,* and *fin* (in the sense of "five-dollar bill") all come from the common Indo-European root for five.

X is ten, possibly from one schematic hand over another (V over Λ) or from your arms crossed across your chest to show the backs of both hands, each with their five fingers; possibly, because ten is a tenth of a hundred, from the Phoenician *teth* (⊗) which is probably the basis for the Roman numeral C (hundred); or possibly because people got tired of scratching single strokes up to ten and crossed the whole thing out when they got to ten (much as we go |, ||, |||, ||||, ⧻). It has also been suggested that X as the Roman numeral for ten is one and the same as the letter of the (Roman) alphabet, the idea being that the letter wasn't really necessary for spelling and so could be spared for numerical work, much as the obsolete letters of the Greek alphabet – *digamma, koppa,* and *sampi* – had been used in Greek after receiving their pink slips as members of the belles-lettres set. But this seems unlikely.

L is fifty and probably does come from the Greek letter that underlies the Roman alphabetical X: West Greek *chi*, a.k.a. Ionic *psi*, ψ, its various variants including ⊥ , ⊥ , ⊥ , and L . Another story has it that L as "fifty" is half of a rather square form of C (100).

C is a hundred and probably, ultimately, from the Phoenician letter *teth* (⊗) that also turned into the letter X. *Teth*, as it slouched into the Etruscan/Roman alphabet, wore several coats – ⊗ , ⊕ , ⊖ among others, and it is not beyond the pale that one could have walked in as the alphabetical letter X while another slipped in under the fence as the numeral C (while yet another could have done an end run as the numeral X while the ticket collectors were scratching their heads). That the Romans, when they thought about it, figured that C stood for *centum* (hundred) was merely dust on the cake or frosting in the eyes.

D is five hundred, probably not, as some have suggested, from a putative Etruscan borrowing of Greek *delta* (Δ) for which the Etruscans had no other immediate use – the Etruscan sign for 500 was △ – but rather from half of CIↃ (1,000) – both IↃ and CI are well attested as Roman shorthand for 500.

M is a thousand and is probably derived not from an abbreviation of Latin *mille* (thousand) but from the Greek letter *phi*, written ⅅ . The Romans had several ways of writing"1,000," actually: I, CIↃ, ∞, ⋈ , and ∾ being chief among them. All but the first, which is fairly transparently a one putting on airs, may be derived from *phi* (φ) with a little orthographic license, and probably were.

Two other theories should be mentioned here, however. The more nearly all-encompassing was put forth by Karl Zangemeister in 1887 and derives all of the Roman numerals from the practice of decussation, i.e., marking with an X (from the Latin verb *decussāre* [to cut crosswise so as to form an X] from the noun *decussis* [coin worth ten (*decem*) *assēs*], the *decussis* being stamped with the Roman numeral X). According to Zangemeister, a single tally is "one," its multiple of ten is a tally with a slash through it (X), half of which gives V for "five," the next multiple of ten is a tally with a slash slashed by a curved slash (Ⅹ) which, when unclutttered by the removal of the straight lines, leaves C = 100, and from the thicket representing the next multiple of ten, Ⱉ , we extract ∞ as "1,000" (its use as a sign for infinity having been proposed in 1665 by an English mathematician named Wallis). Again, half of this gives D for "500." All very ingenious and some of it probably true, but much of it unsupported by the epigraphic evidence.

Priscian, the great Latin grammarian of fifth-century (A.D.) Constantinople, held that ∞ was really a modification of the (Ionic) Greek letter *chi* (χ) which was sometimes used to stand for 1,000 (because the Greek word for a thousand –

chílioi – begins with that letter), but this seems unlikely, especially since the Greeks more commonly used *chi* to represent 600, all of the letters of their alphabet having been pressed into numerical service as part of the job. Priscian goes on to suggest that the CIƆ way of writing 1,000 is to be analyzed as a I in between parentheses – IƆ would be half of this, i.e., I plus only a single parenthesis; IƆƆ would be "5,000," CCIƆƆ would be "10,000," IƆƆƆ would be "50,000," and so on. In this case, what presumably started out as a split *phi* seems to have been reworked into a method with the generative power of multiplying any Roman numeral by five or ten at will. An additional device – drawing a line over a numeral to show that the number that it represented was to be multiplied by a thousand – was also used, chiefly in the world of high finance. An extension of this convention had it that a numeral with a line over it and a line on either side was to be read as 100,000 times its ordinary value: $\overline{|L|}$ = 5,000,000.

Otherwise, though, when it came to marking decimal places, the Romans had a hard time of it, since zero hadn't been invented yet. This indispensable item didn't make its way from India to Europe until the first full blossoming of Arab-Muslim culture in the early Middle Ages, at which time, speakers of Late Latin seized upon the Arabic *ṣifr* with both hands, the one grasping the word as *cifra* (whence English *cipher/cypher*) and the other as *zephirum* (whence English *zero* but not *zephyr* [western wind] which breezed its way through Latin from Greek *zéphyros*, a derivative of *zóphos* [darkness, west]). To be sure, the English meanings of *cipher* and *zero* overlap – both words designate the mathematical sign variously represented as capital O, zero o, or one or the other of these with a slash through it – but this is perhaps no more than might have been expected even in the absence of the notion of decussation, though the relationship between X and capital O/zero has been a long and fruitful one, witness XOXOX as love (or hugs) and kisses (the X presumably representing the sound of osculation while the O stands for the osculatory orifice itself or, perhaps, for the empty interlude for breath), X's and O's as the primitives of tick-tack-toe (known in England as *naughts and crosses* or *noughts and crosses* or *oughts and crosses*, *aught*, *ought*, *naught*, and *nought* being something of an etymological snarl: *aught*, as in "for aught I know" means "all" and comes from Old English *ā wiht* [all things, everything]; *aught* in the sense of "nothing, zero" comes from the missegmentation of *a naught* [a nothing, a zero] into *an aught*, much as *a norange* was sliced up into *an orange*; *naught* comes from Old English *nā wiht* [no thing] and forms the basis of *naughty*, whose original sense was something on the order of worthless, worth nothing; *nought* is from *no wiht*, whose basic meaning was not all that different from that of *nā wiht*: "in no way"; and *ought* – as in *oughts and crosses* – was a misguided extrapolation from *nought*, signifying, as the man said, "nothing"), and the X and O with which Christians and Jews none too familiar with the Roman alphabet affixed their respective signatures to legal documents, Christians making an X as the sign of the Christian cross, and Jews, aware of the Christian convention, opting, instead of an X, for a circle, the Yiddish word for which being *kikel* or *kykel* (from Greek *kýklos* [circle] plus the diminutive *-el*), from which the now derogatory term *kike* is most probably derived, all part of the irony, as one scholar of Yiddish has suggested, that having to learn the Palmer Method of penmanship with its rounded letters entailed for immigrants to America who were used to the utterly angular Hebrew script.

Numbers might have been simpler, and, indeed, all societies in possession of the alphabet have had a whack or two at imbuing their letters with numerical argle-bargle, the practice being known as *gematria* (a quick rendering of Greek *geōmetría*, which originally referred to the measurement – *metría* – of the earth – *gē* – but which got to refer to the measurement of other things as well, as people got into it). The biblical Apocalypse makes much of the number 666, which is glossed as the (Greek) summing of the numerical values of the letters of name NERON KAISAR, i.e., the emperor Nero. In addition, Suetonius records a lampoon in circulation in Rome during Nero's time to the effect that if you counted up the values of the letters in the emperor's name, on the one hand, and those in the phrase "murdered his own mother" on the other, the numbers would be equal. And in our own time, people drive around with vanity plates that say 10Q and I12B12, CBers say "10–4, rear door," and, in the most literate restaurants, cooks use "86" as a signal to the floor staff – "86 the *grenouille à la pêche flambée*" – that the item just ordered is all sold out.

Bibliography

The reader hungry for more information will find lots of it in the books listed below. Some are translations into particularly felicitous English of the classics mentioned in the preceding pages; some are sources we have found particularly helpful in illuminating the lives and times of speakers of Latin and its Romance offspring, while others discuss at length topics we have managed to touch on more briefly than we might like given worlds enough and time, not to mention the forbearance of our kind publishers.

Except where otherwise indicated in the text, translations are our own; those wishing to have a crack at it themselves are directed to the perennial Loeb Library editions which reproduce original text with facing translations into English where suitable, and into Italian (usually) where scurrilous, which at least lets one know where the naughty parts are. The Loeb Library series, formerly published by Heinemann of New York and London, is now issued by Harvard University Press in Cambridge, Massachusetts.

Another series not to be missed is the Penguin Classics, which are translations only – and very good ones – of much of the best Latin literature; Penguin's main office is in Harmondsworth, Middlesex County, England, but the company has branches all over the English-speaking world, including an office in New York City, and most titles are available in the United States.

Since many of the following books have run to several editions, we have chosen to list the publication date of the latest edition available to us. Complete bibliographical information may be found in *Books In Print* for books still published; out-of-print titles will still be listed in the *Union Catalogue* of the Library of Congress, with the able assistance of your local librarian.

Bibliography

▓▓▓

248

Abbott, Frank Frost, *Roman Politics* (Boston: 1923).

Allen, W. Sidney, *Vox Latina: The Pronunciation of Classical Latin* (Cambridge, England: 1965).

Apuleius, Lucius, *The Golden Ass*, William Adlington Collier, trans. (New York City: 1962).

Armour, Richard, *It All Started with Stones and Clubs* (New York City: 1967).

Attwater, Donald, *The Penguin Dictionary of Saints* (Harmondsworth, England: 1965).

Balsdon, J. P. V. D., *Roman Women* (New York City: 1962).

Benveniste, Emile, "Problèmes sémantiques de la reconstruction," in *Word* (Vol. 10: 1954).

Berger, Phillipe, *Histoire de l'écriture dans l'antiquité* (Paris: 1892).

Biblia Sacra, Desclée et Cie. (Paris: 1927).

Bickerman, E. J., *Chronology of the Ancient World* (Ithaca, NY: 1968).

Birley, Anthony, "Nerva," in *Lives of the Later Caesars* (Harmondsworth, England: 1976).

Black, Henry Campbell, *Black's Law Dictionary* (St. Paul, Minn.: 1979).

Bloch, Raymond, *The Etruscans* (New York City: 1963).

Bok, Sissela, *Lying* (New York: 1979).

Bonnefoy, Yves, ed., *Dictionnaire des mythologies et des religions des sociétés traditionnelles et du monde antique* (Paris: 1981).

Boyd-Bowman, Peter, *From Latin to Romance in Sound Charts* (Kalamazoo, Mich.: 1954).

Boyer, Paul, and Stephen Nissenbaum, *Salem Possessed* (Cambridge, Mass.: 1974).

Bradford, William, *Of Plymouth Plantation* (New York City: 1962).

Bramont, Jules, ed., *The Travels of Sir John Mandeville and the Journal of Friar Odoric* (London: 1928).

Buck, Carl Darling, *Comparative Grammar of Greek and Latin* (Chicago: 1933).

———, *A Dictionary of Selected Synonyms in the Principal Indo-European Languages* (Chicago: 1949).

Caesar, Gaius Julius, and Aulus Hirtius, *The Battle for Gaul*, Anne and Peter Wiseman, trans. (Boston: 1980).

Cajori, Florian, *A History of Mathematical Notation* (Chicago: 1928).

Carcopino, Jérôme, *Daily Life in Ancient Rome*, E. O. Lorimer, trans. (New Haven: 1940).

Castiglioni, Arturo, *A History of Medicine*, E. B. Krumbhaar, trans. and ed. (New York City: 1969).

The Century Dictionary: An Encyclopedic Lexicon of the English Language, prepared under the direction of William Dwight Whitney (New York City: 1891).

Chadwick, Henry, *The Early Church* (Harmondsworth, England: 1967).

Chomsky, Carol, *The Acquisition of Syntax in Children from 5 to 10* (Cambridge, Mass.: 1969).

Conklin, Harold C., "Hanunóo Color Categories," in *Language in Culture and Society*, Dell Hymes, ed. (New York City: 1964).

Copley, Frank O., and Moses Hadas, eds., *Roman Drama* (Indianapolis: 1965).

Crawford, Michael, *The Roman Republic* (Cambridge, Mass.: 1982).

Dauzat, Albert, Jean Dubois and Henri Mitterand, *Nouveau dictionnaire étymologique et historique* (Paris: 1971).

De Sola, Ralph, *Abbreviations Dictionary* (New York City: 1967).

Diringer, David, *Writing* (New York City: 1962).

Dorland's Illustrated Medical Dictionary, Leslie Brainerd Arey *et al.*, eds. (Philadelphia: 1957).

Einarson, Benedict, "Notes on the Development of the Greek Alphabet," *Classical Philology* (Vol. 62, no. 1: Jan. 1967).

Ernout, A., and A. Meillet, *Dictionnaire étymologique de la langue latine: histoire des mots* (Paris: 1959).

Evans, Ivor H., ed., *Brewer's Dictionary of Phrase and Fable* (New York City: 1981).

Fergusson, Peter, *The Architecture of Solitude* (Princeton: 1984).

Fisher, David, and Reginald Bragonner, Jr., *What's What: A Visual Glossary of the Physical World* (Maplewood, N.J.: 1981).

Fowler, W. Warde, *Social Life at Rome in the Age of Cicero* (New York City: 1909).

Freud, Sigmund, *A General Introduction to Psychoanalysis* (New York City: 1960).

Frontinus, Sextus Julius, *The Stratagems* and *The Aqueducts*, Charles E. Bennett, trans. (Cambridge, Mass.: 1925).

Frumke, Lewis Burke, *How to Raise Your I.Q. by Eating Gifted Children* (New York City: 1983).

Garlan, Yvon, *War in the Ancient World: A Social History*, Janet Lloyd, trans. (New York City: 1975).

Glare, P. G. W., ed., *Oxford Latin Dictionary* (London: 1983).

Goffman, Erving, *Strategic Interaction* (Philadelphia: 1969).

Gómara, Francisco López de, *Cortés: The Life of the Conqueror by his Secretary*, Lesley Byrd Simpson, trans. (Berkeley: 1966).

Gordon, Benjamin Lee, *Medicine Throughout Antiquity* (Philadelphia: 1949).

Gordon, Cyrus H., *Forgotten Scripts* (New York City: 1982).

Gould, Stephen Jay, *The Mismeasure of Man* (New York City: 1981).

Grandgent, C. H., *An Introduction to Vulgar Latin* (New York City: 1962).

Grant, Michael, *Roman Myths* (New York City: 1971).

Greenough, J. B., A. A. Howard, G. L. Kittredge and Benjamin L. D'Ooge, eds., *Allen and Greenough's New Latin Grammar for Schools and Colleges* (Boston: 1903).

Hammond, N. G. L. and H. H. Scullard, eds., *The Oxford Classical Dictionary* (Oxford, England: 1970).

Hecker, Linda, "Runic Song," in *Panache* (Sunderland, Mass.: 1976).

Heer, Friedrich, *The Medieval World*, Janet Sondheimer, trans. (New York City: 1962).

Heller, Louis, Alexander Humez and Malcah Dror, *The Private Lives of English Words* (Henley on Thames, England: 1984).

Hoban, Russell, *Riddley Walker* (New York City: 1980).

Holmes, Oliver Wendell, *The Autocrat of the Breakfast Table* (New York City: 1957).

Horace (Quintus Horatius Flaccus) and Aules Persius Flaccus, *The Satires of Horace and Persius*, Niall Rudd, trans. (Harmondsworth, England: 1973).

Humez, Alexander, and Nicholas Humez, *Alpha to Omega: The Life and Times of the Greek Alphabet* (Boston: 1981).

————, *Latin for People/Latina pro Populo* (Boston: 1976).
James, E. O., *Seasonal Feasts and Festivals* (New York City: 1961).
Jespersen, Otto, *A Modern English Grammar on Historical Principles* (Heidelberg: 1909).
Justinian (Flavius Anicius Justinianus), ed., *The Digest of Roman Law*, Colin F. Kolbert, trans. (Harmondsworth, England: 1979).
Juvenal (Decimus Junius Juvenalis), *The Sixteen Satires*, Peter Green, trans. (Harmondsworth, England: 1967).
Kafka, Franz, *Parables and Paradoxes/Parabeln und Paradoxe*, Clement Greenberg *et al.*, trans. (New York City: 1961).
Kastner, Joseph, *A Species of Eternity* (Bloomington, Ind.: 1969).
Kinder, Hermann, and Werner Hilgemann, *The Anchor Atlas of World History, Vol. I*, Ernest A. Menze, trans., with maps designed by Harald and Ruth Bukor (New York City: 1974).
Las Casas, Bartolomé de, *History of the Indies*, Andrée M. Collard, trans. (New York City: 1971).
Latham, R. E., *Revised Medieval Latin Word-List from British and Irish Sources* (London: 1965).
Leach, Edmund R., *Rethinking Anthropology* (London: 1961).
Lévi-Strauss, Claude, *The Elementary Structures of Kinship* (Boston: 1969).
Ley, Willy, *The Lungfish and the Unicorn: An Excursion into Romantic Zoology* (New York City: 1941).
Liber Usualis, with introduction and rubrics in English, Solesmes Benedictines, eds. (New York: 1962).
Linnaeus, Carolus, *Systema Naturae* (Holm: 1759)
Livy (Titus Livius), *The Early History of Rome*, Aubrey de Sélincourt, trans. (Harmondsworth, England: 1960).
————, *The War with Hannibal*, Aubrey de Sélincourt, trans. (Harmondsworth, England: 1965).
————, *Rome and the Mediterranean*, Henry Bettenson, trans. (Harmondsworth, England: 1976).
Lounsbury, Floyd G., "The Formal Analysis of Crow- and Omaha-type Kinship Terminologies," in *Explorations in Cultural Anthropology*, Ward E. Goodenough, ed. (New York City: 1964).
Lucan (Marcus Annaeus Lucanus), *Pharsalia*, Robert Graves, trans. (Harmondsworth, England: 1957).

Lum, Peter, *Fabulous Beasts* (New York City: 1951).

Maine, Henry Sumner, *Ancient Law* (New York City: 1864).

Martial (Marcus Valerius Martialis), *Epigrams*, Walter Ker, trans. (Cambridge, Mass.: 1925).

Martin, Judith, *Miss Manners' Guide to Excruciatingly Correct Behavior* (New York City: 1982).

McEvedy, Colin, *The Penguin Atlas of Ancient History* (Harmondsworth, England: 1967).

Meillet, A. and J. Vendryes, *Traité de grammaire comparée des langues classiques* (Paris: 1966).

Menninger, Karl, *Number Words and Number Symbols*, Paul Broneer, trans. (Cambridge, Mass.: 1969).

Meyer-Lübke, W., *Romanisches Etymologisches Wörterbuch* (Heidelberg: 1911).

Mirsky, Jeannette, ed., *The Great Chinese Travelers* (Chicago: 1964).

Mossé, Claude, *The Ancient World at Work*, Janet Lloyd, trans. (New York City: 1969).

Nandris, Grigore, *Colloquial Rumanian* (London: 1945).

Ober, J. Hambleton, *Writing: Man's Great Invention* (Baltimore: 1965).

O'Brien, Flann, *The Third Policeman* (New York City: 1976).

Ogg, Oscar, *The 26 Letters* (New York City: 1961).

Onions, C. T., ed., *The Oxford Dictionary of English Etymology* (Oxford, England: 1966).

Ovid (Publius Ovidius Naso), *Fasti*, Sir James George Frazer, trans. (Cambridge, Mass.: 1931).

———, *Tristia* and *Ex Ponto*, Arthur Leslie Wheeler, trans. (Cambridge, Mass.: 1924).

Palmer, L. R., *The Latin Language* (London: 1954).

Parkinson, C. Northcote, *East and West* (Boston: 1963).

Partridge, Eric, *A Dictionary of Slang and Unconventional English* (London: 1961).

———, *Origins: A Short Etymological Dictionary of Modern English* (New York City: 1958).

———, *Words, Words, Words!* (London: 1933).

Pedersen, Holger, *The Discovery of Language: Linguistic Science in the 19th Century*, John Webster Spargo, trans. (Cambridge, Mass.: 1931).

Pei, Mario, *The Story of the English Language* (New York City: 1967).

Petronius Arbiter, Gaius, *The Satyricon*, William Arrowsmith, trans. (New York City: 1959).

Plautus, Titus Maccius, *Amphitron*, Paul Nixon, trans. (Cambridge, Mass.: 1961).

Pliny the Elder (Gaius Plinius Secundus), *Natural History*, H. Rackam *et al.*, trans. (Cambridge, Mass.: 1938–1963).

Pliny the Younger (Gaius Plinius Caecilius Secundus), *The Letters of the Younger Pliny*, Betty Radice, trans. (Harmondsworth, England: 1963).

Polybius, *The Rise of the Roman Empire*, Ian Scott-Kilvert, trans. (Harmondsworth, England: 1979).

Pomeroy, Sarah B., *Goddesses, Whores, Wives, and Slaves* (New York City: 1975).

Pulgram, Ernst, *The Tongues of Italy* (Cambridge, Mass.: 1958).

Quintilian (Marcus Fabius Quintilianus), *Institutio Orationis*, A. E. Butler, trans. (Cambridge, Mass.: 1922).

Radcliffe-Brown, A. R., *Structure and Function in Primitive Society* (New York City: 1965).

Rawson, Hugh, *A Dictionary of Euphemisms and Other Doubletalk* (New York City: 1981).

Riley, H. T., ed., *Dictionary of Latin Quotations, Proverbs, Maxims, and Mottos* (London: 1856).

Robins, R. H., *A Short History of Linguistics* (Bloomington, Ind.: 1967).

Rybot, Doris, *It Began Before Noah* (London: 1972).

Sallust (Gaius Sallustius Crispus), *The Jugurthine War* and *The Conspiracy of Cataline*, S. A. Handford, trans. (Harmondsworth, England: 1963).

Schneider, David M., *American Kinship: A Cultural Account* (Chicago: 1980).

Seneca, Lucius Annaeus, *The Pumpkinification of the God Claudius*, Robert Graves, trans., in Graves, *Claudius the God* (New York City: 1962).

Shepherd, Walter, *Shepherd's Glossary of Graphic Signs and Symbols* (London: 1971).

Sherk, William, *500 Years of New Words* (Toronto: 1983).

Simpson, D. P., ed., *Cassell's New Latin Dictionary* (New York City: 1960).

Smith, David Eugene, *History of Mathematics* (New York City: 1925).

Smith, William, William Wayte, and G. E. Marindin, eds., *A Dictionary of Greek and Roman Antiquities* (London: 1901).

Snowden, Frank M., *Blacks in Antiquity* (Cambridge, Mass.: 1970).

Southern, R. W., *Western Society and the Church in the Middle Ages* (Harmondsworth, England: 1970).

Spears, Richard, *Slang and Euphemisms* (New York City: 1981).

Suetonius Tranquillus, Gaius, *The Twelve Caesars*, Robert Graves, trans. (Harmondsworth, England: 1957).

Tacitus, Cornelius, *On Britain and Germany*, H. Mattingly, trans. (Harmondsworth, England: 1948).

Varro, Marcus Terentius, *De Lingua Latina*, Roland G. Kent, trans. (Cambridge, Mass.: 1958).

Warmington, E. H., trans., *Remains of Old Latin* (Cambridge, Mass.: 1967).

Wheeler, Arthur Leslie, *Catullus and the Traditions of Ancient Poetry* (Berkeley: 1934).

Zall, P. M., ed., *A Hundred Merry Tales and Other English Jestbooks of the Fifteenth and Sixteenth Centuries* (Lincoln, Neb.: 1963).

Zook, David H., Jr., and Robin Higham, *A Short History of Warfare* (New York City: 1966).

Zwicky, Arnold M. *et. al.*, *Studies Out in Left Field: Defamatory Essays presented to James D. McCawley on the occasion of his 33d or 34th Birthday* (Edmonton, Alberta: 1971).

Index

Hertz, Heinrich Rudolf, 121
Hesiod, 119
Hieron of Syracuse, 51
Hilaria, 68
Himera, battle of, 51
Himilco, 88
Hindu, 96
Historian, 41
Histrionic, 53
Hitler, Adolf, 39
Hoban, Russell, 3
Hobbes, Thomas, 229
Hoffman, Albert, 196
Holiday, 61
Homer, 167
Homo erectus, 209
Homo habilis, 210
Homo troglodytus, 207
Hood, 33–34
Hoodlum, 34
Hoodwinking, 35
Hoplites, 18
Hostis, Mattheus, 241–42
Horace (Quintus Horatius Flac-
cus), 103, 139
Horn, 238
Horn Syllogism, 41
Hour, 117, 119–20
Hull, John, 154
Humor, Roman, 98–109
Hyphen, 181

IANATRIX, 10
Ianus, 114, 153, 165
Iarbas, 86
Ibid., 54
I, Claudius (Graves), 99
Idean Mother, 67–68. *See also*
Cybele
Ides, 112, 116
I.e., 57
I GRAECA, 239
Illuminated Doctor, 43
Impale, 173
Incest, 9, 14
Inch, 216, 223
Incitatus, 95, 103
Indict, 40

Indigo, 96
Indoanaline, 96
Indo-Europeans, 95–96, 146–47,
158
Indus River, 96
Injury, 127
Ink, 197
Institutio Orationis (Quintilian),
41, 99
INSVLAE, 154
Intercalary days, 115, 116, 117
Intercalary months, 116–17, 119
Interrobang, 186–87
Interrogative pronouns, 177–78
Invidious, 238
Invincible Doctor, 44
10!, 178
IOCVS, 97, 98–99
*Ipsomobile, 212
Irrefragable Doctor, 43
Isham, Sir Gyles, 138
Ishtar, 85
Isidore of Seville, 180–86 *passim*
Isis, 68–69, 106
Island, 228
Island of Aesculapius, 46, 154, 166
Istanbul, 72
Italicization, 57
Iugurtha, 17, 96
Iulus, 167
Iuno, *see* Juno
Iunonia, 93
Iuppiter, *see* Jupiter
IVS, 124–25; GENTIVM, 132

James I, 220
James II, 220
Janitor, 153
January, 114
Janus, *see* Ianus
Jarns, 189
Jealous, 238
Jefferson, Thomas, 33
Jerome, Saint, 224–25
Jest, 98
Jesus, 69, 169
Jewish calendar, 116–17
Jezebel, 85

Acknowledgments

A number of invaluable friends have contributed directly to the writing of this book, and we would like to thank them here, in alphabetical order: Jane V. Anderson, Francis Judd Cooke, Glenn Corwin, the late Warren Cowgill, Jo Diggs, Peter Fergusson, George Gibson, David Godine, Edward Goldfrank, William Goodman, Judy Grant, Carol Grayson, Betsy Handley, Jerold Harmatz, Dorian Hastings, Bertha Hatvary, Linda Hecker, David Hildebrand, Frank Holan, Ilse Holan, Jenny Holan, Andrea Humez, David Humez, Elisabeth Gleason Humez, Jean McMahon Humez, David Jones, John Larkins, Tom McMahon, Elizabeth Michaud, Karen Motylewski, Nan Myerson, Nate Raymond, William Revis, William Sarill, Jennifer Savary, William J. Slattery, Dorothy Straight, Robert Wallace, Malcah Yaeger-Dror.

A·B·C Et Cetera

has been set in Electra by Graphic Composition, Inc., of Athens, Georgia. Designed by William Addison Dwiggins for the Mergenthaler Linotype Company and first made available in 1935, Electra is impossible to classify as either "modern" or "old-style." Not based on any historical model or reflecting any particular period or style, it is notable for its clean and elegant lines, its lack of contrast between the thick and thin elements that characterize most modern faces, and its freedom from all idiosyncrasies that catch the eye and interfere with reading.

Haddon Craftsmen, Scranton, Pennsylvania, was the printer and binder.